U0596109

跨文化交际

主　编　李晓红

副主编　吴　倩　唐黎卿

编　者　张晓青　陈　玥　佘雄飞

　　　　邱　玥　傅周丹

INTERCULTURAL COMMUNICATION

ZHEJIANG UNIVERSITY PRESS
浙江大学出版社

图书在版编目（CIP）数据

跨文化交际：英文 / 李晓红主编. -- 杭州：浙江大学
出版社，2020.8
ISBN 978-7-308-20478-1

Ⅰ．①跨⋯ Ⅱ．①李⋯ Ⅲ．①文化交流－英语－高等职
业教育－教材 Ⅳ．①G115

中国版本图书馆CIP数据核字(2020)第153351号

跨文化交际

李晓红　主　编
吴　倩　唐黎卿　副主编

责任编辑	郑成业	
责任校对	李　晨	
封面设计	春天书装	
出版发行	浙江大学出版社	
	（杭州市天目山路148号　　邮政编码　310007）	
	（网址：http://www.zjupress.com）	
排　　版	杭州林智广告有限公司	
印　　刷	浙江省邮电印刷股份有限公司	
开　　本	787mm×1092mm　1/16	
印　　张	17	
字　　数	443千	
版 印 次	2020年8月第1版　2020年8月第1次印刷	
书　　号	ISBN 978-7-308-20478-1	
定　　价	55.00元	

FOREWORD

前　言

　　随着世界经济的全球化、信息技术的飞速发展、国际文化交流的日益频繁，中国与世界接轨的步伐不断加快，不同文化背景的个体和群体之间的交流在深度和广度上实现着前所未有的突破，跨文化交际已经成为"地球村"的普遍现实。然而，文化之间的差异往往会导致交际的困惑、误解、矛盾和冲突，因此，培养对文化差异的敏感度和宽容度、发展跨文化意识是"地球村"公民的共识，跨越交际障碍、构建人类命运共同体是当今世界的迫切诉求，跨文化交际人才培养是21世纪人才培养至关重要的任务。

　　本教材介绍跨文化交际知识，指导学生进行跨文化交际实践，明晰文化冲突原因，克服文化冲突障碍，提高对异文化的适应能力，学会有效传播中国故事。

　　教材以提升高职学生知识、能力和态度为设计宗旨，充分考虑知识性、趣味性和实用性的结合，富有多模态资源。全书以模块串联内容，共分六个模块：第一模块介绍了文化、交际和跨文化交际的基本概念；第二模块分析了两个最具影响力的文化价值理论；第三和第四模块阐释了跨文化语言交际和非语言交际的内涵；第五模块讨论了跨文化交际中的障碍和如何搭建跨越障碍的桥梁；第六模块讲述了三大跨文化交际情境——商务情境、旅游情境和教育情境。各模块相互独立，又层层递进。

　　每个模块下设单元，共十五单元，每个单元包含影视片段、阅读材料和案例听力三部分，同时，教材适应互联网+教学和碎片化学习的时代需求，设有二维码，二维码中的内容与各单元主题相关，便于学生实现时时学和处处学，拓展知识和能力。影视片段和教学视频能够帮助学生构建跨文化交际的真实情境，形成对跨文化交际的具象认知；阅读材料是对跨文化交际的理论介绍，深入浅出，简洁精练；案例听力是理论联系实际和解决问题的过程。每一单元的练习都设有主观题和客观题，便于学生理解和思考。每一单元的教学大约需要4课时，完成整本教材大约需要60课时。

　　教材可以与跨文化交际在线课程配套使用，跨文化交际课程在智慧树平台上的网址是：https://www.zhihuishu.com/。此外，本教材提供配套课件，可扫描右方二维码下载以供学习使用。

扫一扫
下载配套课件

FOREWORD

　　教材是集体智慧和劳动的结晶，主编是浙江旅游职业学院的李晓红教授，她编写了第三、六、七、八、十一、十二、十三、十四和十五单元，浙江同济科技职业学院的吴倩副教授编写了第一单元和第二单元，浙江旅游职业学院的唐黎卿老师编写了第四单元和第五单元，浙江旅游职业学院的陈玥老师和佘雄飞老师编写了第九单元和第十单元，浙江义乌工商职业学院的张晓青副教授、浙江经贸职业技术学院的邱月副教授、浙江君威国际旅行社有限公司董事长助理兼市场部总监傅周丹、浙江旅游职业学院的外教福迪尔·塞尔穆尼（Fodil Selmouni）对教材的部分内容进行了材料整理和练习设计。二维码中的教学视频由浙江旅游职业学院的外教和中国教师共同完成，他们是中国的李晓红、唐黎卿、边宇琪、杨志超、陈积峰、佘雄飞，加拿大的福迪尔·塞尔穆尼（Fodil Selmouni），美国的安东尼奥·古铁雷斯（Antonio Gutierrez）和格兰特·托马斯（Grant Thomas），英国的安娜·帕里（Anna Parry）、劳伦·安德森（Lauren Anderson）和格雷戈瑞·索耶（Gregory Sawyer），俄罗斯的奈利·波拉托娃（Nelli Bulatova），西班牙的布鲁诺·桑切斯（Bruno Sánchez）和韩国的洪玹熙（Hong Hyunhee）。教材在编写过程中，参考了大量的国内外专著、教材和论文，得到了有关专家的倾心指导，也得到了浙江大学出版社李晨编辑的大力协助，敬请接受本人的深深谢意。

　　教材可以作为高职院校英语专业学生的用书，也可以作为大学生人文素养通识课程的参考用书，还可以供对跨文化交际感兴趣的社会人士阅读。

　　由于编者的水平和能力有限，书中疏漏和谬误仍在所难免，尽请使用者批评指正，便于今后完善、提高。谢谢！

编者

2020年8月

CONTENTS

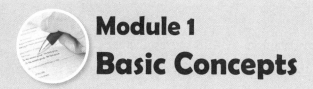

Module 1
Basic Concepts

Unit 1   Culture

Video Clip Appreciation

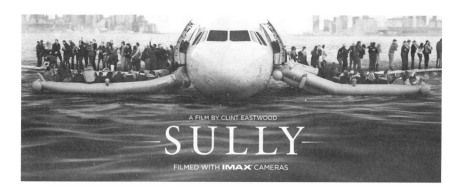

I. Introduction to the Movie *Sully*

Based on a real event, the movie follows Sullenberger's emergency landing of the US Airways Flight 1549 on the Hudson River, in which all passengers and crew survived with only minor injuries, and the subsequent publicity and investigation. On January 15, 2009, pilot "Sully" (the affectionate nickname of Sullenberger) and the first officer Jeff Skiles took off for Charlotte Douglas. Barely three minutes before the flight, the plane hit a group of geese, which crippled both engines of the plane. Without engine power and any airport within range, Sully glided his disabled plane onto the frigid waters of the Hudson River, saving the lives of all 155 aboard. However, even as Sully was dubbed a hero by the press for his actions, an unfolding investigation threatened to destroy his reputation and career.

II. Introduction to the Video Clip

Although Sully was being heralded by the public and the media for his unprecedented feat of aviation skill, the National Transportation Safety Board believes that the accident may have been pilot error. Because preliminary data from ACARS suggest that the port engine was still running at idle power. Theoretically, this would have left him with enough power to return to LaGuardia or land at Teterboro. Furthermore, the Board claims that several confidential computerized simulations show that the plane could have landed safely at either airport without engines. Sully has to defend himself to the commission. Will he succeed?

III. Script of the Video Clip

Video Clip

Investigator 1: Multiple airports, runways, two successful landings. We are simply mimicking what the computer already told us.

Investigator 2: A lot of toes were stepped on in order to set this up for today. And frankly, I really don't know what you gentlemen plan to gain by it.

Sully: Can we get serious now?

Investigator 2: Captain?

Sully: We've all heard about the computer simulations and now we are watching actual sims. But I can't quite believe you still have not taken into account the human factor.

Investigator 2: Human piloted simulations showed that you could make it back to the airport.

Sully: No, they don't. These pilots were not behaving like human beings, like people who are experiencing this for the first time.

Investigator 2: Well, they may not like be reacting like you did.

Sully: Immediately after the bird strike, they are turning back for the airport. Just as in the computer sims, correct?

Investigator 2: That is correct.

Sully: They obviously knew the turn and exactly what heading to fly. They did not run a check. They did not switch on the APU.

Investigator 2: They had all the same parameters that you faced.

Sully: No one warned us. No one said, "You are going to lose both engines at a lower altitude than an jet in history. But be cool. Just make a left turn for LaGuardia like you're going back to pick up the milk." This was dual engine loss at 2,800 feet followed by an immediate water landing with 155 souls on board. No one has ever trained for an incident like that. No one. The Teterboro landing, with its unrealistic bank angle, we were not the Thunderbirds up there. I'd like to know how many times the polit practiced that maneuver before he actually pulled it off. I'm not questioning the pilots. They're good pilots. But they've clearly been instructed to head for the airport immediately after the bird strike. You're allowed no time for analysis or decision-making. In these simulations, you've taken all of the humanity out of the cockpit. How much time did the pilots spend planning for this event? For these simulations? You're looking for human errors. Then make it human.

Skiles: This wasn't a video game. It was life and death. Sully's right. That's worth a few seconds.

Sully: Please ask how many practice runs they had.

Elizabeth: Seventeen.

Sully: Seventeen?

Elizabeth: The pilot who landed at Teterboro had seventeen practice attempts before the simulation we just witnessed.

Investigator 2: Your reaction decision time will be set at 35 seconds.

Skiles: Thirty-five seconds. That's not enough time.

Sully: We only had 208 seconds total, so I'll take it.

Investigator 1: Upload the link. Return to LaGuandia. Now with an added 35-second delay in response time.

Pilot 1: Birds.

Pilot 2: Okay, I saw them. Give me 35 seconds.

Pilot 1: Thirty-five seconds. Time's up.

Pilot 2: Here we go. Flight path vector. Going for 1-3.

Pilot 1: Okay.

Pilot 2: Activate confirm.

Pilot 1: All right—You are confirmed.

Pilot 2: We are heading right for the airport.

Broadcast: Caution, obstacle. Caution, obstacle.

Pilot 1: We're about seven miles from the runway.

Broadcast: Caution, obstacle. Terrain, terrain. Pull up. Pull up. Pull up. Pull up. Too low, terrain. Too low, terrain.

Pilot 1: We got a little extra speed. You want some flaps? (Too low, terrain. Too low, terrain.)

Pilot 2: No, leave the flaps up. Too low, terrain. (Too low, terrain. Too low, terrain. Too low, terrain.)

Investigator 2: Let's try Teterboro.

Investigator 1: Upload the link, please.

Pilot 3: Birds.

Pilot 4: Auto pilot off. Flight Director off. Hack the time.

Pilot 3 & 4: Thirty-five seconds.

Pilot 3: Engine one and two fail. Turn.

Pilot 4: Okay. Let's see if we can make it.

Pilot 3: Heading sub 2-9-8. You seeing Teterboro out there?

Pilot 4: I do. Way too low.

Broadcast: Obstacle. Obstacle. Pull up. Pull up. Pull up. Pull up. Pull up. Pull up.

Pilot 4: Not gonna work, not gonna work. (Pull up. Pull up. Pull up. Pull up.)

Sully: Does anyone need to see more simulations?

Skiles: Now that we've seen what could have happened, can we, uh, listen to what actually we did?

Investigator 2: We will look at all the results at a later date. Elizabeth.

Elizabeth: For the record, this is the CVR of US Airways Flight 1549, January 15th, 2009. Gentlemen, headsets.

Sully: Birds.

Skiles: Shit.

Sully: Oh, yeah. We got one rolling back. We have both of them rolling back. Ignition start. I'm starting the APU. My aircraft.

Skiles: Your aircraft.

Sully: Get out the QRH.

Skiles: Priority left.

Sully: Loss of thrust on both engines. Mayday, mayday, mayday. This is Cactus 1549. Hit birds. We've lost thrust on both engines. We are turning back towards LaGuardia.

Patrick: Okay, you need to return to LaGuardia? Turn left heading 2-2-0.

Sully: 2-2-0.

Patrick: Which engine did you lose?

Sully: Both. Both engines.

Skiles: If fuel remaining, engine mode, select your ignition. Ignition.

Sully: Ignition.

Skiles: Thrust levers, confirm idle.

Sully: Idle.

Skiles: Airspeed. Optimum relight, 300 knots. We don't have that.

Sully: No, we don't.

Patrick: Cactus 1549, if we can get it for you, do you wanna try to land runway 1-3?

Sully: We are unable. We may end up in the Hudson.

Skiles: Emergency electrical power, emergency generator not online.

Sully: Online.

Skiles: ATC notified. Squawk 7700. Distress message transmit. We did that.

Patrick: Cactus 1549, it's gonna be left traffic, runway 3-1.

Sully: Unable.

Patrick: Okay, where do you need to land?

Broadcast: Wind shear.

Skiles: FAC 1 off, then on.

Patrick: Been 10 seconds. Captain. Come on. Talk to me. Cactus 1549, runway 4's available if you wanna make left traffic to runway 4.

Sully: I don't think we can make any runway. Uh, what about over to our right? Anything in New Jersey? Maybe Teterboro?

Patrick: Okay, yeah. Off your right side is Teterbor Airport. LaGuardia Departure, got an emergency inbound.

Airport Traffic Controller: This is Teterboro tower. Go ahead.

Patrick: Cactus 1549 over the GW Bridge needs to go to the airport right now.

Airport Traffic Controller: Check. Does he need assistance?

Patrick: Yes. Bird strike. Can I get him in for runway 1? Cactus 1549, you wanna try and go to Teterboro? Obstacle.

Broadcast: Obstacle. Obstacle. Obstacle. Pull up. Clear of conflict.

Skiles: No relight after 30 seconds, engine master one and two, confirm off.

Sully: Off.

Skiles: Wait 30 seconds.

Broadcast: Too low, terrain. Too low, terrain. Too low, terrain. Too low, terrain.

Sully: This is the captain. Brace for impact.

Patrick: Cactus 1549, turn right 2-8-0. You can land runway 1 Teterboro.

Sully: We can't make it.

Patrick: Okay. Which runway would you like at Teterboro?

Sully: Go ahead. Try number one.

Skiles: Number one. No relight.

Sully: We're gonna end up in the Hudson. (Too low, terrain.)

Patrick: I'm sorry. Say again. Cactus? (Too low, terrain. Too low, terrain.)

Sully: All right, let's put the flaps out. Put the flaps out.

Skiles: Flaps out.

Patrick: Cactus 1549, radar contact lost. You also got Newark off your two o'clock in about seven miles.

Skiles: Got flaps out. Two hundred fifty feet in the air. 170 knots. Got no power on either one. Try the other one.

Sully: Try the other one.

Patrick: 1549? Still up?

Skiles: One hundred and fifty knots. Got flaps two. You want more?

Sully: No, let's stay at two.

Patrick: You got runway 2-9 available at Newark. It'll be two o'clock in seven miles.

Sully: You got any ideas?

Skiles: Actually not.

Broadcast: Terrain. Terrain. Pull up. Pull up. Pull up. Pull up. Pull up. Pull up. Pull up. Pull up.

Sully: We're gonna brace. (Pull up.) Thirty. (Pull up.) Twenty. (Pull up.)

Sully: I need to take a quick break. What did you think? Hearing the CVR just now? Let me tell you what I think. I'm just so damn proud. And you, you were right there, through all that distraction. With so much at stake. We did it together. We were a team.

Skiles: Thanks, Sully.

Sully: We did our job.

Skiles: We did our job.

Larry: Hey, you did good.

Investigator 2: I'd like to call this hearing back to order. If we could settle, please? Take your seats.That is honestly the first time that I have listened to a crash recording while actually sitting with the captain and the first officer. It's extraordinary.

Skiles: That was no simulation.

Investigator 2: No, it wasn't.

Elizabeth: Gentlemen, I want to inform you that the left engine has been recovered. We just received a comprehensive report. There was extensive damage to both the guide vanes and fan blades of the engine. Five compressor blades were fractured and eight variable gudie vanes missing.

Sully: So, no thrust?

Elizabeth: As you testified, it was completely destroyed. The ACARS data was wrong. I'd like to add sth on a personal note. I can say with absolute confidence that after speaking with the rest to the flight crew, with bird experts, aviation engineers, after running through every scenario, after interviewing each player, there is still an "X" in this result and it's you, Captain Sullenberger. Remove you from the equation, and the math just fails.

Sully: I disagree. It wasn't just me. It was all of us. It was Jeff and Donna and Sheila and Doreen and all of the passengers, the rescue workers, air traffic control, ferry boat crews and the scuba cops. We all did it. We survived.

Elizabeth: First Officer Skiles, is there anything you'd like to add? Anything you would have done differently if you had to do it again?

Skiles: Yes, I would have done it in July.

New Words

simulation [ˌsɪmjuˈleɪʃn] *n.* a model of a set of problems or events that can be used to teach someone how to do sth, or the process of making such a model 模拟 , 模仿

parameter [pəˈræmɪtə] *n.* a set of facts or a fixed limit that establishes or limits how sth can or must happen or be done 参量 , 参数 ; 决定因素 ; 界限

maneuver [məˈnuːvə] *n.* a movement or set of movements needing skill and care 精巧动作

humanity [hjuˈmænɪtɪ] *n.* people in general （统称）人 , 人类

activate [ˈæktɪveɪt] *v.* to cause sth to start 启动 , 开动 ; 激活

caution [ˈkɔːʃ(ə)n] *n.* great care and attention 谨慎 , 小心 , 慎重

obstacle [ˈɒbstək(ə)l] *n.* a situation, an event, etc. that makes it difficult for you to do or achieve sth 障碍 ; 阻碍 , 妨碍

upload [ˌʌpˈləʊd] *v.* to copy or move programs or information to a larger computer system or to the Internet 上传（程序或信息）

ignition [ɪgˈnɪʃ(ə)n] n. the electrical system of a vehicle that causes the fuel to burn or explode in order to start the engine 点火器

Mayday [ˈmeɪdeɪ] *n.* a special radio signal sent from a ship or an aircraft when it needs help（船只、飞机发出的）无线电求救信号

knot [nɒt] *n.* a measure of the speed of ships, aircrafts, or movements of water and air. One knot is one nautical mile per hour. 节 , 飞机或轮船的航速以及流速单位 ;1 节约等于 1

海里 / 小时

distress [dɪ'stres] *n.* a situation in which you are suffering or are in great danger and therefore in urgent need of help 受苦；遇难，遇险

testify ['testɪfaɪ] *v.* to speak seriously about sth, especially in a law court, or to give or provide proof 作证；声明，证明

Phrases and Expressions

pull off: to leave the road in order to stop for a short time 驶向路边短暂停靠

at stake: sth that is valuable in a situation where it might be lost 有风险；处于危急关头

Notes

gonna: It is used in spoken English, meaning "going to." 将要（等于 going to）

APU: Abbreviation for auxillary power unit. It is a small jet engine housed in the tail of the aircraft used to provide a source of electricity to power the aircraft on the ground when the engines are switched off and as a source of air in order to start the engines. 辅助动力装置

CVR: Abbreviation for cockpit voice recorder. It is installed to help reconstruct the events leading to an aircraft accident. 驾驶舱话音记录器，即"黑匣子"

QRH: Abbreviation for quick reference handbook. It contains all the procedures applicable for abnormal and emergency conditions in an easy-to-use format. In addition, performance data corrections are also provided for specific conditions. 快速检查单

ATC: Abbreviation for air traffic control. It is a service provided by ground-based air traffic controllers who direct aircrafts onto the ground and through controlled airspace, and can provide advisory services to aircraft in non-controlled airspace. The primary purpose of ATC worldwide is to prevent collisions, organize and expedite the flow of air traffic, and provide information and other support for pilots. 空中交通管制

GW Bridge: It represents George Washington Bridge. The Bridge is a double-decked suspension bridge spanning the Hudson River, connecting the Washington Heights neighborhood of Manhattan in New York City with the borough of Fort Lee in New Jersey. 乔治·华盛顿大桥，位于哈德逊河之上，为纽约的一条交通要道

ACARS: Abbreviation for aircraft communications addressing and reporting system. In aviation, ACARS is a digital datalink system for transmission of short messages between aircraft and ground stations via airband radio or satellite. 飞机通信寻址与报告系统

IV. Exercises for Understanding

1. Decide whether the following statements are true or false according to the video clip you have just watched. Write a "T" for true or an "F" for false.

_____(1) Originally, the men of the National Transportation Safety Board thought it was not necessary to settle on the Hudson River.

_____(2) The computer simulations indicated that the plane could have landed at LaGuardia or Teterboro safely.

_____(3) Elizabeth claimed that the left engine was idle and still functioning.

_____(4) Sully argued that what the Board did not take into account was the "human factor."

_____(5) Sully failed to defend his reputation and career.

2. Put the following sentences in the right order according to the video clip you have just watched.

_____(1) Sully made his only announcement to the passengers "Brace for impact."

_____(2) The plane hit a flock of Canada geese, which crippled both of the engines.

_____(3) With its nose raised, Flight 1549 completed an unpowered ditching in the Hudson.

_____(4) With no thrust and little altitude Sully decided that gliding back to LaGurardia was not possible.

_____(5) Without thrust Sully began his glide towards the Hudson.

_____(6) Sully decided that landing at Teterboro was not viable.

3. Explore interculturally.

_____(1) Do you think Sully is a hero? Why or why not?

_____(2) What are the similarities and differences between Chinese and American hero? What are the cultural factors underlying it?

Section B   Reading

Definitions of Culture

E. B. Tylor, the forefather of culture study, conceived culture as "the complex whole which includes knowledge, belief, art, morals, law, custom, and any other capabilities and habits acquired by man as a member of society." Another scholar, Edward Hall, defined culture very simply. He proposed that culture is communication and communication is culture.

E. Sapir defined culture as what a society does and thinks. According to R. Benedict, what really binds men together is their culture—the ideas and the standards they have in common.

In the eyes of Clyde Kluckhohn, an anthropologist, culture means the total life way of a people, the social legacy the individual acquires from his group. Or culture can be regarded as that part of the environment that is the creation of man.

D. Brown regarded culture as a collection of beliefs, habits, living patterns, and behaviors which are held more or less in common by people who occupy particular geographic areas. In 1981, I. Robertson thought the culture of every society is unique, containing combinations of norms and values that are found nowhere else.

The definition by G. Hofestede is as follows: I treat culture as the collective programming of the mind that distinguishes the members of one group or category of people from another. The "mind" stands for the head, heart, and hands—that is, for thinking, feeling, and acting, with consequences for beliefs, attitudes, and skills.

Simply put, culture is a system of meaning.

Metaphors of Culture

Culture is like an iceberg. Like an iceberg, only some of culture is visible. Aspects of culture that we can easily observe are often referred to as objective culture. This includes things like history, literature, and customs. When we learn the facts about our own or other cultures, we are learning the objective culture. Most of culture is below the surface of our awareness. It is not easily observable. This is referred to as subjective culture. It includes feelings and attitudes about how things are and how they should be. When we only learn objective culture, we are missing the bigger part that is below the surface.

Liangzhu Ancient City—The First City in China

Culture is our software. Culture is the basic operating system that makes us human around the world physically pretty much the same. There are variations in body size, shape and color, but the basic equipment is universal. We can think of our physical selves as the hardware, but we cannot be said to be human until we are programmed and each of us is programmed by our home culture.

Humans are unique among all the animals on earth in that the infant is weak and incapable of survival for an exceptionally long period of time. At birth the infant is only a potential human. It must learn how to be human and it learns that in a culturally specific way. It is the culture that provides the software. As with any good software, we are only vaguely aware of it as we use it. It fades into the background and we just know that we can be, that the computer works,

Introduction to America

or perhaps sometimes does not work because it is incompatible with someone else's software.

Culture is like the water a fish swims in. Like any creature a fish scans its environment to find food, reproduce and protect itself from danger. It notices everything except the water it is swimming in. The fish takes the water for granted because it so totally surrounds the fish that it really cannot imagine another environment. The same is true for us. Our culture is so much a part of who we are and what the world is like for us that we do not notice it, we take it for granted. For most people for most of their lives, everything they see and do takes place in the same culture. Everyone is swimming in the same water. They couldn't describe the water even if they wanted to.

Culture is the story we tell ourselves about ourselves. Every cultural group has a story that provides a way for members of the group to understand who they are and what the world is like. People tell themselves their story in their folklore, arts, in politics and in intimate conversations among friends and family members. The stories may be very old and include legends of how the group was created, but stories also change to adapt to changing circumstances.

For instance, Chinese often say that China is an old country while the United States is very young. This seems to be true if American culture is assumed to begin with the European settlement of North America or American independence. In fact, American culture is an extension of Western culture and that dates back to the ancient Greeks or even the ancient Egyptians. It can be argued that American culture is just as old as Chinese culture, but that is not what is important. What is significant is that the Chinese tell this story and use it to define who they are as Chinese in comparison to other groups.

Similarly, Americans often say they are an immigrant nation. If you ask an American about his culture, he will probably tell you something about his ethnic or religious background. He may tell you where his ancestors came from and how they happened to go to America. He will tell you how his life and his family's life are unique. This story emphasizes the diversity within American culture. In fact, many visitors comment that the United States is remarkably similar from coast to coast. It is recognizably American no matter which part of the country they visit. It can be argued that the United States is culturally rather uniform with the same language, similar social attitudes and lifestyles throughout the country, while Chinese culture is remarkably diverse. People speak different languages or dialects in different areas and identify strongly with their local region or hometown. Again, it is not important whether the story is true or not. What is significant is that people tell the story to show themselves and others who they are.

Culture is the grammar of our behavior. Culture is what people need to know in order to behave appropriately in a society. It includes all the rules that make actions meaningful to those acting and to the people around them. In learning to speak, everyone learns to use the grammar of their native language, but they use it automatically with little or no awareness of the rules of grammar.

Introduction to Great Britain

Similarly, people learn their cultural grammar unconsciously and apply its rules automatically. Just as native speakers of a language are usually unable to describe the grammatical rules of that language unless they have specifically studied grammar, most people find it difficult to describe the meaning system of their own culture. Like the grammar of a language, cultural grammars are repetitive. They are made up of basic patterns that occur again and again. For instance, an important pattern in Chinese culture is the distinction between inside and outside. This pattern shows up in the language, traditional architecture and in social relationship.

Exercises for Understanding

1. Answer the following questions according to the passage you have just read.

(1) Which of the metaphors of culture given above do you prefer? Why?

(2) Brainstorm examples of culture. Then classify them into the visible and invisible parts of the iceberg.

2. Choose the correct answers to the following questions.

(1) To _____, culture is learned.

   A. E. B. Tylor and Clyde Kluckhohn

   B. Edward Hall and R. Benedict

   C. E. B. Tylor and D. Brown

   D. I. Robertson and Clyde Kluckhohn

(2) Which of the statements of culture is not true?

   A. Culture is transmissible.

   B. Culture is adaptive.

   C. Culture is dynamic.

   D. Culture is static.

(3) Culture is our software implies except that _____.

   A. The physical body is like the hardware of the computer.

   B. It is programmed by our own culture.

   C. An infant learns how to be human in a culturally specific way.

D. We are strongly aware of the "software" as we use it.

3. Decide whether the following statements are true or false according to the passage you have just read. Write a "T" for true or an "F" for false.

_____(1) Culture is innate as soon as a person is born.

_____(2) Culture is acquired through socialization.

_____(3) Man is the producer of culture and the product of culture.

_____(4) Culture can be seen as shared knowledge, what people need to know in order to act appropriately in a given culture.

_____(5) One's actions are totally independent of his or her culture.

Section C　Case

Scan and Listen

The Scenario

Dinner with Friends

Janice is a young American engineer working for a manufacturing joint venture near Nanjing. She and her husband George, who is teaching English at a university, are learning Chinese and enjoying their new life. They have been eager to get to know Chinese people better so were pleased when Liu Lingling, Janice's young co-worker invited them to her home for dinner.

When Janice and George arrived, Lingling introduced them to her husband Yang Feng, asked them to sit down at a table containing 8 plates of various cold dishes, served them tea and then disappeared with her husband into the kitchen. After a few minutes, Lingling came back and added water to their tea. Janice offered to help in the kitchen but Lingling said she didn't need help. She invited the couple to look at their new CD player and their color TV and then disappeared again.

A halfhour later she came back and sat down and the three began to eat. Yang Feng came in from time to time to put dish after dish on the table. Most of the food was wonderful but neither George nor Janice could eat the fatty pork in pepper sauce or the sea cucumbers, and there was much more than they could eat. They kept wishing Yang Feng would sit down so they could talk to him. Finally, he did sit down to eat a bit, but quickly turned on the TV to show them all its high-tech features. Soon it was time to go home.

George and Janice felt slightly depressed by this experience, but returned the invitation two weeks later. They decided to make a nice American meal and felt lucky to find olives, tomato juice, crackers and even some cheese in the hotel shops. They put these out as appetizers. For the main course they prepared spaghetti and a salad with dressing made from oil, vinegar, and some spices they found in the market.

When Liu Lingling and Yang Feng arrived, they were impressed by the apartment and asked the price of the TV, video player, vacuum cleaner and other things. Janice politely refused to answer their questions. They took small tastes of the appetizers and seemed surprised when both George and Janice sat down with them. They ate only a little spaghetti and did not finish the salad on their plates. George urged them to eat more but they refused and looked around expectantly. Janice and George talked about their families and jobs and asked the Chinese couple about theirs. After a while, George cleared the table and served coffee and pastries. Yang Feng and Lingling each put four spoons of sugar into their coffee but did not drink much of it and ate only a bite or two of pastry.

After they left, George said that at least they had a chance to talk, but Janice was upset. "We left their place so full that we couldn't walk and they're going to have to eat again when they get home.

Exercise

Listen to the case above and answer the following questions.

(1) Who are Janice and Liu Lingling?

(2) How did Janice and her husband feel when Liu Lingling invited them to have dinner at home?

(3) What were Liu Lingling and her husband busy with for most of the time? How did Janice and her husband feel?

(4) How did the American couple treat Liu Lingling and her husband when they returned the invitation?

(5) What's the difference between Chinese and American food culture?

Unit 2　Communication

Video Clip Appreciation

I. Introduction to the Movie *La La Land*

La La Land tells the story of Mia, an aspiring actress, and Sebastian, a dedicated jazz musician, who meet and fall in love in Los Angeles while pursuing their dreams. Set in modern day, Los Angeles, this original musical about everyday life explores the joy and pain of pursuing dreams.

II. Introduction to the Video Clips

Sebastian, a pianist who holds on to an ideal version of jazz, wants to open his own club. Mia, an incurable romantic, is fascinated by the allure of the old Hollywood. These two proper L. A. dreamers are simply meant for each other despite getting off to a bad start. Soon they are blissfully in love and move in together. In Clip 1, Sebastian is playing the piano at home. Mia comes home, and Sebastian begins singing *City of Stars* as he plays. Mia joins him on the piano bench and joins in, making the song a duet. Later, Mia is on the phone with her mother. She is being asked about Sebastian and defensively tells her mom that he's going to open a jazz club but admits he doesn't have the money yet. The truth of the comment hits home for Sebastian and he takes the job offered by Keith, his old friend, to play in a newer-style jazz band that he doesn't really believe in. After that, Sebastian is always on tour. In Clip 2, when Mia gets home, Sebastian is back making a meal as a surprise for her. They talk with each other happily at first but end up with a quarrel. On the following night, Sebastian misses Mia's performance because of a photoshoot of the band. After that, Mia breaks off the relationship, saying she's going to move back to her hometown and give up acting. A casting agent contacts Sebastian, looking for Mia for a film audition. Sebastian tracks her down to her hometown and drives her to the meeting. In Clip 3, Sebastian and Mia are discussing their future after the audition. In Clip 4, both are successful with their careers. Sebastian opens his own jazz club and Mia has her desired career as a famous actress and married someone else. The two former lovers encounter each other five years later when Mia's husband takes her to Sebastian's jazz club.

III. Script of the Video Clips

Clip 1

Video Clip 1

[*Lyrics of the song*]

City of stars

Are you shining just for me?

City of stars

There's so much that I can't see

Who knows?

I felt it from the first embrace I shared with you

That now our dreams

They've finally come true

City of stars

Just one thing everybody wants

There in the bars

And through the smokescreen of the crowded restaurants

It's love

Yes, all we're looking for is love from someone else

A rush

A glance

A touch

A dance

To look in somebody's eyes

To light up the skies

To open the world and send them reeling

A voice that says

I'll be here and you'll be alright

I don't care if I know

Just where I will go

'Cause all that I need's this crazy feeling

A rat-tat-tat on my heart

I Think I want it to stay

Clip 2

Sebastian: I thought... Surprise! I gotta leave first thing in the morning, but I just—I had to see you. It's so nice to be home.

Mia: I'm so glad you're home.

Video Clip 2

Sebastian: How's the play going?

Mia: I'm nervous.

Sebastian: You are? Why?

Mia: Because... what if people show up?

Sebastian: Pishi Kaka. You're nervous about what they think?

Mia: I'm nervous to do it. I'm nervous to get up on that stage and perform for people. I mean, I don't need to say that to you.

Sebastian: It's gonna be incredible.

Mia: You don't get it but I'm terrified.

Sebastian: They should be lucky to see it. I can't wait.

Mia: I can. When do you leave? In the morning?

Sebastian: 6:45. Boise.

Mia: Boise?

Sebastian: Boise.

Mia: To Boise.

Sebastian: You should come.

Mia: To Boise?

Sebastian: Yeah. You can knock it off your bucket list.

Mia: Oh. That would be really exciting. I wish I could. What are you doing after the tour?

Sebastian: Why can't you?

Mia: Come to Boise?

Sebastian: Yeah.

Mia: 'cause I have to rehearse.

Sebastian: Yeah, but can't you rehearse anywhere?

Mia: Anywhere you are?

Sebastian: I mean—I guess.

Mia: Well, all my stuff is here and it's in two weeks. So I don't think really think that would be...

Sebastian: Okay.

Mia: The best idea right now, but... I wish I could.

Sebastian: We're just gonna have to try and see each other, you know, so that we can see each other.

Mia: I know, but when are you done?

Sebastian: What do you mean? I mean...

Mia: When you finish with the whole tour?

Sebastian: After we finish, we're gonna go to recording and then we'll go back on tour. You know, we tour so we can make the records so we can go back to tour the record.

Mia: So it's like the long haul?

Sebastian: What do you mean the "long haul"?

Mia: I mean the long haul that you're gonna stay in this band for a long time. On tour.

Sebastian: I mean, what did you think I was going to do?

Mia: I don't... I hadn't really thought it through. I didn't know the band...

Sebastian: You didn't think we would be successful?

Mia: No, that's not really what I mean. I just mean that y-you... I mean... you'll be on tour for what? Months now? Years?

Sebastian: Yeah, I don't mean—this is it... I mean, this is—it could feasibly be—yeah for... I could be on tour with this... for a couple of years, at least, just this record.

Mia: Do you like the music you're playing?

Sebastian: I don't. I don't know... What—what it matters?

Mia: Well, it matters because if you're going to give up your dream. I think it matters that you like what you're playing on the road for years.

Sebastian: Do you like the music that I play?

Mia: Yeah, I do. I just didn't think that you did.

Sebastian: Yeah well, you know...

Mia: You said Keith is the worst and now you're gonna be on tour with him for years. So I just didn't...

Sebastian: I don't know what—what are you doing right now?

Mia: Know if you were happy?

Sebastian: Why are you doing this?

Mia: I don't...

Sebastian: What do you mean "Why are you doing this?" And it just sounds like now you don't want me to do it.

Mia: What do you mean I wanted you to do this?

Sebastian: This is want you wanted for me.

Mia: To be in this band?

Sebastian: To be in a band to have a steady job. You know, t—to be... you know.

Mia: Of course, I wanted you to have a steady job so that you can take care of yourself and your life and you could start your club.

Sebastian: Yes, so I'm doing that so I don't understand why aren't we celebrating?

Mia: Why aren't you starting your club?

Sebastian: You said yourself no one wants to go to the club. No one wants to go the a club called "Chicken on a Stick."

Mia: So change the name!

Sebastian: Well, no one likes jazz! Not even you!

Mia: I do like jazz just because of you!

Sebastian: And this is what I thought you wanted me to do! What am I supposed to do? Go back to play *Jingle Bells*?

Mia: I'm not saying that! I'm saying why don't you take what you've made and start the club! People will wanna go to it because you're passionate about it and people love what other people are passionate about. You remind people of what they've forgotten.

Sebastian: Not in my experience. Well, whatever alright. It's... it's time to grow up, you know. I have a steady job, this is what I'm doing. And now all of a sudden if you had these problems, I wish you would've said them earlier before I signed on the goddamn dotted line.

Mia: I'm pointing out that you had a dream that you followed, that you were sticking...

Sebastian: This is the dream! This is the dream!

Mia: This is not your dream.

Sebastian: Guys like me work their whole lives to be in sth that's successful, that people like. You know? I mean, I'm finally in sth th-th-th-th-that people enjoy.

Mia: Since when do you care about being liked? Why do you care so much about being liked?

Sebastian: You are an actress! What are you talking about? Maybe you just liked me when I was on my ass because it made you feel better about yourself.

Mia: Are you kidding?

Sebastian: No. I don't know...

Clip 3

Sebastian: When do you find out?

Video Clip 3

Mia: They said the next couple of days. But I'm not expecting to find anything out.

Sebastian: You're gonna get it.

Mia: I really might not.

Sebastian: Yes, you are.

Mia: I don't want to be disappointed.

Sebastian: I know. I know these things.

Mia: Where are we?

Sebastian: Griffith Park.

Mia: Where are we?

Sebastian: I know. I don't know.

Mia: What do we do?

Sebastian: I don't think we could do anything. Because when you get this…

Mia: If I get this.

Sebastian: When you get this, you gotta give it everything you got. Everything. It's your dream.

Mia: What are you gonna do?

Sebastian: I gotta follow my own plan. Stay here and get my own thing doing. You'll be in Paris. Good jazz there. And you love jazz now. Right?

Mia: Yes.

Sebastian: I guess we're just gonna have to wait and see.

Mia: I'm always gonna love you.

Sebastian: I'm always gonna love you too. Look at this view.

Mia: I've seen better.

Sebastian: It's the worst.

Mia: Yeah. I've never been here during the day.

Clip 4

Mia's Husband: Do you wanna check it out?

Mia: Okay.

Mia's Husband: This place is pretty cool.

Video Clip 4

[*Applauce*]

Sebastian: Cal Bennett on the sax! Javier Gonzalez on trumpet. The lovely Nedra Wheeler on

bass. The one and only Cliffon "Fou Fou" Eddie on drums. And a little too good on

the piano. So good that he's gonna own this place if I'm not careful. Khirye Tyler,

everybody. Welcome to Seb's.

[*Sebastian playing the piano*]

Mia's Husband: You want to stay through another?

Mia: No, we should go.

Mia's Husband: Okay.

Sebastian: One, two, one, two, three, four.

New Words
incredible [ɪnˈkredəbl] *adj.* wonderful; unbelievably good 难以置信的，不可思议的
haul [hɔːl] *n.* the act of pulling 拖，拉
feasibly [ˈfiːzɪbəlɪ] *adv.* in a practicable manner; so as to be feasible 可行地
Phrases and Expressions
knock off: get rid of 除去
on my ass: in a tough situation 处境恶劣
Notes
Boise: the capital and most populous city of the US State of Idaho, and the county seat of Ada County 博伊西，美国爱达荷州首府
wanna: used in spoken English, meaning "want to" 想要……（等于 want to）

IV. Exercises for Understanding

1. Fill in the blanks according to the video clips you have watched.

(1) City of stars

Are you 1)_____ just for me?

City of stars

There's so much that I can't see

Who knows?

I felt it from the first 2)_____ I shared with you

That now our dreams

They've finally 3)_____

(2) Sebastian: And this is what I thought you 1)_____ me to do! What am I supposed to do? Go back to play 2)_____?

Mia: I'm not saying that! I'm saying why don't you take what you've made and start the 3)_____! People will wanna go to it because you're passionate about it and people love what other people are 4)_____ about. You 5)_____ people of what they've forgotten.

(3) Sebastian: When you get this, you gotta 1)_____ it everything you got. Everything. It's your 2)_____.

Mia: What are you gonna do?

Sebastian: I gotta 3)_____ my own plan. Stay here and get my own thing doing. You'll be in 4)_____. Good jazz there. And you love jazz now. Right?

Mia: Yes.

Sebastian: I guess we're just gonna have to 5)_____.

Mia: I'm always gonna 6)_____ you.

Sebastian: I'm always gonna 7)_____ you too.

2. Decide whether the following statements are true or false according to the video clips you have just watched. Write a "T" for true or an "F" for false.

_____(1) Sebastian falls in love with Mia because she is a famous actress.

_____(2) Mia quarrels with Sebastian because he can't make enough money.

_____(3) While Mia and Sebastian fight and reconcile, they don't end up together.

_____(4) When Mia returns to L. A., she comes across Sebastian's jazz club.

_____(5) In the end, Sebastian's conveying all his hopes, wishes, and longings about the life Mia and he could've had through every note that he plays.

3. Answer the following questions according to the video clips you have just watched.

(1) Why do Mia and Sebastian fight? What goes wrong in their process of communication?

(2) What do Mia and Sebastian decide to do after Mia's audition?

(3) What's conveyed by the last look Mia and Sebastian share?

Section B   Reading

What is communication? Communication generally refers to the process in which participants create and share information with one another as they move toward reaching mutual understanding. Whether you live in a city of Canada, a village in India, a commune in Israel, or the Amazon jungles of Brazil, you participate in the same activity when you communicate. The results and the methods might be different, but the process is the same.

As to the elements of communication, there are 10 of them. They are: context, sender, encoding, message, channel, receiver, decoding, response, feedback, and noise.

To understand the elements of communication, we have to mention our field of experience, or context. We each carry our own field of experience with us wherever we go. It is culture-specific. Although all aspects of a culture are part of the context, one of the most important aspects of culture is the establishment of the communication norms within the culture. Norms are the guidelines that we establish for conducting transactions. Norms exist at the beginning of a communication encounter and grow, change, or solidify as people get to know one another better. Norms tell us what kinds of message and behaviors are proper in a given context or with a particular person or group of people. Sometimes we don't know the norms. We have to learn them from experience.

Another important element in communication is message. It is the content of a communicative act. Communication takes place through the sending and receiving of messages. Everything a sender says or does has potential message value. The message is usually conveyed by a certain channel. A channel is both the route traveled by the message and the means of transportation. Messages are transmitted through a variety of sensory channels. We may use touch, smell, sound, sight, taste and so on to carry a message. Some channels are more effective at communicating certain messages than others, and the nature of the channels selected affects the way a message will be processed. Experiences show that most of us have channel preferences; that is, we prefer to rely on one or more channel while disregarding others. But in general, the more channels used to carry a message are, the more likely the communication will succeed. Most human communication is a mutual process rather than a one-way message flow. The participants frequently exchange roles as message originators and message receivers in the ongoing process of communication.

But communication is never perfectly effective. The receiver does not always decode a message into exactly the same meaning that the source had in mind when encoding the message. This is because of the noise. Noise is any stimulus, external or internal to the participants, that interferes with the sharing of meaning. Noise can be physical, psychological, perceptual, emotional, linguistic, and cultural. Much of our success as communicators depends on how we cope with these noises. The important point to remember is that noise can function as a communication barrier. As noise increases, the chances for effective communication usually decrease, and as noise decreases, the chances for effective communication usually rise. We must be fully aware of them.

Finally, after receiving the message, the receiver usually gives certain feedback to the sender. Feedback returns information to the sender of a message, thereby enabling the sender to determine whether the message has been received or correctly understood. In any situation, paying attention to both verbal and nonverbal feedback allows us to behave in ways that increase understanding of our message. Feedback serves useful functions for both senders and receivers. It provides senders with the opportunity to measure how they are coming across, and it provides receivers with the opportunity to exert some influence over the communication process.

Exercises for Understanding

1. Answer the following questions according to the passage you have just read.

(1) What channels do you usually prefer to use in communication? Why?

(2) What examples can you find to show that one channel is more effective than others in transmitting certain messages?

(3) What are the things that create noises in the process of communication?

(4) Why is feedback a very important element of communication?

2. Small group task: a contest of English expressions of Chinese culture.

Step 1: Divide the class into 2 groups.

Step 2: In five minutes, each group prepares 5 words or expressions in the Chinese language that represent Chinese culture.

Step 3: Each group hands in the 5 words or expressions to the teacher.

Step 4: Start the contest. Group A expresses in English the words and expressions written by

Group B. Group B expresses in English the words and expressions written by Group A.

The group wins one point when they express one word correctly. Take turns.

Step 5: The group that gets more points wins the game.

3. Choose the correct answers to the following questions.

(1) The process of communication includes _____ elements.

   A. six   B. ten   C. twelve   D. eleven

(2) _____ is the process of putting an idea into a symbol.

   A. Decoding   B. Channel   C. Encoding   D. Response

(3) _____ refers to the response of a receiver to a sender's message.

   A. Noise   B. Channel   C. Context   D. Feedback

(4) Non-verbal communication includes all of the following but _____.

   A. telephone messages   B. gestures   C. facial expressions   D. eye movements

4. Decide whether the following statements are true or false according to the passage you have just read. Write a "T" for true or an "F" for false.

_____(1) People acquire communication norms from their life experiences.

_____(2)There are rules for speakers to follow as to how messages are constructed and interpreted.

_____(3) Communication is a one-way flow.

_____(4) In most cases, intercultural communication is conducted without any cultural "noises."

_____(5) The sender plays a more important role than the receiver in communication.

5. Click (√) your preferable items in the table below and discuss with your partner the reason for your choices.

Test of Communication Skills	
(1) When trying to explain something, I ask my listeners if they are following me.	
○ Almost never	○ Rarely
○ Sometimes	○ Quite often
○ Most of the time	
(2) People do not get what I am saying.	
○ Almost never	○ Rarely
○ Sometimes	○ Quite often
○ Most of the time	

Test of Communication Skills	
(3) I manage to explain my ideas clearly.	
○ Almost never	○ Rarely
○ Sometimes	○ Quite often
○ Most of the time	
(4) I find it difficult to express my opinions when others do not share them.	
○ Almost never	○ Rarely
○ Sometimes	○ Quite often
○ Most of the time	
(5) When I do not understand a question, I ask for additional explanation.	
○ Almost never	○ Rarely
○ Sometimes	○ Quite often
○ Most of the time	
(6) I do not understand what other people are talking about.	
○ Almost never	○ Rarely
○ Sometimes	○ Quite often
○ Most of the time	
(7) I find it easy to see things from someone else's point of view.	
○ Almost never	○ Rarely
○ Sometimes	○ Quite often
○ Most of the time	
(8) I pretend to listen even if my mind drifts away.	
○ Almost never	○ Rarely
○ Sometimes	○ Quite often
○ Most of the time	
(9) I find it hard to express my feelings.	
○ Almost never	○ Rarely
○ Sometimes	○ Quite often
○ Most of the time	
(10) If I have something relevant to add, it is OK to interrupt what someone else is saying.	
○ Almost never	○ Rarely
○ Sometimes	○ Quite often
○ Most of the time	
(11) I can detect the mood of others by looking at them while we are conversing.	

Test of Communication Skills	
○ Almost never	○ Rarely
○ Sometimes	○ Quite often
○ Most of the time	
(12) When I know what the other person is going to say, I answer right away instead of waiting for them to finish.	
○ Almost never	○ Rarely
○ Sometimes	○ Quite often
○ Most of the time	
(13) I get so caught up in what I have to say that I am unaware of the expressions and reaction of my listeners.	
○ Almost never	○ Rarely
○ Sometimes	○ Quite often
○ Most of the time	
(14) My weaknesses are no one else's business and I am better at hiding them.	
○ Almost never	○ Rarely
○ Sometimes	○ Quite often
○ Most of the time	
(15) When I have the impression that I might have hurt someone's feelings, I apologize.	
○ Almost never	○ Rarely
○ Sometimes	○ Quite often
○ Most of the time	

Section C   Case

Scan and Listen

The Scenario

Where's the Bus?

It was National Day and everyone had a long weekend, so the Foreign Affairs Office of a large university in Shanghai arranged a trip for its foreign teachers to the city of Hangzhou. Almost all the foreign teachers decided to go. They were accompanied by a number of mostly monolingual Chinese guides from the Foreign Affairs Office as well as some young teachers from the English, German, French and Russian faculties who accompanied their colleagues to act as interpreters. Altogether about 50 teachers, guides, interpreters and Foreign Affairs Office staff traveled to Hangzhou on a university bus.

When they got to Hangzhou, they were unloaded at a hotel on the outskirts of the city, given a nice dinner, and told to meet in the lobby at 8 the next morning. In the morning, when they were ready to set off sightseeing, the teachers were told that they would be taking the city bus. They didn't understand why they should take the crowded city bus when they had a comfortable touring bus, with a driver, in which they had driven to Hangzhou.

In fact, the Foreign Affairs Office had found out only after they got there that the city of Hangzhou had passed the Emergency Traffic Control Regulation prohibiting buses without Hangzhou registrations from entering the city for the few days before, after, and including the holiday. The interpreters were told NOT to pass this information on to the foreigners, since non-Chinese "wouldn't be able to understand the reasons" for it. The interpreters were instructed simply to insist to the teachers that they had to take the city bus, or if necessary to make up a reason.

The foreign teachers demanded explanations from their interpreters, who tried to explain that they hadn't made the decision and didn't know the reason. When they could get no real answer, the foreigners resigned themselves to taking the city bus. The interpreters, who were also friends and colleagues, could see that not knowing what was going on was affecting their foreign friends' enjoyment of the trip, so one by one they revealed the reason to the foreign teachers. The teachers were then annoyed with the Foreign Affairs Office staff for trying to deceive them. "Why couldn't they just have told us the truth in the first place?" they asked.

The Foreign Affairs Office was annoyed with the interpreters for not following directions. They blamed the interpreters for the fact that the foreigners were annoyed. By evening, everyone was annoyed with someone, and the holiday was turning out to be no fun at all.

Exercise

Listen to the case above and answer the following questions.

(1) When were the foreign teachers in a Shanghai university arranged a trip to Hangzhou?

(2) Who accompanied the foreign teachers?

(3) How did they get to Hangzhou? Where did they stay?

(4) Why did they have to take the city bus to go sightseeing the next morning?

(5) Were they told the truth? Why or why not?

(6) How did they feel when they got the truth?

(7) What are the differences between Chinese and Americans in interpersonal communication?

Unit 3 Intercultural Communication

Section A Video Clip Appreciation

I. Introduction to the Movie *The Second Best Exotic Marigold Hotel*

As the contented residents of the hotel begin settling into their new lives, Sonny Kapoor strives to balance the demands of planning his wedding with the responsibilities of purchasing a new property. Meanwhile, new guests Guy Chambers and Lavinia Beech find themselves in a predicament after arriving at the hotel to find there is only one vacancy. Perhaps with a  little innovation, new co-manager Muriel Donnelly can find a means of accommodating the hotel's latest occupants, but she'll have her work cut out for her as Douglas Ainslie and Evelyn Greenslade begin their new careers in Jaipur while flirting with the idea of a serious romance, like Norman Cousins and Carol Parr. With romance in the air, it's no wonder that Madge Hardcastle has her pick of handsome suitors, and as stalwart Muriel safeguards the many secrets of the vivacious residents, Sonny and Sunaina learn that planning a traditional Indian wedding can be a true test of commitment.

II. Introduction to the Video Clips

Clip 1

As the *Best Exotic Marigold Hotel* has only a single remaining vacancy, posing a rooming predicament for two fresh arrivals, Sonny Kapoor pursues his expansionist dream of opening a second hotel. He and his business partner Muriel flow to America to look for an investor, believing that being a franchise of Evergreen, an American based conglomerate, is the best way to proceed. Evergreen's response is that they will send someone to Jaipur to investigate on their behalf.

Clip 2

The world is seemingly Sonny Kapoor's oyster. He is financially secure enough that he and Sunaina can now get married. The British retirees who hoped to stretch their pensions by relocating to Marigold Hotel in Jaipur, India, begin to pair off romantically. Muriel Donnelly who safeguards many secrets of the vivacious residents, reflects on her old days in the hotel and his thinking about life and death.

III. Script of the Video Clips

Clip 1

Sonny Kapoor: Breathe the air, Mrs. Donnelly!

Video Clip 1

Muriel Donnelly: I'm eating dust.

Sonny Kapoor: The wind in your hair!

Muriel Donnelly: Put the bloody top back on, Sonny!

Sonny Kapoor: I will not hear your negativity. Madam, this is Route 66 and we are most assuredly getting our kicks!

Chet (Bellman): Hi. I'm Chet and I'll be happy to valet your car.

Sonny Kapoor: Not as happy as we are that you are happy to do so, my friend.

Muriel Donnelly: Just tell me... Just tell me there's a cup of tea and a biscuit waiting inside.

Doorman: That's a great accent. Are you from Australia?

Sonny Kapoor: The sound of destiny, Madam... calling us with her siren song. And go to her we must! For this is our moment. If not now, when? And if not us, who?

Muriel Donnelly: Later? Somebody else?

Sonny Kapoor: My hand is powdered, so the shake is firm and dry. My clothes precisely walk the tightrope between casual and relaxed formality.

Muriel Donnelly: Sonny, Sonny. Let me do the talking. Alright?

Sonny Kapoor: Okay.

Sonny Kapoor: Mr. Burley. While I am aware that... convention dictates that I should wait for your assessment of our proposal... please take my interruption less as rudeness than proof... of our profound excitement at the opportunity to meet yourself... and your fine company. And let me say right here and now...

Muriel Donnelly: Alright, that's enough, that's enough.

Sonny Kapoor: We agreed that my colleague would do the speaking and rightly so for... while her language may be... salty, it has great economy and pith.

Mr. Burley: I don't care about any of that.

Muriel Donnelly: No, listen and learn, son. Tea is an herb that's been dried out. So to bring it back to life, you have to infuse it... in boiling water. That is boiling water. Everywhere I've been in this country... they slap down a cup of tepid nonsense... you know with the teabag lying beside it... which means I've got to go through the ridiculous business of dunking it... in the lukewarm piss... waiting for the slightest change of color to occur. And at my age... I haven't got the time.

Sonny Kapoor: This is what I'm talking about.

Mr. Burley: Get her some boiling water. Now, Mrs. Donnelly. Tell me more about your establishment.

Muriel Donnelly: We've been going properly for about eight months now. But phase two of the development is more or less complete. Like life and a tortoise. It's not exactly fast-moving...

Sonny Kapoor: Mrs. Evelyn Greenslade.

Mrs. Evelyn Greenslade: Here.

Muriel Donnelly: ...but you only make progress when you stick your neck out.

Sonny Kapoor: Mr. Douglas Ainslie.

Mr. Douglas Ainslie: Here.

Muriel Donnelly: We have guests that come and go.

Sonny Kapoor: Mrs. Muriel Donnelly.

Mrs. Muriel Donnelly: Here.

Muriel Donnelly: But there's been a hard core of regulars from the beginning.

Sonny Kapoor: Mrs. Madge Hardcastle.

Mrs. Madge Hardcastle: Here.

Sonny Kapoor: Mr. Norman Cousins and Miss Carol Parr.

Mr. Norman Cousins and Miss Carol Parr: Both here.

Muriel Donnelly: We have monthly check-ups at the local clinic... and Sonny takes a rollcall every morning.

Sonny Kapoor: A most valuable precaution to ensure that nobody has died in the night.

Muriel Donnelly: Most of our guests don't just live in India, they now work there.

Evelyn Greenslade: These are lovely.

Dealer Hari: That is why they cost 10,000 rupees each.

Evelyn Greenslade: Every day? We have to do this every day?

Dealer Hari: Process, madam. We must respect the process.

Evelyn Greenslade: Very well. You and I both know that since a fine, genuine pashmina... requires the annual growth of at least three Changra goats... you and everyone in this market blend the yarn to give it more body. The reason I come to this stall is that whereas Bharat over there uses wool... and Mohan goes with the rabbit fur... you at least use a reasonable quality of silk. I'll give you 5,000 for four.

Dealer Hari: Done.

Evelyn Greenslade: Thank you. I'll see you tomorrow, Hari.

Dealer Hari: Tomorrow, Miss Evelyn. And thank you for your respect.

Muriel Donnelly: Two of the guests have made themselves useful at the local expats club, which is, shall we say, a little down on its uppers.

Customer: Norman...

Norman Cousins: Mmm?

Customer: I know the membership's dropping, times are tight, but... do you really have to water down the wine?

Norman Cousins: What?! I uncorked it myself. They're on to us. Let's try the red.

Muriel Donnelly: And others are doing jobs they never thought they could do.

Douglas Ainslie: One Queen was so close to her elephant... that when she passed away, the elephant stood beside her tomb for three days... before dying of grief. We should all know such love, just not necessarily from an elephant.

Muriel Donnelly: And sometimes they're right, they can't.

Tourist: Uh, when were these built?

Douglas Ainslie: I'm sorry?

Tourist: What period are we talking about?

Douglas Ainslie: What, um... period? Ah, uh... yeah. Um...

Boy: 17th... 17th century.

Douglas Ainslie: 17th century.

Tourist: Sure?

Douglas Ainslie: Absolutely positive.

Boy: Wait, wait, wait. Maybe 18th.

Douglas Ainslie: Oh, oh, oh...

Boy: Please admire the beautifully carved...

Douglas Ainslie: Now please admire these beautifully carved pillars...

Boy: that are engraved with typical Rajasthani...

Douglas Ainslie: which are engraved with typical Rajasthani carvings, typical carvings which... And, um, you, you, you can see...

Muriel Donnelly: Look, I could talk and talk... but all that counts in the end is this one had an idea. I know, I know, but it works. The proof of our success is we are victims of it. The Marigold Hotel is full up.

Sonny Kapoor: With nobody checking out. Until the ultimate check-out.

Muriel Donnelly: So we have to expand. There's a local place we've got our eye on.

Sonny Kapoor: The Supreme Quality Hotel.

Muriel Donnelly: You put up the notes, we buy it. And we become the furthest outpost of the Sonny Evergreen franchise.

Sonny Kapoor: Leading to a chain of hotels stretching across India and beyond... for those such as... this great lady... whose face is a map of the world... and whose mind, though failing, still contains many of the secrets of the universe, who had the chance to say, when she left her home for the Best Exotic Marigold Hotel... as others will do... "Why die here... when I can die there?"

Mr. Burley: If you'll indulge me. Evergreen is a different concept. We believe that the... well that the leaves don't need to fall. That these years, the mature years... are an opportunity for travel, for further education... for different work situations. Well, in a word, an opportunity for life. And for passing on the value of that life to others. I take it you would agree with me, Mrs. Donnelly?

Muriel Donnelly: I'm here, aren't I?

Mr. Burley: Are you talking to other companies about this?

Muriel Donnelly: We came to you first.

Mr. Burley: We do have competitors.

Muriel Donnelly: Not in our eyes.

Clip 2

Video Clip 2

Muriel Donnelly: I never understood why anyone would want to get married. I barely found a bugger I could spend a week with... let alone a life. But I've been looking forward to this. And it turns out some things really are worth the wait. I'm not good with special occasions... or the gifts that go with them. So you'll have to make do with this letter instead. Written from the heart to the children I never had. I said at your party, I don't do advice. I do opinions. And my opinion of the groom is this: he gets plenty wrong... but never when it counts. And when he's right... (My friends...) it is something to behold.

Sonny Kapoor: I must tell you, the reception cannot take place at the Best Exotic Marigold Hotel. A bride as radiant as this one... deserves a more splendid setting for her wedding party... and I have just the place. Please, step into Vikram's beautiful minibus. And for those who are less close to it, or just move slower... you may use either of his cousin's and together... We shall ride to my new hotel! Don't look at me. —No, no, no. Don't look at him. Although, as the future unfolds, perhaps we will also take the Supreme Quality Hotel under our wing... and my old friend Kushal shall find himself working but a short distance beneath me... such is the level of my victorious magnanimity. But for now, to your chariots! And let us travel to the new jewel in my crown! The apple of my eye! Let us travel to the pearl in my oyster! No longer the Viceroy Club... but my gift on her wedding day... to the girl of my dreams, where I will welcome you. Ladies and gentle gentlemen... Oh, yes... to the Second Best Exotic Marigold Hotel! That is for you! Come! You see?

Douglas Ainslie: Ladies and Germs... I wonder if I could have your attention just for a moment. I have a few words I'd like to say. I cannot rest from travel: I will drink Life to the lees. All times have I enjoyed greatly... for always roaming with a hungry heart. Much have I seen and known; I am a part of all that I have met; Life piled on life Were all too little, and of one to me. Little remains; But every hour is saved. From that eternal silence, something more. A bringer of new things. A few words of Alfred, Lord Tennyson... speaking to something which we all know, and should never forget that every hour brings new things. And Sonny and Sunaina have today announced... that they want to face those hours... those things, this life together. And it's a privilege to be able... to send them on their way in such remarkable style. Actually, talking of style... I had a fairytale wedding myself. Although mine was Grimm.

Boy: Pause for laugh.

Douglas Ainslie: Moving on... The two things we can give our children, it seems to me... it seems to me, are roots and wings. And Sonny and Sunaina's wonderful families have given them roots... And now... they can take flight.

Evelyn Greenslade: Read this.

Douglas Ainslie: ...together... and as they embark on this...

Boy: Vegetarian, non-vegetarian...

Douglas Ainslie: journey, um, yeah, uh... journey on which we send them with all our love... and, and, and tremendous... you know... um, not obviously...

Boy: This is what the... the young... This is what the young make us remember...

Douglas Ainslie: For this is what the young make us remember...

Boy: that in the end...

Douglas Ainslie: ...that in the end, it's all very simple... that all it takes is to look into someone's eyes... and say... "Yes..." This is what I want. "And for them to reply..." It's what I want, too... And there's nothing to be afraid of. Evelyn and I would like to wish the two of you... all the love and luck in the world. And so say all of us. Sonny and Sunaina!

Carol Parr: If you really want to try monogamy, even though I think it's for the young and very naive... I suppose we could give it a go. Norman?

Chandrima: You lied to me.

Guy Chambers: Well... well, I'm not a hotel inspector anymore and I am gonna write that book. So, actually, everything I said was true... just a few days early, that's all.

Chandrima: What about your wife?

Guy Chambers: Well that, that was true already.

Chandrima: You were my first since my husband died.

Guy Chambers: You weren't the first. But I think you could be the last. Please... come dance with me... Chandrima. Sonny told me.

Chandrima: I'm gonna kill that boy.

Madge Hardcastle: Thank you for coming.

Driver Babul: You called. Left or right, my lady?

Madge Hardcastle: Sorry?

Driver Babul: When we reach the turning, do you want to go left or right?

Madge Hardcastle: What do you do when you're faced with a difficult decision?

Driver Babul: I don't believe there is such a thing. Throw a coin in the air and we always know which side we want it to land. Left or right, my lady?

Sonny Kapoor: Mrs. Donnelly? Mrs. Donnelly? Are you in there, Madam?

Muriel Donnelly: Piss off back to your wedding. I'm having a rest.

Sonny Kapoor: Yes. Of course. Sorry to disturb.

Muriel Donnelly: Did you forget your dancing shoes?

Sonny Kapoor: No, Madam.

Muriel Donnelly: Then go and knock them dead.

Sonny Kapoor: Yes, Madam.

Muriel Donnelly: Sonny...

Sonny Kapoor: I'm going. I'm going.

****

Mr. Burley: Is there no one on reception? I thought this was a hotel?

Muriel Donnelly: What are you doing here?

Mr. Burley: Checking on my investment.

Muriel Donnelly: You've come to the wrong place.

Mr. Burley: I don't think so. I couldn't find you at the party. How are you, Mrs. Donnelly?

Muriel Donnelly: Why did you come here, really?

Mr. Burley: To pay my respects to you. There's nothing I admire more than someone planting trees... under whose shade they may never get to sit.

Muriel Donnelly: Others will. That's what counts. How long are you staying?

Mr. Burley: I fly tomorrow morning. It's a punishing itinerary, I'm afraid. In which of your hotels do you think I should spend the night? Second or the first?

Muriel Donnelly: I don't think you'll get a lot of sleep over there. I... I have to deliver this... then I'll check you in.

Mr. Burley: Thank you, Mrs. Donnelly.

Muriel Donnelly: I know you'll understand me missing the reception... and I hope you'll forgive me for not coming to say goodbye. Go and have the honeymoon you deserve. I'm sure there'll be somebody there to see you off. Thank you. There is no such thing as an ending. Just a place where you leave the story. And it's your story now. I spent 40 years scrubbing floors... and the last months of my life as co-manager of a hotel... halfway across the world. You have no idea now what you will become. Don't try and control it. Let go. That's when the fun starts. Because as I once heard someone say... "There's no present like the time."

New Words

valet ['væleɪ] *v.* to park your car for you at a hotel or restaurant 伺候客人停车

tightrope ['taɪtroʊp] *n.* dangerous situation 危险的处境

dictate ['dɪkteɪt] *v.* to cause or influence 导致，影响

assessment [ə'sesmənt] *n.* the act of judging or assessing a person or situation or event 评价，评定

pith [pɪθ] *n.* the choicest or most essential or most vital part of some idea or experience 精髓，要旨

infuse [ɪn'fjuːz] *v.* to fill, as with a certain quality 倾注

tepid ['tepɪd] *adj.* moderately warm 微温的

dunk [dʌŋk] *v.* to immerse briefly into a liquid so as to wet, coat, or saturate 浸泡

rollcall ['roʊlkɔːl] *n.* the act of reading a list of names to a group of people to check who is there 点名

genuine ['dʒenjuɪn] *adj.* not fake 真的

pashmina [pæʃ'miːnə] *n.* a kind of textile material 羊绒（一种面料）

yam [jæm] *n.* a root vegetable like a potato with orange flesh that grows in tropical regions 山药

expat [,eks'pæt] *n.* a person who is living in a country that is not their own 移居国外者；侨民

grief [griːf] *n.* intense sorrow caused by loss of a loved one (especially by death) 悲痛，悲伤

franchise ['fræntʃaɪz] *n.* a business established or operated under an authorization to sell or distribute a company's goods or services in a particular area 获得特许经销权的机构

victorious [vɪk'tɔːriəs] *adj.* having won 胜利的

magnanimity [,mægnə'nɪməti] *n.* kindness and generosity toward someone, especially after defeating them or being treated badly by them 雅量，高尚

oyster ['ɔɪstər] *n.* marine mollusks having a rough irregular shell; found on the seabed mostly in coastal waters 牡蛎

privilege ['prɪvəlɪdʒ] *n.* a right reserved exclusively by a particular person or group (especially a hereditary or official right) 特权

itinerary [aɪˈtɪnəreri] *n.* an established line of travel or access 行程表

Phrases and Expressions

embark on: to start doing sth 从事；着手

piss off: If someone tells a person to piss off, they are telling the person in a rude way to go away. 滚开，走开

knock sb dead: to strongly impress one (often used as an imperative to give encouragement) 使……倾倒

Bharat: India（梵文）婆罗多，即印度

Exercises for Understanding

1. Decide whether the following statements are true or false according to the video clips you have just watched. Write a "T" for true or an "F" for false.

_____(1) Sonny Kapoor was driving so fast that Muriel Donnelly felt uncomfortable .

_____(2) Sonny Kapoor and the co-manager of the Marigold Hotel Muriel Donnelly, cooperated well with each other that they have finished the second phase of hotel establishment.

_____(3) Douglas Ainslie pretended to be a knowledgeable tour guide and a host with the help of a local Indian boy.

_____(4) Guy Chambers didn't fall in love with Chandrima because Chandrima wasn't the first woman in his life.

_____(5) Muriel Donnelly shows great affection towards Sonny Kapoor.

2. Fill in the blanks according to Video Clip 2 you have just watched.

I never understood why anyone would want to get married. I barely found a bugger I could spend a week with... (1) _____ a life. But I've been looking forward to this. And it turns out some things really are (2) _____. I'm not good with special occasions... or the gifts that go with them. So you'll have to make do with this letter instead. (3) _____ to the children I never had. I said at your party, I don't do advice. I do opinions. And my opinion of the groom is this: he gets plenty wrong... but never when it (4) _____. And when he's right... (My friends...) it is something to (5) _____.

I know you'll understand me missing the (6) _____... and I hope you'll forgive me for not coming to say goodbye. Go and have the (7) _____ you deserve. I'm sure there'll be somebody there to see you off. Thank you. There is no such thing as an ending. Just a place where you (8) _____ . And it's your story now. I spent 40 years scrubbing floors... and the last months of my life as of a (9) _____ hotel... halfway across the world. You have no idea now what you will become. Don't try and control it. Let go. That's when the fun starts. Because as I once heard someone say... "There's no (10) _____ ."

3. Answer the following questions according to the video clips you have just watched.

(1) Why does Muriel Donnelly say to Sonny Kapoor that she will do the talking when they went to the their future investor?

(2) Why does Muriel Donnelly insist that teabag should go together with boiling water?

(3) What does Sonny Kapoor do to ensure the clients in the Marigold Hotel are alive?

(4) How does Muriel Donnelly judge Sonny Kapoor?

(5) Why doesn't Madge Hardcastle tell the driver Babul to turn left or right?

Section B Reading

Intercultural communication is the communication between people whose cultural perceptions and symbol systems are distinct enough to alter the communication event. The need for intercultural communication is as old as humankind. From wandering tribes to traveling traders and religious missionaries, people have encountered others different from themselves. These earlier meetings, like those of today, were often confusing and hostile. The recognition of alien differences, and the human propensity to respond unkindly to them, were expressed more than 2,000 years ago by the Greek playwright Aeschylus, who wrote "Everyone's quick to blame the alien." This sentiment is still a powerful element in today's social and political rhetoric.

Although intercultural contact has a long history, today's intercultural encounters are far more numerous and of greater importance than in any previous time in the past. There are mainly three reasons, namely, the rise of new technology and information systems like communication networks, communication satellite, worldwide transportation, worldwide web, television, and so on; the changes in the world's population; and a shift in the world's economic, political and cultural arena.

First of all, McLuhan characterized today's world as a "global village" because of the rapid expansion of worldwide transportation and communication networks. The popularity of various communication networks, the exploration of communication satellites, the rapid development of worldwide transportation, the expansion of the Internet and all kinds of digital devices all contribute to the possibility and necessity of intercultural communication.

Besides, the swelling and migrating of world's population and changes in immigration patterns have also made it pressing for people to conduct intercultural communication. Within the boundaries of the United States, people are now redefining and rethinking the meaning of the word America. Neither the word nor the reality can any longer be used to describe a somewhat homogeneous group of people sharing a European heritage.

Last but not least, the shift in the world's economic, political and cultural arena after the World War Ⅱ calls for the study of intercultural communication. Globalization of economy especially has further brought people together. This expansion in globalization has resulted in multinational corporations participating in various international business arrangements such as joint ventures and licensing agreements. These and countless other economic ties mean that it would not be unusual for someone to work for an organization that does business in many countries.

With or without your desire or consent, you are now thrusted into contact with countless people who often appear alien, exotic, and perhaps even wondrous. Whether negotiating a major contract with the Chinese, discussing a joint venture with a German company, being supervised by someone from Mexico, counseling a young student from Cambodia, or working alongside some who speak no English, you encounter people with cultural backgrounds that are often strikingly different from your own.

Yet there is a fact that when people of different nationalities and ethnic origins who frequently speak different languages and hold different convictions attempt to work and live together, conflicts can easily arise.

The ineffectiveness of many international development projects, the failure to conduct American government programs designed to offer economic and scientific expertise to aid the developing countries in the 1950s were mainly due to the ignorance about the vital role culture plays in the process of communication. Intercultural communication study thus became important to address the problem of cultural illiteracy.

As intercultural communication study is of great significance nowadays, then how to study intercultural communication well? We should be fully aware of the four variables in intercultural communication study: perception, verbal processes, nonverbal processes, and contextual elements.

The variable of Perception , for example, includes beliefs, attitudes, values, and world views. These cultural value systems serve as message filters that determine, to a certain extent, the meaning each person assigns to the messages he/she encounters and thus, how to perceive the events these messages describe.

Take verbal processes or language for example. Language is a major means of communication, heavily influenced by the culture in which it is developed. It can be a great stumbling block in intercultural communication. A great language problem is the tenacity with which some people will cling to one meaning of a word or a phrase in the new language, regardless of connotation or context. The variations in possible meaning, especially when inflection and tone are varied, are so difficult to cope with that they are often waved aside. This complacency will stop a search for understanding.

For example, in American English, to be "embarrassed" is to feel mildly uncomfortable, but to Spanish speakers, to be "embarrassed" connotes "to be pregnant." That's why the Spanish translation of the English advertisement of the bottled ink produced by Parker Pen Company "To avoid embarrassment, use Parker SuperQuink" was decoded into "To avoid pregnancy, use Parker SuperQuink."

Another variable in intercultural communication study is nonverbal process. Learning the language, which most visitors to foreign countries consider their only barrier to understanding, is actually the beginning. To enter into a culture is to be able to hear its special "hum and buzz of implication." People from different cultures inhabit different sensory realities. They see, hear, feel, and smell only that which has some meaning or importance for them. They abstract whatever fits into their personal world of reorganization and then interpret it through the frame of reference of their own culture. The misinterpretation of observable nonverbal signs and symbols—such as gestures, postures, and other body movements—is a definite communication barrier. But it is possible to learn the meanings of these observable messages usually in informal rather than formal ways.

Culture strongly influences our subjective reality and there are direct links among culture, perception, and behavior.

Exercises for Understanding

1. Answer the following questions according to the passage you have just read.

(1) What are the reasons that bring about intercultural communication?

(2) What are the 4 variables in intercultural communication?

(3) How do Spanish people understand the meaning of being "embarrassed"?

(4) How do you understand a culture's hum and buzz of implication?

(5) Why is our subjective reality affected by culture?

2. Small group task.

In *Teaching Culture: Strategies for intercultural Communication*, Ned Seelye tells the following story: Some years ago some scholars conducted a research study to see how well American students studying abroad in Colombia (Latin America) could communicate with their Colombian hosts. The result of the study was that American students who already spoke better Spanish when they arrived in Colombia were more likely to have miscommunication problems with their hosts. Surprisingly, there were fewer communication problems between hosts and American students who didn't speak Spanish very well.

In groups, please discuss why the students who could speak better Spanish miscommunicate with their hosts.

Section C   Case

The Scenario

Scan and Listen

Are You Mad at Me?

Jeff was pleased to have been assigned an international student as his roommate in his second year at a small liberal arts college in the US. Ji Bing was an easy-going guy, a good listener, warm-hearted, and always ready for a new experience. He apprenticed Jeff's explanations of American life and unfamiliar language. Jeff didn't think Ji Bing was any more difficult to get along with than the American roommate he had the year before, except that he seemed to want to study more that Jeff was used to and he sometimes borrowed Jeff's things without asking first.

One night, Jeff was working on a project that required some artwork. Ji Bing was at his desk studying for a test. Jeff's scissors were just too dull to do the job, so he asked Ji Bing, "Sorry to bother you while you're studying, but could I use your scissors for a while?"

Ji Bing said, "Sure," opened his desk drawer and handed Jeff the scissors. "Thanks, thanks a lot," Jeff said. A few minutes later, Jeff decided that his crayons were not going to do the trick. He addressed his roommate again, "Sorry to bug you again, but these crayons make this look like kindergarten. You know those colored pencils you have? Would it be OK if I used them for my project?"

Ji Bing got up and got them off the shelf and said, "Help yourself," and went back to reading as Jeff thanked him.

After another few minutes, Jeff said, "I must be driving you crazy, but have you got any glue or tape? Promise I will buy you another roll."

Ji Bing handed Jeff a role of tape that was on his desk saying, "Use as mush as you want. I don't need it." "Appreciate it," mumbled Jeff as he went back to his project.

Ji Bing went back to reading. As Jeff was finishing his project, he noticed that Ji Bing was watching him. He looked up and was surprised to hear his Chinese roommate ask him in a plaintive tone, "Are you mad at me?"

"Of course not," Jeff replied, "What makes you think like that?"

Exercise

Listen to the case above and answer the following questions.

(1) What is Ji Bing like in terms of characteristics in the eyes of Jeff when they first become roomates?

(2) Why does Ji Bing suspect that Jeff is mad?

(3) What answer will Ji Bing give to Jeff's question?

(4) What are the differences in what American and Chinese young people expect from their friends?

(5) Give advice to both Jeff and Ji Bing on how to handle their relationship.

Module 2
Cultural Value Orientations

Unit 4　Hofstede's Cultural Dimensions

　Video Clip Appreciation

I. Introduction to the movie *Monsoon Wedding*

It's a story set in the modern upper-middle class of India, where telecommunications and a western lifestyle mix with old traditions. Young Aditi accepts the arranged wedding when she ends the affair with a married TV producer. The groom, Hermant Rai, is an Indian living in Houston, Texas, US. All relatives from both families, some from distant places like Australia, come to New Delhi during the monsoon season to attend the wedding. The four-day arrangements and celebrations will see clumsy organization, family parties and drama, dangers to the happy end of the wedding, lots of music and even a new romance for the wedding planner Dubey with the housemaid Alice.

II. Introduction to the Video Clips

Clip 1

Aditi's father is calling P. K. Dubey, a wedding contractor, who is running far behind schedule.

Clip 2

The groom's family and guests begin to arrive, from all over India, US and Australia. The whole family comes together from all corners of the globe for the wedding.

Clip 3

The Verma family and guests are sitting around a table and chatting.

Clip 4

Pimmi Verma talks to her husband, hoping he could reconsider his decision to send their son to boarding school.

III. Script of the Video Clips

Clip 1

Video Clip 1

Lalit Verma: Dubey! Dubey!

Pimmi Verma: Not here.

Lalit Verma: Not here yet? He's an impossible fellow! Nearly 11:00. How to fix this? Pimmi, please bring the phone.

Pimmi Verma: Darling, you want something else? Tea? Nimbu pani?

Lalit Verma: No, no. That bloody bastard Dubey hasn't come yet. He wants money but doesn't want to work. Dubeyji? Lalit Verma, who else? Very kind of you to answer. What's going on? No sign of anyone.

Pimmi Verma: Alice? Alice? Fry the pakoras. Tea for the master. Hurry!

Shashi Chadha: Pimmi, I'm sorry to say. Lalit takes on too much tension. It's not good. You see all these young men getting heart attacks these days.

Ria's Mother: God forbid it! The wedding is so soon. And Lalit is doing everything single-handedly. Hundreds of things to get tense about.

Lalit Verma: The marigold gate is falling apart. The flowers are everywhere. What's going on?

P. K. Dubey: No need to get so upset, sir. Flowers? What's a few flowers? For you, I'll bring Kashmir's Mughal garden. Just say the word. I'm stranded in a traffic jam.

Lalit Verma: Enough! Get here on the double.

P. K. Dubey: Ten minutes, exactly and approximately. I can't phone and drive.

Lalit Verma: What's the idiot up to? Left, left, you idiot! Stop the car! You'll spoil the decorations also. Don't you even know how to drive?

Rahul Chadha: I've only got one hand to drive with.

Lalit Verma: Who told you to break your hand at this time, idiot? Where were you?

Rahul Chadha: I went to the airport to get your sister and her husband.

Lalit Verma: Where are they?

Rahul Chadha: I didn't see them.

Lalit Verma: You are incredible. What do you mean, you didn't see them?

Rahul Chadha: I don't even know what they look like.

Lalit Verma: Hold up a placard: "Mr. and Mrs. Tej Puri from USA." They could have seen you. Why are you yawning so much?

Rahul Chadha: I've hardly slept. Not to mention I got back from Australia just yesterday.

Lalit Verma: You young people! What do you need to sleep so much for? What time is the flight coming?

Rahul Chadha: About 9:00.

Lalit Verma: Make sure you're there on time. And take this car, okay?

Rahul Chadha: Okay.

Lalit Verma: Don't run the AC when you're going to receive them. And only run the AC when you've received them. And park this car somewhere else!

Rahul Chadha: Chill.

Lalit Verma: And take off that stupid topi.

****

Pimmi Verma: Oh, God, Varun, what are you doing with that? Why haven't you got ready? Didn't you hear Papa? He's getting so angry.

Varun Verma: It's the last step! Coconut curry, Ma.

Pimmi Verma: No, no. Now, hurry up. Don't give me a hard time. And this TV, I'm so sick of it! Take this off. Hurry up.

Varun Verma: Ma, what are you doing? I'll do it myself.

Pimmi Verma: What "wear it yourself"? I'll wear it myself. The guests are on their way. Did you change your underwear?

Varun Verma: Ma!

Pimmi Verma: Did you? Out with the truth! Are you wearing dirty ones from yesterday? I just hope they're not smelling. You're such a silly little boy.

Varun Verma: "Little"?

Pimmi Verma: Oh, God!

Clip 2

[*In the garden*]

Lalit Verma: Pimmi, come on!

Video Clip 2

Alice: The groom! The groom is here!

Aditi Verma: Oh, shit.

Lalit Verma: Welcome, welcome. Congratulations, Mr. Rai!

Mohan Rai: Thank you, thank you.

Lalit Verma: This is Pimmi's brother from Muscat. Rahul, come here!

Hermant Rai: It's okay, it's okay.

Lalit Verma: So, excited? Soon to be in family way! So, you like India?

Hermant Rai: Yeah.

Lalit Verma: Better than Houston, no? Good, good, good. India needs young men like you. Yes, computer engineers are India's biggest export.

Varun Verma: Am I a coolie or what?

[*In the house*]

Lalit Verma: Bhai-sahab, what would you like to drink?

Mohan Rai: Scotch, please on the "rockiolis."

Lalit Verma: "Rockiolis" means ice?

Mohan Rai: Two lumps, exactly.

Lalit Verma: Exactly.

Saroj Rai: I'll have the same, thanks.

Lalit Verma: Rahul, two whiskies here. Two cubes of ice exactly.

Mohan Rai: Oh, my goodness. Look at you! How lovely you look.

C. L. Chadha: Rockioli, rockioli. Mrs. Rai over there.

Lalit Verma: Pay your respects to Grandmother.

Ria Verma: Hi. Congratulations.

Hermant Rai: Hi.

Grandmother: Look what I have for you. Know why God arranged your marriage in a hurry? I told him I had to see a great-grandson before dying. He heard me! How beautiful! So fair and lovely.

Pimmi Verma: Say hello to Hermant.

Hermant Rai: Hi. How are you?

Aditi Verma: Fine.

Shashi Chadha: Enough! Give them some privacy. I met C. L. only once, and we got married right away!

Ria's Mother: Don't you feel like getting married?

Lalit Verma: Rahul, idiot, come here. Come here and hold the camera. Listen. Come on, put it on. Camera on! On the ring!

D. L. Chadha: Sweeten your mouths, my dears.

Lalit Verma: Just in time! My dear brother-in-law! Look at hime.

Vijaya: This is Varun? He's almost a young man.

Lalit Verma: How did you manage? I sent Rahul to airport, told me flight was late.

Tej Puri: No, it was not late. Nobody was there at the airport, so we took a cab.

Lalit Verma: You had to take a cab?

Tej Puri: It's okay.

Lalit Verma: Rahul, you idiot, I sent you to the airport to receive them. You come back and tell me the flight was late? What a complete idiot!

Shashi Chadha: He's been working day and night. He doesn't know India.

Lalit Verma: But he's number one most stupid duffer.

Shashi Chadha: I'm sorry to say, but I don't like this! Calls my son an idiot, then calls him a duffer. Who does he think he is? I'm not coming back to India.

Lalit Verma: Bhai-sahab, this is Mr. Tej Puri, married to my sister Vijaya. After my older brother Surinder bhai-sahab passed away, Tej bhai has been the hero of the family. He has really looked after us. Come and meet Hermant.

Tej Puri: Yes. Excuse me.

Lalit Verma: Excuse me.

Vijaya: My naughty niece, couldn't you wait? You know how difficult it was to get tickets at this time of the year?

Lalit Verma: Difficult or not, we would have brought you here first-class if we had to. We couldn't have had the shadi without you, my darling sister.

Tej Puri: Nothing would have stopped us.

Tej Puri: Ria? Is that you? Come here, come here, come here. God bless. Very good.

Clip 3

Lalit Verma: Paaji, would you like a cigar?

Tej Puri: I quit.

Lalit Verma: America makes everyone quit smoking.

Vijaya: The Rais are so cultured.

Lalit Verma: Speak a little English and you become a very cultured family.

Video Clip 3

Lalit Verma: Tej bhai-sahab, I wanted to talk to you about Ria's plans. Ria, come here a minute, please. Ria wants to study in America.

Tej Puri: Is that so?

Lalit Verma: We're hoping you could give us some advice.

Vijaya: What do you want to do?

Ria Verma: I'm applying for creative writing programs.

Lalit Verma: She wants to be a writer.

Tej Puri: Very good.

Ria's Mother: Have you thought of the budget? Where will the money come from? My teacher's salary? Make her understand. Why can't she be like Aditi and do the right thing at the right time?

C. L. Chadha: Lots of money in writing these days. That girl who won the Booker Prize became an overnight millionaire!

Lalit Verma: Absolutely! Just one book. Who knows? It might happen.

Shashi Chadha: You must go to the States. You Know saada Umang is also there.

Tej Puri: You must give us his phone number.

Shashi Chadha: He's coming here tonight. We're hoping Ria and Umang will like each other.

C. L. Chadha: Two weddings in one!

Lalit Verma: Umang? What are the chances of getting hooked?

Ria Verma: Bad.

D. L. Chadha: I have another joke. Nonvegetarian!

Lalit Verma: Save the jokes for the sangeet. He'll be the MC at the sangeet.

E. L. Chadha: Let me start rehearsing, then.

Aditi Verma: Varun, out!

Varun Verma: What's your problem anyway?

Aditi Verma: Out! I can't have some privacy in my own house?

Lalit Verma: Varun, what happened to you?

Tej Puri: Okay, okay, I have an announcement to make. I'm thinking that if Ria wants to study in America... I will fund her entire education. No, no arguments. This is my family. I won't listen to you or Ria's mother. You see, Lalit, Ria is a sensible girl, If she wants to write, we must encourage her.

Lalit Verma: I can still work.

Tej Puri: This is final! We'll talk about it later, okay? Now you tell us what needs to be done for the wedding.

Vijaya: Absolutely. Now you don't have to worry about anything. We're here, we take care of everything.

Tej Puri: Anything.

Lalit Verma: My God, I don't know what to say. This is enough for me that we are all here together. My God! Pimmi, it's wonderful, no? After so many years. After Surinder bhai-sahab passed away... I think this is the fisrt time the whole family's here together. Ria, Ria, Ria. Don't cry. I know you are missing him. We are all missing your father. But he is here with us. Your papa is always blessing our family.

Clip 4

Pimmi Verma: I've been thinking, Lalit. I don't want to send Varun to boarding school.

Lalit Verma: Don't start again.

Pimmi Verma: I don't want to lose both my children.

Lalit Verma: Pimmi, don't start over again, huh? We've been through all this. He's going to boarding school, and that's final. He's wasting his life, staying here watching TV the whole day. There's no one here to discipline him. He doesn't listen. I give up. I don't know what to do.

Video Clip 4

Pimmi Verma: He also needs love and affection. He's such a sensitive boy and he's so wonderful with all these creative things.

Lalit Verma: Creative things like singing and dancing, cooking sesame chicken. Let's find him a nice boy.

Pimmi Verma: Don't say that. Why do you always look at everything like that?

Lalit Verma: You know what he told Tej bhai-sahab he wants to be when he grows up?

Pimmi Verma: What?

Lalit Verma: He said he wants to be a chef. I tell you. Our son will be a cook. A cook!

Pimmi Verma: He's just a kid. It doesn't mean anything.

Lalit Verma: He's a fool. My son will be a man when he grows up, understand? He'll be an educated professional. He won't be singing and dancing in people's shadis.

Varun Verma: Mama. Can you do this for me? Make a mucchi and on my eyes?

Pimmi Verma: Why, beta?

Varun Verma: For my dance with Ayesha tonight.

Pimmi Verma: Okay.

Lalit Verma: Why can't you do sth useful? Like some exercise or reading your schoolbooks for a change. Look at you, a big huge hulk. Can't spend your whole life singing and dancing.

Varun Verma: Why not?

Lalit Verma: What do you mean, why not? You want to be an entertainer? You don't do any exercise. You don't even play cricket. You don't read a book. Just sleeping all day and watching TV... and now this new nonsense, dancing!

Varun Verma: Why? You also took Mama's dupatta and danced the night.

Lalit Verma: Don't compare yourself with me. You're just a kid.

Varun Verma: But right now you said I'm big now.

Lalit Verma: That's it. You're going to boarding school. Decided!

Varun Verma: Since when?

Pimmi Verma: Beta, Papa and I are only talking about it.

Lalit Verma: No, I have made up my mind. We are not...

Pimmi Verma: Let me talk to him. It's going to be good for you. Soon Aditi's going away. You'll be so lonely at home. So we thought you'd go to boarding school. You'll have so much fun.

Varun Verma: You also have been trying to send me away to boarding school.

Pimmi Verma: No, beta. Nothing has been decided. That school is much better than this school. We thought you'll go there and there'll be so many boys your age. You'll really enjoy yourself.

Varun Verma: No, I don't want to go. I won't go. You do what you want.

Lalit Verma: We're just doing this for your own good. It'll make you a bit tougher. It'll be good for you.

Varun Verma: I hate you! I hate you both! You don't even understand one thing about me.

Lalit Verma: Don't you talk to me like that!

Varun Verma: Fine! I just won't talk to you at all.

Pimmi Verma: Varun.

Varun Verma: No.

Pimmi Verma: Please, son. Listen to me.

Varun Verma: Leave me alone!

Pimmi Verma: Happy now? Happy with what you've done?

Lalit Verma: I didn't mean to upset him like that. Why couldn't you say sth?

Pimmi Verma: Don't talk to me, okay? Just don't talk to me.

New Words

monsoon [ˌmɑːnˈsuːn] *n.* a period of heavy rain in summer in South Asia （南亚地区的）雨季

contractor [ˈkɑːntræktər] *n.* a person or company that has a contract to do work or provides goods or services for another company 承包商；承包公司

pakora [pəˈkɔːrə] *n.* a flat piece of spicy South Asian food consisting of meat or vegetables fried in batter （南亚）油炸辣肉菜片

strand [strænd] *v.* to leave sb in a place from which they have no way of leaving 使滞留

placard [ˈplækɑːrd] *n.* a large written or printed notice that is put in a public place or carried on a stick in a march 标语牌；广告牌

topi [ˈtoʊpi] *n.* a light hard hat worn to give protection from the sun in very hot places 遮阳帽

lump [lʌmp] *n.* a piece of sth hard or solid, usually without a particular shape 块

sesame [ˈsesəmi] *n.* a tropical plant grown for its seeds and their oil that are used in cooking 芝麻

hulk [hʌlk] *n.* a large, clumsy-looking person 身躯巨大且笨重的人

dupatta [dʊˈpʌtə] *n.* a long piece of material worn around the head and neck by women in South Asia 围巾，头巾

Phrases and Expressions

nimbu pani: lemonade 柠檬水

AC: air conditioner 空调

MC: master of ceremony 司仪，仪式主持人

Notes

marigold flower: Marigolds are one of the traditional flowers used in garlands and offerings in South Asia. Marigolds are widely used in all kinds of rites and rituals. It represents and symbolizes marriages, celebrations, romance and more. 万寿菊；金盏花

Exercises for Understanding

Video Clip 1

1. Answer the following questions according to the video clip you have just watched.

(1) Is Lalit satisfied with Dubey's service? Why or why not?

(2) Why is Lalit so tense and angry?

(3) What's wrong with the marigold gate?

(4) Why does the mother help her son change clothes?

2. Decide whether the following statements are true or false according to the video clip you have just watched. Write a "T" for true or an "F" for false.

_____(1) The father of the bride-to-be is stressed making arrangements for his daughter's wedding.

_____(2) The wedding contractor is driving when he gets Lalit's phone call.

_____(3) The young man Rahul came back from America for the wedding.

_____(4) Varun is watching a cooking show on TV when his mother walks in.

Video Clip 2

1. Answer the following questions according to the video clip you have just watched.

(1) Has Aditi met Hermant before? How do you know?

(2) Do the groom's family like Aditi? How do you know?

(3) After watching this video clip, could you describe the engagement ceremony?

2. Decide whether the following statements are True or False according to the video clip you have just watched. Write a "T" for true or an "F" for false.

_____(1) The groom works as a computer engineer in Houston, US.

_____(2) Lalit's sister and brother-in-law had to take a taxi because their flight was late and nobody was at the airport to meet them.

_____(3) Rahul's mother is not happy about what Lalit said about her son.

_____(4) Lalit's brother-in-law has helped the Verma family a lot since Lalit's big brother passed away.

Video Clip 3

1. Answer the following questions according to the video clip you have just watched.

(1) What does Ria want to do in America?

(2) What do the Verma family think of the idea of becoming a writer?

(3) What does Lalit think of his brother-in-law's proposal to fund Ria's education in America?

2. Decide whether the following statements are true or false according to the video clip you have just watched. Write a "T" for true or an "F" for false.

_____(1) Lalit wants to talk to his brother-in-law about the wedding preparation.

_____(2) Ria is the daughter of Lalit's old brother who passed away years ago.

_____(3) The MC begin to rehearse for the wedding and everybody in the house joins the singing and dancing.

Video Clip 4

1. Answer the following questions according to the video clip you have just watched.

(1) Why doesn't Pimmi want to send Varun to boarding school?

(2) Why does Lalit want to send Varun to boarding school?

(3) What does Varun want to do when he grows up?

(4) What does Lalit want his son to be when he grows up? Why?

(5) Who has the final say over whether to send Varun to boarding school? How do you know?

2. Decide whether the following statements are true or false according to the video clip you have just watched. Write a "T" for true or an "F" for false.

_____(1) The mother thinks her son is sensitive and creative.

_____(2) The father likes his son's hobbies of singing, dancing and cooking.

_____(3) Varun wants to be a chef when he grows up, but his parents don't like the idea.

_____(4) Varun doesn't want to go to boarding school and is angry at his parents.

Section B **Reading**

In 1970s, Dutch researcher Geert Hofstede conducted opinion surveys of employees of IBM, a large multinational business organization around the world. He then used statistical methods to analyze the responses to the surveys. From the analysis he identified four pairs of contrasting values that he used to compare values across cultures. He found a way to assign each country a score for each pair of contrasting values, and a rank was assigned according to the scores. Hofstede's study was later expanded by replication studies of the IBM research and the extended IBM models: the Chinese Value Survey and the World Values Survey. In this unit, the data about the ranks of the countries and regions are based on the IBM research and its replications, which give scores for seventy-six countries and regions.

The four pairs of contrasting values Hofstede identified are: individualism vs. collectivism, high and low power distances, masculinity vs. femininity, strong and weak uncertainty avoidance. Hofstede used the term "dimension" to refer to the contrasting values. A dimension is an aspect of a culture that can be measured relative to other cultures. More recently abundant research has shown that Hofstede's dimensional model applies not only to work-related values but also to cultural values in general.

Individualism vs. Collectivism

In Hofstede's research there are two pairs of contrasting values to describe social relationships, power distance and individualism vs. collectivism.

According to Hofstede, individualism pertains to societies in which the ties between individuals are loose: everyone is expected to look after himself or herself and his or her immediate family. Collectivism as its opposite pertains to societies in which people from birth onward are integrated into strong, cohesive in-groups, which throughout people's lifetime continue to protect them in exchange for unquestioning loyalty.

According to Hofstede's research, Western cultures tend to be individualist, and the countries in Hofstede's study that received the highest scores for individualism were (in order): the United States, Australia, Great Britain, Canada, Hungary, the Netherlands, and New Zealand. In contrast, the cultures of Asian countries such as China, Singapore, Thailand and Vietnam (all the four countries had an index of 20, and ranked No.58 out of 76 countries and regions) ranked much lower on the individualism scale, so were considered much more collectivist.

A minority of people in our world live in societies in which the interests of the individual prevail over the interests of the group, societies that we call individualist. An individualist culture is one in which people tend to view themselves as individuals and to emphasize the needs of individuals. It has the following components. First, the individual is the single most important unit in any social setting. Westerners tend to believe that individuals should make decisions for themselves, and that individuals should take credit and responsibility for what they have personally done. Second, independence rather than interdependence is stressed. Westerner tend to believe that people should rely on themselves as much as possible—and they usually expect other people to do the same. Third, individual achievement is rewarded. Lastly, the uniqueness of each individual is of paramount value. A person's rights and privacy prevail over group considerations in an individualistic culture. Westerners generally feel that the rights of individuals should not be subordinated to the needs of a large group, or at least that individuals should have the right to decide for themselves whether to sacrifice their personal benefit for the sake of the group. Individualists are likely to belong to many groups but retain only weak ties, changing membership when desired.

The majority of the world's population live in societies in which the interest of the group prevails over the interest of the individual. We call these societies collectivist. A collectivist culture is one in which people tend to view themselves as members of groups (families, work units, tribes, nations), and usually consider the needs of the group to be more important than the needs of individuals. In collective cultures, relationships form a rigid social framework that distinguishes between in-groups and out-groups. People rely on their in-groups (e.g. family, tribe, clan, organization) to look after them, and in exchange they believe they owe loyalty to that group. In collective cultures, the individual is emotionally dependent on organizations and institutions, and group membership is emphasized. The importance of the group in collective societies is shown by a Chinese proverb: "No matter how stout, one beam cannot support a house."

The individualism-collectivism dimension produces variations in family structures, how classroom activities are conducted, the way organizations manage work groups, and even how the individual conducts social relations. In a learning environment, a collective classroom will stress harmony and cooperation rather than competition.

There are two very important things we need to remember about the difference between individualist and collectivist cultures. First, saying that Western culture is individualist does not mean that all Westerners are always individualist. For example, in many Western countries there is a strong emphasis on teamwork, and we can see this in the popularity of team sports, through which young people are taught to work together and make sacrifices for the good of the team. So, while it is generally true that Westerners think and act in individualist ways more than people in collectivist cultures do, the difference between individualist and collectivist cultures is relative rather than absolute. Second, not all Western countries are equally individualist, and some Western countries tend to be more individualist than others. Likewise, while the cultures of East Asia all tend to be more or less collectivist, they also differ from each other in many important ways.

Power Distance

Another cultural values dimension about social relationship revealed by Hofstede's research is power distance, which classifies cultures on a continuum of high and low power distance. Every society has hierarchy to some degree. In other words, some people have a higher rank and more power than others. Power distance is concerned with how societies manage the fact that people are unequal. According to Hofstede, power distance refers to the extent to which the less powerful members of institutions and organizations within a country expect and accept that power is distributed unequally. In this sense, institution refers to family, school, and community, while organizations are the places where people work. So power distance is described based on the value system of the less powerful members. The way power is distributed is usually explained from the behavior of the more powerful members, the leaders rather than those led.

According to Hofstede's research, among the countries that received the highest scores for power distance were (in order) Malaysia, the Philippines, Russia, Mexico, China (ranked No.14), Indonesia, India, and Singapore. The countries that received the lowest scores for power distance included Ireland, Switzerland, New Zealand, Denmark, Israel and Austria, with Austria at the lowest end.

Individuals from high power distance cultures accept power as part of society. Superiors consider their subordinates to be different from themselves and vice versa. People in high power distance countries or regions believe that power and authority are facts of life. Both consciously and unconsciously, these cultures teach their members that people are not equal in this world and that everybody has a rightful place which is clearly marked by countless societal hierarchies. In organizations in high power distance cultures, there is a greater centralization of power, more recognition and use of rank and status, and adherence to established lines of authority.

Low power distance countries or regions hold that inequality in society should be minimized. Cultures referred to as "low power distance" are guided by laws, norms, and everyday behaviors that make power distinctions as minimal as possible. Subordinates and superiors consider each other as equals. People in power, be they supervisors, managers, or government officials, often interact with their constituents and try to look less powerful than they really are. In low power distance work centers, you might observe decisions being shared, subordinates being consulted, bosses relying on support teams, and status symbols being kept to a minimum.

We can observe signs of power distance dimension in nearly every social setting, for example, in family, at school and in the workplace. In the high-power-distance situation, children are expected to be obedient toward their parents while in low-power-distance situation, children are more or less treated as equals as soon as they are able to act. In the high-power-distance situation, teachers are treated with respect, and seldom publicly contradicted or criticized, while in the low-power-distance situation, teachers are supposed to treat the students as basic equals and expect to be treated as equals by the students.

In North American companies there are always differences in position and power, but in daily conversation many North Americans try to interact as if there were no such differences.

So, for example, in many US organization the norm is for people to address each other by first names, thus minimizing the appearance of rank differences. Also, a boss is generally more liked by employees if he or she acts like "one of the guys" and doesn't "pull rank" too often.

Masculinity vs. Femininity

According to Hofstede, the words masculinity and femininity refer to the degree to which masculine or feminine traits are valued and revealed. His rational is that many masculine and feminine behaviors are learned and mediated by cultural norms and traditions. For better understanding, we can use the terms "career success" and "quality of life" to convey the meaning behind this dimension.

According to Hofstede's research, the countries that received the highest masculinity-index scores were (in order): Slovakia, Japan, Hungary, Austria, Venezuela, Switzerland, Italy, Mexico, Ireland, Jamaica, China (ranked No.11 out of 76 countries), Germany, Great Britain, and the Philippines. The countries with the lowest masculinity-index scores were Denmark, the Netherlands, Latvia, Norway and Sweden, with Sweden at the lowest end.

Masculinity is the extent to which the dominant values in a society are male-oriented. A society is masculine when emotional gender roles are clearly distinct: men are supposed to be assertive, tough, and focused on material success, whereas women are supposed to be more modest, tender, and concerned with the quality of life. Masculine, or career success, oriented cultures have highly defined gender roles and promote achievement in the workplace. Assertiveness and the acquisitive of money are emphasized and often take precedence over interpersonal relationships.

Cultures that value femininity as a trait stress nurturing behaviors. A society is feminine when emotional gender roles overlap: both men and women are supposed to be modest, tender, and concerned with the quality of life. A feminine worldview maintains that men need not be assertive and that they can assume nurturing roles. It also promotes sexual equality and holds that people and the environment are important. Interdependence is ideal and people sympathize with the less fortunate.

In all cultures, men and women adopt distinct norms of socialization and tend to play differentiated roles in society. However, different cultural expectations of male and female occur across cultures. We can observe signs of masculinity-femininity dimension in family and school settings.

In the family, the stability of gender role patterns is almost entirely a matter of socialization. Socialization means that both girls and boys learn their place in society, and once they have learned it, the majority of them want it that way. Boys in a masculine society are socialized toward assertiveness, ambition, and competition. When they grow up, they are expected to aspire to career advancement. The family within a feminine society socializes children toward modesty and solidarity, and in these societies both men and women may or may not be ambitious and may or may not want a career.

In feminine cultures, teachers will rather praise weaker students, in order to encourage them, than openly praise good students. As Hofstede noticed in his own teaching experience with students from all over the world, students from masculine countries may ask to take an exam again after passing with a mediocre grade, while Dutch students almost never do so. He concluded that in the more feminine cultures, the average students are considered the norm, while in more masculine countries, the best students are the norm. Parents in these masculine countries expect their children to try to match the best. The "best boy in class" in the Netherlands is a somewhat ridiculous figure.

Uncertainty Avoidance

All human beings have to face the fact that we do not know what will happen tomorrow: the future is uncertain. However, cultures vary in their ability to tolerate ambiguity and unpredictability. As the term is used in Hofstede's research, uncertainty avoidance refers to the extent to which the members of a culture feel threatened by ambiguous or unknown situations.

According to Hofstede's research, the countries that received the highest uncertainty avoidance index scores included Greece, Portugal, Belgium, Russia, Poland, Japan. Countries with the lowest uncertainty avoidance index scores included the United States, the Philippines, India, Malaysia, Great Britain, Ireland, China (ranked No.70 out of 76 countries), Vietnam, Sweden, Denmark, Jamaica and Singapore, with Singapore in the lowest end. High uncertainty avoidance cultures endeavor to reduce unpredictability and ambiguity through intolerance of deviant ideas and behaviors, emphasizing consensus, resisting changes, and adhering to traditional social protocols. These cultures are often characterized by relatively high levels of anxiety and stress. People with this orientation believe that life carries the potential for continual hazards, and to avoid or mitigate these dangers, there is a strong need for laws, written rules, planing, regulations, rituals, ceremonies, and established societal, behavioral, and communication conventions, all of which add structure to life. Social expectations are clearly established and consistent. For example, Japan is a high uncertainty culture with many formal social protocols that help to predict how people will behave in almost every social interaction.

Low uncertainty avoidance cultures more easily accept the uncertainty inherent in life, tend to be tolerant of the unusual, and are not as threatened by different ideas and people. They prize initiative, dislike the structure associated with hierarchy, are willing to take risks, are flexible, think that there should be as few rules as possible, and depend not so much on experts as on themselves. As a whole, members of low uncertainty avoidance cultures are less constrained by social protocol.

Every human society has developed ways to alleviate anxiety from uncertainty, including technology, law and religion. Technology helps people to avoid uncertainties caused by nature. Laws and rules try to prevent uncertainties in the behavior of other people. Religion is a way of relating to the transcendental forces that are assumed to control people's personal future. Religion helps followers to accept the uncertainties against which one cannot defend oneself. The difference between strong and weak uncertainty avoidance sentiment can be summarized as "What is different is dangerous" versus "What is different is curious."

As with other value dimensions, differences in uncertainty avoidance influence communication and activities in varied contexts. In a classroom composed of children from a low uncertainty avoidance culture, such as Britain, you would expect to see students feeling comfortable dealing with unstructured learning situations, being rewarded for innovative approaches to problem solving, and learning without strict timetables. A different behavior is the case in high uncertainty avoidance cultures like Germany, where you find that students expect structured learning situations, firm timetables, and well-defined objectives.

As we discuss the above four value dimensions, it is important to keep in mind that Hofstede's work measured cultural dimensions at a national rather than individual level, which means that his value dimensions characterize the dominant culture in that society. Within every culture you will find individuals all along a particular value continuum. For example, in the United States, some members of the dominant culture possess strong collective tendencies. Conversely, in a group-oriented culture such as ROK, you can find individuals that assert individuality. Therefore, in any intercultural encounter, you must be mindful that the other person or persons may not adhere to the norm for their culture.

Exercises for Understanding

1. Answer the following questions according to the passage you have just read.

(1) What does the proverb "No matter how stout, one beam cannot support a house" mean in Chinese? Can you think of other Chinese proverbs that demonstrate the collective sense in

Chinese culture?

(2) Can you explain in your own words the four pairs of contrasting values identified in Hofstede's research? Can you find examples across countries to support Hofstede's findings?

(3) In *Cross-Cultural Communication*, the authors draw readers' attention to the following fact:

There are numerous US co-cultures that can be classified as collective. African Americans, for instance, exhibit many of the traits attributed to collective societies, and Hispanics and Asian Americans place great value on their extended families.

What does the above paragraph tell you about American culture? What did Hofstede say about American culture in terms of the individualism-collectivism dimension? What can you learn about the cultural values mentioned in Hofstede's research?

2. Small group task.

In *Cultures and Organizations*, the authors describe the use of words "no" and "yes" in collectivist cultures. Read the description and discuss in groups whether it fits your culture, and then share your personal experience in this aspect.

In most collectivist cultures, direct confrontation of another person is considered rude and undesirable. The word no is seldom used, because saying "no" is a confrontation; "you may be right" and "we will think about it" are examples of polite ways of turning down a request. In the same vein, the word yes should not necessarily be inferred as an approval, since it is used to maintain the line of communication: "yes, I heard you."

Section C Case

Scan and Listen

The Scenario

Chinese Culture is Built into the Furniture

As an American teacher at a Chinese university, I find the arrangement of classrooms a problem. Most of them have large raised podiums with students sitting in rows below and in front. This design reinforces the authority of the teacher and encourages a teacher-centered style of learning. I prefer classrooms with movable tables and chairs that would make it easier to arrange the students into work groups. I would like to move among the groups monitoring their work and offering advice as needed. As a teacher I prefer the role of facilitator, a person who defines tasks and goals and arranges activities to achieve them. I am not the main source of knowledge for the students but the leader of their learning activities. I do not want students to sit below and in front of me listening to what I have to say, at least not all the time. I want the students to learn cooperatively with each other and to depend on peers as much as the teacher as resources for their learning. To do this in China, I have to work against the physical structures.

Exercise

Listen to the case above and answer the following questions.

(1) What does the author do in China?

(2) What's the problem with the Chinese classroom according to the author?

(3) What kind of classroom arrangement does the author prefer? Why?

(4) What does a facilitator do in a classroom? Why does the author prefer the role of facilitator?

(5) Use Hofstede's power distance dimension to analyze the case.

Unit 5　Hall's Culture Context Model

Video Clip Appreciation

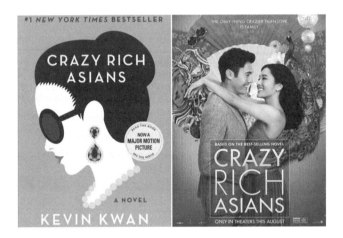

I. Introduction to the Movie *Crazy Rich Asians*

Crazy Rich Asians is a 2018 US romantic comedy based on the 2013 novel of the same name by Singaporean American novelist Kevin Kwan. It was directed by Chinese American filmmaker Jon M. Chu and praised in the United States since its release for its all-Asian cast. In the movie, Rachel Chu, an American-born Chinese economics professor who lives in New York, has been dating her boyfriend Nick Young for over a year when he invites her on a trip to his home country of Singapore to attend his friend Colin's wedding and meet his family. She's surprised to learn that Nick's family is extremely wealthy and he's considered one of the country's most eligible bachelors. Thrusted into the spotlight, Rachel must now contend with jealous socialites, quirky relatives and something far, far worse—Nick's disapproving mother.

II. Introduction to the Video Clips

Clip 1

Nick Young brings his girlfriend Rachel to meet his mother for the first time. They are having a brief talk in the kitchen.

Clip 2

Nick brings Rachel to his family gathering where people are wrapping dumplings. Later Rachel is kind of lost in the big building and Eleanor finds her.

III. Script of the Movie Clips

Video Clip 1

Clip 1

Nick: Mum.

Eleanor: You need a haircut. So unkempt. And you look tired from your trip. I'm gonna ask the cook to make you some herbal soup. I'll send it to the hotel later.

Nick: Mum, this is Rachel Chu.

Rachel: Oh, my gosh! I'm so happy to meet you, Mrs. Young. Or Auntie. Right? I'm learning the lingo.

Eleanor: I'm very glad to finally meet you, too. And I'm sorry Nick's father couldn't be here. He was called to business in Shanghai.

Nick: I told Rachel when duty calls, Dad answers.

Eleanor: As it should be. Nick tells me you're a professor, too. What do you teach?

Rachel: Um, I teach economics.

Nick: And she's brilliant. NYU's youngest faculty member.

Eleanor: So, economics... Sounds challenging. Are your parents academics as well?

Rachel: No. Well, my dad actually died before I was born, and my mom didn't even go to college. She actually hardly spoke any English when she immigrated to the United States. But she worked really hard, and she studied, and she earned her real estate license while she was waiting tables to support us. Now, she likes to say that she's Flushing's top real estate broker.

Eleanor: Self-made woman. She must be so proud of you.

Rachel: Well, she knows that I'm passionate about what I do, and she's always wanted that for me.

Eleanor: Pursuing one's passion. How American. Well, your mother's very open-minded, not like here, where parents are obsessed with shaping the life of their children.

Nick: That's dinner.

Eleanor: Go ahead. I'll be out in a minute. Rachel, it was lovely meeting you.

Rachel: Thank you. You, too. Okay, she hates me.

Nick: She takes a little minute to warm up, but we'll get there.

Rachel: A minute?

Clip 2

Aunt Alix: This is too much. We're hosting a rehearsal dinner, not feeding an army.

Eleanor: Better too many than have people say we're stingy.

Video Clip 2

Nick: So, right. You put the baby in bed. You tuck, tuck, tuck. Same on the other side. You give him a kiss good night.

Rachel: That's so cute.

Nick: How's that?

Rachel: And then you eat the baby.

Nick: Then you eat the baby after he's cooked.

Rachel: No, you gotta make sure he's cooked. Did your Ah Ma teach you that?

Nick: She did.

Oliver: I, on the other hand, was taught by Grand-Auntie Mabel. You put the Botox in the face, and then you pinch, pinch, pinch. Then, voila!

Rachel: Did you guys all learn when you were kids?

Astrid: We didn't have a choice.

Aunt Felicity: We taught you so you'd know the blood, sweat, and tears it took to raise and feed you monkeys.

Aunt Alix: Not like the ang-mohs microwaving macaroni and cheese for their own children. No wonder they put their parents in the old folks' home when they all grow up.

Aunt Felicity: I know!

Eleanor: Ah Ma says if we don't pass traditions down like this, they'll disappear.

Astrid: God forbid, we lose the ancient Chinese tradition of guilting your children.

Nick: It's totally worth it. Mother used to wait for me after school with a nice basket of these.

Astrid: Hey, I never got after-school dumplings.

Oliver: Well, that's because Auntie Felicity was doing after-school micro dermabrasion. Auntie, this is Dolce.

Aunt Alix: You speak Cantonese?

Rachel: No, I don't. It's just great seeing you guys all like this. When I was growing up, it was just me and my mom, which I loved. But we didn't really have a big family like this. It's really nice.

Oliver: Oh, that's so lovely of you to say, Rachel. We are all very lucky to have each other.

Rachel: That's a beautiful ring, Auntie Eleanor. I've never seen anything like it.

Eleanor: Nick's father had it made when he proposed to me.

Rachel: That's very romantic. How did you guys meet?

Nick: Actually, they met at Cambridge. They were both studying law together.

Rachel: Oh, I didn't know you were a lawyer.

Eleanor: I wasn't. I withdrew from university when we got married. I chose to help my husband run a business and to raise a family. For me, it was a privilege. But for you, you may think it's old-fashioned. It's nice you appreciate this house and us being here together wrapping dumplings. But all this doesn't just happen. It's because we know to put family first, instead of chasing one's passion.

Ah Ma: Ah, everyone's here!

Nick: Ah Ma... Thank you.

Ah Ma: Oh, Nick.

Nick: Come and sit.

Ah Ma: Oh, Nicki. You brought Rachel. Good. I can see you more clearly in the day. The shape of your nose is auspicious. Let me have a look, come closer... very nice looking. Sit. Sit.

Ah Ma: You made those dumplings? They don't look very good. You lost your touch.

****

Rachel: Oh, hi. I think I'm a little lost. This house is pretty big.

Eleanor: I'm glad I found you. I am afraid that I've been unfair.

Rachel: Oh, no, you know what? I'm sorry I made an assumption. I didn't mean to offend you.

Eleanor: Not at all. You asked about my ring. The truth is Nick's father had it made when he wanted to propose to me because Ah Ma wouldn't give him the family ring. I wasn't her first choice. Honestly, I wasn't her second.

Rachel: Gosh, I'm so sorry. I had no idea.

Eleanor: I didn't come from the right family, have the right connections. And Ah Ma thought I would not make an adequate wife to her son.

Rachel: But she came around, obviously.

Eleanor: It took many years, and she had good reason to be concerned. Because I had no idea the work and the sacrifice it would take. There were many days when I wondered if I would ever measure up. But having been through it all, I know this much. You will never be enough. We should head back. I wouldn't want Nick to worry.

New Words

unkempt [ˌʌn'kempt] *adj.* not neatly combed 乱蓬蓬的；不整洁的

herbal ['hɜːrbl] *adj.* connected with or made from herbs 草药的

lingo ['lɪŋgəʊ] *n.* (informal) a characteristic language of a particular group (as among thieves) 语言；术语；行话

academics [ˌækə'demɪks] *n.* an educator who works at a college or university 大学教师；学者

real estate ['riːəl ɪs'teɪt] *n.* property consisting of houses and land 地产；不动产

broker ['brəʊkə(r)] *n.* a businessman who buys or sells for another in exchange for a commission (房产)经纪人

self-made ['self'meɪd] *adj.* having achieved success or recognition by your own efforts 自力更生的；独力奋斗的

stingy ['stɪndʒi] *adj.* (informal) not given or giving willingly; not generous, especially with money 小气的；吝啬的

tuck [tʌk] *v.* to push, fold or turn the ends or edges of clothes, paper, etc. 塞进；折叠；卷起

botox ['bəʊtɒks] *n.* a substance that is injected into the face in order to make the skin look smoother 肉毒杆菌

pinch [pɪntʃ] *v.* to take in a tight grip between the thumb and finger 捏；掐

voila ['vɔɪlə] *int.* <法> 那就是；瞧（表示事情成功或满意之感叹用语）

macaroni [ˌmækə'rouni] *n.* a type of pasta in the shape of small tubes 通心粉；通心面

guilt [gɪlt] *n.* a strong feeling of shame and sadness because you know that you have done sth wrong 内疚；自责

dermabrasion [ˌdɜːmə'breɪʒən] *n.* removal of scars or tattoos by anesthetizing the skin surface and then sanding or scraping off some of the outer skin layer 磨皮法

propose [prə'pəuz] *v.* to ask sb to marry you 求婚

withdraw [wɪð'drɔː] *v.* to stop taking part in an activity, belonging to an organization etc. 退出（活动、组织等）

privilege ['prɪvəlɪdʒ] *n.* sth enjoyable that you are honored to have the chance to do 荣幸；光荣

auspicious [ɔː'spɪʃəs] *adj.* showing that sth is likely to be successful 吉利的；幸运的

assumption [ə'sʌmpʃn] *n.* sth that is taken as a fact or believed to be true without proof 假定，臆测

adequate [ˈædɪkwət] *adj*. having the necessary ability or qualities 适当的；能胜任的

Phrases and Expressions

lose your touch: If you lose your touch, you can no longer do sth as well as you could before. 不如以往；变得不擅长

come around: to change one's position or opinion 转而接受

measure up: If you do not measure up to a standard or to someone's expectations, you are not good enough to achieve the standard or fulfil the person's expectations. 合格；符合标准

Notes

NYU: NYU stands for New York University. Founded in 1831, New York University is one of the largest private universities in the United States. Its enrolment has grown to more than 50,000 students at three degree-granting campuses in New York City, Abu Dhabi, and Shanghai, and at study away sites in Africa, Asia, Australia, Europe, North and South America. Today, its students come from every state in the US and from 133 foreign countries. 纽约大学，一所位于美国纽约州的世界顶尖私立研究型大学，为"常春藤"名校之一

Dolce & Gabbana: Dolce & Gabbana is an Italian luxury fashion house founded in 1985 in Legnano by Italian designers Domenico Dolce and Stefano Gabbana. The two met in Milan in 1980 and designed for the same fashion house. In 1982, they established a designer consulting studio; in time it grew to become "Dolce & Gabbana." They presented their first women's collection in 1985 in Milan, and opened their store a year later. 杜嘉班纳，总部位于意大利米兰，为奢侈品领域中最主要的国际集团之一

University of Cambridge: It is a university at Cambridge in England, founded in 1230. It is one of the world's oldest universities and leading academic centers, and a self-governed community of scholars. Its reputation for outstanding academic achievement is known worldwide and reflects the intellectual achievement of its students, as well as the world-class original research carried out by the staff of the university and the colleges. With more than 18,000 students from all walks of life and all corners of the world, over 11,000 staff, 31 colleges and 150 departments, faculties, schools and other institutions, no two days are ever the same at the University of Cambridge. 牛津大学，一所位于英国牛津的世界顶尖公立研究型大学，在多个领域拥有崇高的学术地位及广泛的影响力，被公认为当今世界最顶尖的高等教育机构之一

Exercises for Understanding

Video Clip 1

1. Answer the following questions according to the video clip you have just watched.

(1) What does Rachel say about her family? How did Rachel feel about her family?

(2) What does Nick's mother think of Rachel's mother?

(3) Why does Rachel think Nick's mother hates her?

(4) Does Nick's mother like Rachel? Why or why not?

2. Decide whether the following statements are true or false according to the video clip you have just watched. Write a "T" for true or an "F" for false.

_____(1) Rachel is very happy to see Nick's mother.

_____(2) Nick's father is not at home.

_____(3) Rachel's mother spoke English well when she immigrated to the United States.

_____(4) Rachel is proud of her mother.

_____(5) Nick's mother likes the idea of pursuing one's passion.

3. Fill in the blanks according to the video clip you have just watched.

Eleanor: So, economics... Sounds (1) _____. Are your parents academics as well?

Rachel: No. Well, my dad actually died before I was born, and my mom didn't even go to college. She actually hardly spoke any English when she (2) _____ to the United States. But she worked really hard, and she studied, and she earned her real estate (3) _____ while she was (4) _____ to support us. Now, she likes to say that she's Flushing's top real estate (5) _____.

Eleanor: Self-made woman. She must be so (6) _____ of you.

Rachel: Well, she knows that I'm passionate about what I do, and she's always wanted that for me.

Eleanor: Pursuing one's (7) _____. How American. Well, your mother's very (8) _____, not like here, where parents are obsessed with shaping the life of their children.

Video Clip 2

1. Answer the following questions according to the video clip you have just watched.

(1) What does Ah Ma say about the dumplings made by Nick's mother?

(2) Does Ah Ma like her daughter-in-law? How do you know?

(3) Why didn't Ah Ma give her son the family ring when he proposed to Eleanor?

(4) Why does Eleanor tell Rachel about the story behind the ring?

(5) What does Ah Ma say about Rachel? Does Ah Ma like Rachel?

2. Decide whether the following statements are true or false according to the video clip you have just watched. Write a "T" for true or an "F" for false.

_____(1) Nick and his cousins learned to make dumplings when they were kids.

_____(2) Both Nick and Astrid had after-school dumplings when they were children.

_____(3) Rachel didn't grow up in a big family, and she felt sorry for that.

_____(4) Eleanor went to Cambridge to study law and became a lawyer after graduation.

_____(5) Eleanor thought Rachel would not make an adequate wife to her son.

3. Fill in the blanks according to the video clip you have just watched.

Eleanor: I didn't come from the right family, have the right connections. And Ah Ma thought I
        would not make an (1) _____ wife to her son.

Rachel: But she came around, obviously.

Eleanor: It took many years, and she had good reason to be (2) _____. Because I had no idea
        the work and the (3) _____ it would take. There were many days when I wondered
        if I would ever (4) _____. But having been through it all, I know this much. You
        will never be enough. We should head back. I wouldn't want Nick to (5) _____.

Section B Reading

Context is important in all kinds of communication, but it is relatively more important in some situations than in others. There are significant differences across cultures in the ways and the extent to which people communicate through context.

In 1976, the well-known US anthropologist Edward Hall, the father of intercultural communication, originated the concepts of high-context culture and low-context culture. Hall based his concepts on the degree to which meaning comes from the context or from the words being exchanged.

In high-context cultures, much information is implied in the context. Context includes the situation or surrounding circumstances, relationships of the communicators, their family background, title, age, sex, education, status, and social networks. Relatively, little is provided in the verbal message itself. In low-context cultures, however, the majority of the information is contained in the verbal code, and the message is stated clearly and explicitly without depending on the context of the communication.

In high-context cultures, most of the meaning exchanged during an encounter is often not communicated through words. Information is provided through inference, gestures, and even silence. One reason that meanings frequently do not have to be stated verbally in high-context cultures is because there is normally a strong level of similarity among the people. Everyone, no matter what their culture is, communicates in this way in some situations. The most common example is communication between close friends and family members. Husbands and wives, and parents and children in all cultures typically communicate in this way. They are so familiar with one another, that a glance, a turn of the head, or a slight change in facial expression carries more meaning than many words possibly could. In the intimacy of these relationships, people even discount what the other person is saying if what is said is not consistent with the context.

In low-context cultures, lack of a large pool of common experiences means that each time they interact with others they need detailed background information. In low-context cultures, the verbal message contains most of the information and very little is embedded in the context or the participant's nonverbal activity. This characteristic manifests itself in communication. For example, the Asian mode of communication (high-context) is often vague, indirect and implicit, where as Western communication (low-context) tends to be direct and explicit. Americans depend more on spoken words than on nonverbal behavior to convey messages. They think it is important to be able to "speak up" and "say what's on their mind." They admire a person who has a large vocabulary and who can express himself or herself clearly and cleverly.

The following table shows cultures arranged along the high-context and low-context dimension found by Edward Hall.

High-Context Cultures

Japanese
|
Chinese
|
Korean
|
African American
|
Native American
|
Arab
|

Greek
|
Latin
|
Italian
|
English
|
French
|
North American
|
Scandinavian
|
German
|
German/Swiss

Low-Context Cultures

Source: Adapted form E.T. Hall. *Beyond Culture*. NY: Doubleday, 1976: 91.

From the table we can see Asian cultures incline towards high-context communication that emphasizes role hierarchy and relations rather than the expression of self through direct communication. The high-context nature of Asian cultures is a result of Confucian philosophy.

Direct and Indirect Communication

An important difference between high-context and low-context communication is that with high-context communication, the burden of interpreting the meaning falls on the listener, while with low-context communication the speaker has the responsibility for making the meaning clear.

In the low-context cultures, such as American and British cultures, people are usually from diverse background and do not share much common information. So the way Westerners communicate tends to be relatively explicit and direct. In other words, Westerners tend to put most of their ideas and feelings into words, and then state these ideas and feelings plainly and openly. It is generally considered a good thing to "get to the point" to ensure that his/her message is stated in a way that is clear and easy to understand. They expect others to "take them at their word," i.e. to believe that what they say is what they mean.

Collectivist cultures are usually high-context cultures. In these cultures, such as Japanese, African-American, and Latino cultures, people are very homogeneous and share much background information. Therefore, it is not necessary to articulate every detail of the information explicitly. High-context communication style is more indirect and subtle, and listeners are expected to take more responsibility for interpreting messages correctly. People are expected to pay much attention to the context in which communication takes place—who the speaker is, where and why the conversation is taking place, body language, and so forth—and when people interpret what others mean, they often give more weight to the context than to the actual words said. In fact, people in high-context cultures often view direct, explicit communication as unsophisticated or even rude.

Differences in communication styles sometimes cause misunderstandings between Chinese and Westerners. Often in China when someone answers, "We must give it more thought" to a request, he is refusing a request that cannot be met. He does not want to disrupt the relationship with the person making the request and expects the other person to interpret his answer as a polite refusal. The Westerner may assume that there is a good chance that the answer will be "yes." (In fact, there is a better chance that the implied answer is "no.") In a similar situation many Westerners would not hesitate to say, "Sorry, it can't be done."

Differences in communication styles may also cause bad feelings between Chinese and Westerners. Westerners tend to dislike indirect communication, and often feel that Chinese "beat around the bush" too much rather than being direct. In contrast, Chinese often find Westerners too blunt and direct.

It is important to note that Westerners are not all equally direct in their communication styles. For example, the direct low-context communication style described above is more typical of Western men than of Western women. Furthermore, even in Western culture it is generally not considered good to communicate so directly and bluntly that you hurt other people's feelings, offend them, or create conflicts.

Silence is often regarded as a very important nonverbal code highly valued by people in high-context cultures. Just as a proverb says, "Empty cans clatter the loudest," high-context people may perceive talkative low-context people as less credible. However, in the eyes of people in low-context cultures, who hate ambiguity and value clarity, silence is usually associated with negative meanings such as indifference, anger, hostility, disagreement, shyness, embarrassment, ignorance, boredom or coldness.

In-groups and Out-groups

In addition to differences in communication styles, the differences between in-groups and out-groups is another manifestation of high-context and low-context cultures. "In-groups" are the people we have the most in common with and identify most closely with, such as our family, classmates, or co-workers. We also have larger in-groups such as people who are from our own region, religious group, ethnic group, or nation. In contrast, "out-groups" are those groups of people who we do not identify with, people from other families, regions, ethnic groups, or nations.

The way we relate to in-groups tends to differ from how we relate to out-groups in a number of ways. We generally have more positive feelings toward members of our in-groups than we do toward outsiders. When we are with our in-groups, we have a relatively strong sense of belonging and familiarity, and also usually feel more at ease and comfortable. We also usually trust other in-group members more than we trust outsiders. We tend to have a stronger sense of obligation to insiders than to outsiders. We tend to judge in-groups and out-groups by different standards. We are usually biased in favor of our in-groups and more generous in the ways we judge the behavior of in-group members. Toward outsiders, we tend to be more critical, suspicious, and willing to pass harsh judgments.

Exercises for Understanding

1. Answer the following questions according to the passage you have just read.

(1) What is high-context culture and what is low-context culture?

(2) What are the differences between high-context communication and low-context communication?

(3) The proverb "Empty cans clatter the loudest" is used to illustrate the point that people in low-context culture may be perceived as less credible by high-context people. Can you think of some Chinese proverbs or sayings concerning Chinese people's view on silence or eloquence?

2. Small group task.

In *Cross-cultural Communication*, the authors listed the most common cultural patterns and their influences on behavior and communication in a table. Study the following table carefully and discuss in groups your understanding of the relationship between cultural patterns and communication styles.

Cultural Patterns	
Individualism vs. Collectivism	
Individualism (e.g., the US, Australia, Canada) * Focus is on the individual & self-promotion * Independency * Task dominates relationship * Social obedience through sense of guilt	Collectivism (e.g., Korea, China, Mexico) * Focus is on the group & self-criticism * Interdependency * Relationship dominates task * Social obedience through sense of shame
Egalitarian vs. Hierarchical (Power Distance)	
Egalitarian (e.g., Australia, Canada, the US) * Horizontal relationships * Subordinates consulted * Equality expected	Hierarchial (e.g., Mexico, India, Korea) * Vertical relationships * Subordinates informed * Inequality accepted
Low vs. High Uncertainty Avoidance	
Low Uncertainty Avoidance (e.g., India, the US) * Change is normal and good * Few behavioral protocols * Greater cultural diversity	High Uncertainty Avoidance (e.g., Japan, Spain) * Change is disruptive and disliked * Many behavioral protocols * Less cultural diversity
Low vs. High Context Communication	
Low Context (Direct) (e.g., Germany, the US) * Meaning reliant on verbal message * Nonverbal communication low importance * Silence is avoided	High Context (Indirect) (e.g., Korea, Japan) * Meaning can be derived from context * Nonverbal communication high importance * Silence is normal
Low vs. High Face Concerns	
Low Face Concerns (e.g. Canada, the US) * Conflict / disagreement is constructive * Concern for self-face	High Face Concerns (e.g., Korea, China) * Conflict / disagreement is threatening * Concern for mutual / other-face

Source: L. A. Samovar, R. E. Porter, E. R. McDaniel et al. *Cross-Cultural Communication*. Beijing: Beijing University Press, 2007.

Section C Case

The Scenario

Scan and Listen

Scene 1: Two European American neighbors are having a conversation.

Jane: (knocks on her neighbor's open window) Excuse me, it is 11 o'clock already, and your high-pitched opera singing is really disturbing my sleep. Please stop your gargling noises immediately! I have an important job interview tomorrow morning, and I want to get a good night's sleep. I really need this job to pay my rent!

Diane: (resentfully) Well, this is the only time I can rehearse my opera! I've an important audition coming up tomorrow. You're not the only one that is starving, you know. I also need to pay my rent. Stop being so self-centered!

Jane: (frustrated) I really think you're being very unreasonable. If you don't stop your singing right now, I'm going to file a complaint with the apartment manager and he could evict you...

Diane: (sarcastically) OK, be my guest... Do whatever you want. I'm going to sing as I please.

Scene 2: Two Japanese housewives are having a conversation.

Mrs. A: Your daughter has started taking piano lessons, hasn't she? I envy you, because you can be proud of her talent. You must be looking forward to her future as a pianist. I'm really impressed by her enthusiasm—every day, she practices so hard, for hours and hours, until late at night.

Mrs. B: Oh, no, not at all. She is just a beginner. We don't know her future yet. We hadn't realized that you could hear her playing. I'm so sorry you have been disturbed by her noise.

Exercise

Listen to the case above and answer the following questions.

(1) Why did Jane knock on her neighbor's window at 11 o'clock at night? Did she reach her goal?

(2) Why did Mrs. A comment on Mrs. B's daughter's piano performance? What's her real purpose?

(3) Which dialogue exemplifies the low-context communication interaction?

(4) Which dialogue exemplifies the high-context communication interaction?

(5) What are the characteristics of high-context communication as is shown in the case?

(6) What are the characteristics of low-context communication as is shown in the case?

Module 3
Verbal Communication

Unit 6   Language and Culture

Video Clip Appreciation

I. Introduction to the Movie *The King's Speech*

At the official closing of the British Empire Exhibition at Wembley Stadium, Prince Albert, Duke of York, the second son of King George V, addresses the crowd with a strong stammer. His search for treatment has been discouraging, but his wife, Elizabeth, persuades him to see the Australian-born Lionel Logue, a non-medically trained Harley Street speech defects therapist. "Bertie," as he is called by his family, believes the first session is not going well, but Lionel, who insists that all his patients address him as such, has his potential client recite Hamlet's "To be, or not to be" soliloquy while hearing classical music played on a pair of headphones. Bertie is frustrated at the experiment but Lionel gives him the acetate recording that he has made of the reading as a souvenir.

After Bertie's father, King George V, broadcasts his 1934 Royal Christmas Message, he explains to Bertie that the wireless will play a significant part in the role of the royal family, allowing them to enter the homes of the people, and that Bertie's brother's neglect of his responsibilities make training in it necessary. The attempt at reading the message himself is a failure, but that night Bertie plays the recording Lionel gave him and is astonished at the lack of stutter there. He therefore returns for daily treatments to overcome the physical and psychological roots of his speaking difficulty.

George V dies in 1936, and his eldest son David ascends the throne as King Edward VIII. A constitutional crisis arises with the new king over a prospective marriage with the twice-divorced American socialite Wallis Simpson. Edward, as head of the Church of England, cannot marry her, even if she receives her second divorce, since both her previous husbands are alive.

At an unscheduled session, Bertie expresses his frustration that, while his speech has improved when speaking to most people, he still stammers when talking to David. When Lionel insists that Bertie himself could make a good king, Bertie accuses Lionel of speaking treason and quits Lionel in anger. Bertie must now face the Accession Council without any assistance.

Bertie and Lionel only come together again after King Edward decides to abdicate in order to marry. Bertie ascends the throne as King George VI and visits Lionel's home with his wife before their coronation.

Bertie and Lionel's relationship is questioned by the King's advisors during the preparations for his coronation in Westminster Abbey. It comes to light that George never asked for advice from his advisors about his treatment and that Lionel has never had formal training. Lionel explains that at the time he started with speech defects there were no formal qualifications and that the only known help that was available for returning Great War shell-shocked Australian soldiers was from personal experience.

As the new king, Bertie is in a crisis when he must broadcast Britain's declaration of war with Nazi Germany in 1939. Lionel is summoned to Buckingham Palace to prepare the king for his address to Britain and the Empire. He delivers his speech with Logue conducting him, but by the end he is speaking freely.

As the Royal Family step onto the palace balcony and are applauded by the crowd, a title card explains that Logue was always present at King George VI's speeches during the war and that they remained friends for the rest of their lives.

The King's Speech is a 2010 film about King George VI of Britain, his impromptu ascension to the throne, and the speech therapist who helped the unsure monarch become worthy of it.

II. Introduction to the Video Clips

Clip 1

The film focuses on the professional and personal relationship between Prince Albert, (Bertie who later becomes King George VI), and Lionel Logue, his speech therapist. Structurally this scene signifies a key transition in Bertie's psychological journey to become an effective speaker. But beyond being an important scene, it is also a hugely entertaining moment seeing a King breaking into an emotional frustration anger that has been roiling around for years, just waiting to emerge. As a result, we then find Bertie sitting in the office of a speech therapist who's trying all sorts of unconventional ideas to cure his stutter.

Clip 2

In the movie's final scene, Logue steps into a broadcasting room with Bertie and helps him get through his first wartime speech. With the support of Lionel Logue and his family, the King will overcome his stammer and deliver a radio-address that inspires his people and unites them in battle. The end of the movie is about as heartwarming as it gets. Although Bertie hasn't exactly cured his speech impediment, he has learned to live with it in a more constructive way. A final goodbye tells us that Bertie and Logue would go on to be friends for the rest of their lives and that Logue would help Bertie with all of his wartime speeches.

III. Script of the Video Clips

Clip 1

Video Clip 1

Bertie: Strictly business. No... personal nonsense.

Elizabeth: Yes, I thought I'd made that clear in our interview.

Lionel: Have you got the shilling you owe me?

Bertie: No, I haven't.

Lionel: Didn't think so.

Bertie: Besides, you... you tricked me.

Lionel: Physical exercises and tricks are important. But what you're asking will only deal with the surface of the problem.

Elizabeth: Is that that's sufficient? Ah, no. As far as l see it, my husband has mechanical difficulties with his speech.

Bertie: I...

Elizabeth: Maybe just deal with that.

Bertie: I... I'm willing to work hard, Dr. Logue...

Lionel: Lionel.

Bertie: [*Stammering*] Are you... Are you willing to do your part?

Lionel: All right. You want mechanics? We need to relax your jaw muscles, strengthen your tongue, by repeating tongue twisters. For example, "I'm a thistle-sifter. I have a sieve of sifted thistles and a sieve of unsifted thistles. Because I am a thistle-sifter."

Bertie: Fine.

Lionel: And you do have a flabby tummy, so we'll need to spend some time strengthening your diaphragm. Simple mechanics.

Elizabeth: That's all we ask.

Lionel: All that's about a shilling's worth.

Bertie: Forget about the blessed shilling! Perhaps, upon occasions, you might be requested to assist in coping with... with some minor event. Would that be agreeable?

Lionel: Of course.

Elizabeth: Yes, and that would be the full extent of your services.

Bertie: Shall I see you next week?

Lionel: I shall see you every day.

Lionel: Feel the looseness of the jaw. Good. Little bounces. Bounces. Shoulders loose, shoulders loose. Beautiful, beautiful, beautiful. Now, loose.

Lionel: Take a nice deep breath. Expand the chest. Put your hands onto your ribs. Deeper. Good. How do you feel?

Bertie: Full of hot air.

Lionel: Isn't that what public speaking's all about?

Bertie: My wife and I are glad to visit this important...

Lionel: Take a good deep breath, and up comes Your Royal Highness. And slowly exhale, and down comes Your Royal Highness.

Elizabeth: You all right, Bertie?

Bertie: [*Groaning*] Yes.

Elizabeth: It's actually quite good fun.

Bertie: Mmm... Mother.

Lionel: Shorten the humming each time.

Bertie: Mmm... Mother. Mmm...

Bertie: ... manufacturing the district...

Lionel: Another deep breath. And Jack and Jill.

Bertie: Jack and Jill.

Lionel: Went up the hill.

Bertie: Went up the hill.

Lionel: Now, just sway. Perfect.

Bertie: ... will not permit us to...

Lionel: Loosen the shoulders.

Bertie: Ding dong bell, pussy's in the well. Who put her in? Little Tommy Tin.

Lionel: You have a short memory, Bertie. Come on.

Bertie: A cow, a cow...

Lionel: A... a king... Anyone who can shout vowels at an open window can learn to deliver a speech.

Elizabeth: 14, 15!

Lionel: Good. Deep breath, and...

Bertie: It is...

Lionel: Let the words flow.

Bertie: Mine doesn't bloody work.

Lionel: Come on, one more time, Bertie. You can do it.

Bertie: A sieve of thisted siphles. Gah! Mah! Bah!

Lionel: Father.

Bertie: Father.

Lionel: Father. Aim for the a-t-h. Father. Father. Father.

Bertie: Father. Father.

Clip 2

Man 1: Forty seconds, sir.

Bertie: Logue. However this turns out, I don't know how to thank you for what you've done.

Lionel: Knighthood?

Video Clip 2

Man 1: Twenty seconds.

Lionel: Forget everything else, and just say it to me. Say it to me as a friend.

Bertie: In this grave hour, perhaps the most fateful in our history, I send to every household of my (a-)peoples both at home and overseas this message spoken with the same depth of feeling for each one of you as if I were able to cross your threshold and speak to you myself. For the second time in the lives of most of us, we are at... [*Lionel mouthing*] … at war.

Lionel: [*Whisper*] Very good.

Bertie: Over and over again we have tried to find a peaceful way out of the differences between ourselves and those who are now our enemies. But it has been in vain. We have been forced into a conflict, for we are called to meet the challenge of a principle, which, if it were to prevail, would be fatal to any civilized order in the world. Such a principle, stripped of all disguise, is surely the mere primitive doctrine that might is right. For the sake of all that we ourselves hold dear, it is unthinkable that we should refuse to meet the challenge. It is to this high purpose that I now call my people at home and my peoples across the seas, who will make our cause their own. I ask them to stand calm and firm and united in this time of trial. The task will be hard. There may be dark days ahead, and war can no longer be confined to the battlefield. But we can only do the right as we see the right, and reverently commit our cause to God. If one and all we keep resolutely faithful to it, then, with God's help, we shall prevail.

[*Applause*]

Lionel: That was very good, Bertie. You still stammered on the "W."

Bertie: Well, I had to throw in a few, so they knew it was me.

Wood: Congratulations, Your Majesty. A true broadcaster.

Bertie: Thank you, Mr. Wood.

Man 2: Congratulations, Your Majesty.

Man 3: Sir.

Man 4: Congratulations, Your Majesty.

Bertie: Thank you.

Man 5: Congratulations, Your Majesty.

Bertie: Thank you.

Bertie: Ready. Good?

Man 6: Perfect, sir.

Lionel: Your first wartime speech. Congratulations.

Bertie: I expect I shall have to do a great deal more. Thank you, Logue. Well done. My friend.

Lionel: Thank you. Your Majesty.

Elizabeth: I knew you'd be good. Thank you... Lionel.

Bertie: Onwards.

Man 7: Congratulations, sir.

Man 8: Well done, sir.

Man 9: Couldn't have said it better myself, sir.

Man 10: Your Majesty, I am speechless.

Man 11: Congratulations, sir.

Bertie: Gentlemen.

Bertie: So how was Papa, Elizabeth?

Princess Elizabeth: Halting at first, but you got much better, Papa.

Bertie: Well, bless you.

Bertie: And how about you, Margaret?

Princess Margaret: You were just splendid, Papa.

Bertie: Of course I was.

Bertie: Are we all ready?

Elizabeth: Come on, girls.

New Words

thistle ['θɪsəl] *n.* a wild plant which has leaves with sharp points and purple flowers 蓟

sifter ['sɪftə] *n.* a household sieve (as for flour) 筛子；负责筛选的人

sieve [sɪv] *n.* a tool used for separating solids from liquids or larger pieces of sth from smaller pieces 筛子；过滤器

flabby ['flæbi] *adj.* not strong or robust; incapable of exertion or endurance 松弛的

tummy ['tʌmi] *n.* the part of the front of your body below your waist 肚子

diaphragm ['daɪəfræm] *n.* a muscle between your lungs and your stomach 横膈膜（位于肺和胃之间的肌肉，呼吸时起作用）

exhale [eks'heɪl] *v.* to breathe out the air that is in your lungs 呼气

pussy ['pʊsɪ] *n.* an informal name for a cat 猫咪

knighthood ['naɪthʊd] *n.* a title that is given to a man by a British king or queen for his achievements or his service to his country. A man who has been given a knighthood can put "Sir" in front of his name instead of "Mr." (英国的) 爵士称号及身份

threshold ['θreʃəʊld] *n.* the floor in the doorway, or the doorway itself 门口

prevail [prɪ'veɪl] *v.* to win in a battle, contest, or dispute 获胜

strip [strɪp] *v.* to remove everything that covers sth 剥离

disguise [dɪs'gaɪz] *v.* to hide sth or make sth appear different so that people will not know about it or will not recognize it 掩饰

doctrine ['dɒktrɪn] *n.* a set of principles or beliefs, especially religious ones (尤指宗教的) 信条；学说

cause [kɔːz] *n.* an aim or principle which a group of people support or are fighting for 奋斗目标；事业

reverently ['rəvərəntli] *adv.* piously, prayerfully 虔诚地，恭敬地

stammer ['stæmə] *v.* to speak with difficulty, hesitating and repeating words or sounds 结结巴巴地说

Phrases and Expressions

in vain: for nothing, of no effect 徒然，无效

be confined to: be limited to 局限于；限制于

Exercises for Understanding

1. Decide whether the following statements are true or false according to the video clips you have just watched. Write a "T" for true or an "F" for false.

_____(1) When Bertie and Elizabeth came to receive training from Lionel, they didn't want to talk about personal affairs.

_____(2) Lionel thought that physical exercises and tricks could completely solve Bertie's problem of stammering.

_____(3) Tongue twisters was one of the mechanical ways used by Lionel to improve Bertie's speaking skills.

_____(4) Bertie promised to give Lionel knighthood after he succeeded in delivering a speech against the Nazis.

_____(5) Margaret thought that his father Bertie gave a wonder public speech without any halting.

2. Fill in the blanks according to the video clips you have just watched.

Video Clip 1

Bertie: Strictly business. No... (1) _____.

Elizabeth: Yes, I thought I'd made that clear in our interview.

Lionel: Have you got the shilling you owe me?

Bertie: No, I haven't.

Lionel: Didn't think so.

Bertie: Besides, you... you (2) _____ me.

Lionel: Physical exercises and tricks are important. But what you're asking will only deal with the surface of the problem.

Elizabeth: Is that that's sufficient? Ah, no. As far as I see it, my husband has (3) _____ difficulties with his speech.

Bertie: I...

Elizabeth: Maybe just deal with that.

Bertie: I... I'm willing to work hard, Dr. Logue…

Lionel: Lionel.

Bertie: [*Stammering*] Are you... Are you willing to (4) _____?

Lionel: All right. You want mechanics? We need to relax your jaw muscles, (5) _____, by repeating tongue twisters. For example, "I'm a thistle-sifter. I have a sieve of sifted thistles and a sieve of unsifted thistles. Because I am a thistle-sifter."

Video Clip 2

Over and over again we have tried to find a peaceful way out of the differences between ourselves and those who are now our enemies. But it has been (1) _____. We have been forced into a conflict, for we are called to meet the challenge of a principle, which, if it were to prevail, would be fatal to any civilized order in the world. Such a principle, (2) _____, is surely the mere primitive doctrine that might is right. For the sake of all that we ourselves hold dear, it is unthinkable that we should refuse to meet the challenge. It is to this high purpose that I now call my people at home and my peoples across the seas, who will (3) _____. I ask them to stand calm and firm and united (4) _____. The task will be hard. There may be dark days ahead, and war can no longer be confined to the battlefield. But we can only do the right as we see the right, and reverently commit our cause to God. If one and all we keep resolutely it, then, with God's help, we shall (5) _____.

3. Explore interculturally.

(1) Do you think language is powerful? Why or why not?

(2) What do you think are the reasons for Bertie to make a successful public speech against the Nazis?

Section B Reading

Language is extremely important to human interaction because it is how we reach out to make contact with our surroundings. We may use language when we are first awake and say "Good morning!" to unite with the outside world. We may use words to share an unpleasant experience and to get support from others: "Let me tell you about the horrible dream I had last night." We use words so that we can exercise some control over the present: "Please pass the salt and pepper." We also use words to form images of the future: "I have to meet with Jane at work today, but I dread seeing her, because I know she's going to be upset about the changes I'm making in her work schedule."

Austrian philosopher Ludwig Wittgenstein once said that "The limits of my language are the limits of my world."

According to Erza Pound, an American poet, the sum of human wisdom is not contained in any one language, and no single language is capable of expressing all forms and degrees of human comprehension.

The language we use and the culture in which we live are closely related. Some scholars compare language and culture to a living organism: life is flesh, and culture is blood. Without culture, language would be dead; without language, culture would have no shape. In other words, they cannot be separated and exist alone.

Some other scholars consider language and culture as two sides of the same coin. Language embodies the products, perspectives, communities, and persons of a culture. To fully reveal the culture, we must examine the language. Language is a product of the culture, as any others, but it also plays a distinct role. Members of the culture have created the language to carry out all their cultural practices, to identify and organize all their cultural products, and to name the underlying cultural perspectives in all the various communities that comprise their culture. Language, therefore, is a window to the culture.

To practice culture, we also need language. We need to be able to express ourselves and to communicate with members of the culture as we engage with them in the myriad practices and products that make up their way of life. Moreover, we need to do this appropriately, using the right language in the right way, according to the expectations of the members of the culture. This is the language of self-expression, communication, and social interaction.

Language shapes our lives. The advertising world is a prime example of the use of language to shape, persuade, and dissuade. "Weasel words" tend to glorify very ordinary products into those that are "sparkling" or "refreshing." In the case of food that has been shaped of most its nutrients by the manufacturing process, we are told that these products are now "enriched" and "fortified." A foreigner in the United States once remarked that in the United States, there are no "small" eggs, only "medium" "large" "extra-large" and "jumbo." Euphemisms—or telling it like it isn't—abound in American culture where certain thoughts are taboo or certain words connote sth less than desirable. Garbage men are "sanitary engineers"; toilets are "rest rooms"; slums are "substandard dwellings." Even a common word like "family" has for some social scientists been replaced by a "micro cluster of structured role expectation."

Conversational Skills—Idioms & Expressions in North America

The words in a language have meanings. When we use words, sometimes we use their denotative meanings, that is, the basic meaning of the words. Yet, sometimes, we use the implied meaning of words. This kind of implied meaning is also known as the connotation. Connotations are in general closely related to the culture they are rooted in. When we learn about another culture or communicate with people from another culture, the "culturally loaded" aspect of the words they use require our special attention.

More often than not, the problem is that the seeming equivalents in two languages may have same denotations but their connotations differ greatly.

For example, "dog" in English has positive connotations. The expressions like "Love me, love my dog." "Every dog has his day." and so on convey Westerners' special love of dogs. This is totally a different picture in China. In Chinese, "dog" has a lot of negative connotationslike "狗胆包天" "狗急跳墙" "狼心狗肺" "狗仗人势" "狗皮膏药" "狗头军师" "狗血喷头" "狗尾续貂" "丧家之犬" and so on.

Words of color also connote differently. To the Chinese, Japanese, and Koreans, red represents a color of longevity, splendor, and wealth. The color black is very much welcome in the Caribbean and Africa. Yellow is a noble color for the Chinese and Indians. White is a wedding color in the United States, but a funeral color in India. Red is a wedding color in parts of India, but suggests sexual impurity (i.e. a "scarlet woman") in a US wedding.

Besides, Chinese kinship terms are so complicated that they are beyond the understanding of foreigners. Mostly, they don't have equivalents in English. Uncle in English is used to indicate all of the father's and mother's brothers. It could refer to what we call 叔叔, 伯父, 舅

舅，姨夫 and so on. In the same way, aunt is used to refer to all of father's and mother's sisters. This difference is not only linguistic. It is fundamentally cultural. This kind of difference can pose great problems to intercultural understanding. Look at this example of translation. How can it be done in English!

Clyde Kluckhohn once said that every language is a special way of looking at the world and interpreting experiences.

It is impossible to master the connotation of every word when we communicate with people from different cultures. However, we should at least be aware that the words we choose to use may lead to misunderstandings and misinterpretations. To achieve successful intercultural communication, we should certainly NOT overlook cultural connotations.

Exercises for Understanding

1. Answer the following questions according to the passage you have just read.

(1) How do you understand Ludwig Wittgenstein's saying that "The limits of my language are the limits of my world"?

(2) What is the metaphor that is used to describe the relationship between language and culture?

(3) What are the functions of language when practicing culture?

(4) Can you list 5 other examples of the use of English weasel words?

(5) What is the difference between denotative and connotative meaning?

2. Samll group task: please analyze the following cases in groups.

Case 1: Scandinavian vacuum cleaner manufacturer Electrolux raised more than a few eyebrows when one of its most expensive marketing efforts in the US market was spearheaded by an ad claiming that "Nothing Sucks Like an Electrolux!" In the US, "sucks" means bad or terrible.

Case 2: Catering to the needs of small farmers (farmers of small-size farms), a farming implement plant carried out a large scale advertisement campaign in the US, while it didn't enjoy the same popularity in Europe. Why? Because in Europe, small farmers refer to the bumpkins who are supposed to be short-sighted and illiterate.

Case 3: When the salesperson of General Motors promoted the latest model Chevrolet Noya in Puerto Rico, there wasn't the expected attention to this model. Finally, the salesperson was informed that in Spanish, "Nova" meant "immobile." Of course, it is not an ideal name for an automobile. "Nova" was changed into "Caribe."

3. Fill in the following blanks with the appropriate color terms. Each term can be used more than once.

black   blue   brown   green   red   white   yellow

(1) He is just a _____ recruit fresh from college.

(2) I tried to call her many times but she was in a _____ study and didn't hear me.

(3) One day, out of the _____, a girl rang up and said she was my sister.

(4) The new office block has unfortunately become an expensive _____ elephant.

(5) Mary was always regarded as the _____ sheep of the family.

(6) You'd better do something to prove you are not _____.

(7) Can you see the _____ in her eyes?

(8) The mere thought of her husband with the secretary made her see _____?

(9) I got some _____ looks from the shopkeeper when I canceled my order.

(10) When I am feeling _____, all I have to do is to take a look at you, and then I am not so blue.

(11) Don't tell me any _____ lie to make me feel good.

(12) It may cost over a week to go through all the _____ tape to get the permission.

(13) His type of humor is a bit too _____ for my tastes.

(14) Are you all right? You look absolutely _____.

(15) He based his judgment on headline and _____ journalism.

4. Find the connotations of the following words and phrases.

(1) lover   (2) busboy

(3) busybody   (4) dry goods

(5) heartman   (6) blind date

(7) dead president   (8) sweet water

(9) confidence man   (10) criminal lawyer

(11) dressing room   (12) horse sense

(13) familiar talk   (14) black stranger

(15) white man   (16) yellow book

(17) red tape   (18) blue stocking

(19) American beauty   (20) English disease

(21) Indian summer   (22) Greek gift

(23) Spanish athlete   (24) French chalk

Section C Case

The Scenario

Scan and Listen

Practicing English

One night, a Chinese student majoring in English sat on the steps of the foreign student's residence and talked with two young male foreign students, one German and one American. They didn't speak a word to her on their own initiative, but she asked many questions to get a conversation started. Every time they answered her with only one or two words. But she was determined to practice her English so she tried to keep the conversation going.

"How do you spend you weekend?" she asked.

The German boy answered immediately, "Fishing," and the two boys looked at each other meaningfully.

"Fishing?" She was really confused. "But where do you fish?" she asked.

"Fishing has two meanings. One if the literal meaning. The other is just sitting here and walking on the street and waiting for some girls to come up to us." Then they both burst out laughing.

She was annoyed. She sat there silently and then suddenly stood up and walked without saying goodbye.

Exercise

Listen to the case above and answer the following questions.

(1) Why did the Chinese student sit on the steps of foreign students' building?

(2) Were the two foreign students eager to talk with the Chinese student? Why or why not?

(3) Why was the Chinese student determined to keep the conversation going?

(4) What is the implied meaning of fishing?

(5) What cultural differences are shown in this case?

Unit 7   Norms of Social Interaction

Video Clip Appreciation

I. Introduction to the Movie *My Big Fat Greek Wedding 2*

In *My Big Fat Greek Wedding 2*, Toula and Ian are still happily married and still live right next door to Toula's family, and are in fact now sandwiched by the clan. The couple's daughter, Paris, is now 17 and ready to go off to college, and her heart is set on any school that can get her hundreds, if not thousands, of miles away from her overbearing Greek family. The economic downturn has forced Toula to abandon her travel agency business, but the family restaurant is still going strong. The family schemes to find a way to make Paris stay close to home rather than travel for college. Another important thing in the movie is that Toula's father Gus makes a shocking discovery: he's not actually married to

Maria, the woman he has called "wife" for half a century. They plan on "officially" tying the knot, but only if Gus will properly court her, ask for her hand in marriage, and put on a big fat Greek wedding. But do they still share that spark they need for happily-ever-after, and can the ceremony go off without a hitch?

II. Introduction to the Video Clip

It's a cold, fall morning in Chicago. We are introduced to the Portokalos family one by one as Gus, the grandfather, picks up his grandchildren to take them to school. Gus harps on Paris to get married before she gets too old and tells his daughter, Toula, to find Paris a Greek boyfriend. After stopping at his daughter's house, he drives to two other houses which belong to Toula's brother Nick and Toula's sister Athena. When Athena gets to the car, she tells Paris to come by the family restaurant and then criticizes Toula for letting Paris wear too much mascara. A few minutes later, Gus drops all the kids off at school and as Paris jumps out, Gus tells her to find a nice Greek boy and have babies. As Gus drives through Greektown, Toula realizes that she is now taking care of her parents instead of her daughter. Paris gazes out the hallway window alone, as other students talk together. She runs into her dad, Ian, at the library. Ian is concerned that she's not in class and Paris goes off on him for being another family member that smothers her. Toula is volunteering at the College Fair where the whole family comes around, including Maria, Gus, Uncle Taki, Aunt Voula, Angelo, Nikki, and all the kids and cousins. Gus and Uncle Taki run through available Greek boys for Paris. Paris then tells her family that she's applying to schools that are far away from them and storms off. Gus argues that everyone is a descendent of Alexander the Great and that he is determined to find Paris a Greek boyfriend.

III. Script of the Video Clip

Video Clip

Gus: You better get married. You're starting to look old.

Toula: Dad! You can't say that to her!

Paris: Pappou!

Toula: That's a family tradition. My dad used to say that to me, and now he just said it to my daughter. She's 17. My family worries about each other because we're close. Very close. Extremely close. We see no difference between hugging and suffocation.

Gus: Toula, find your daughter a Greek boyfriend before she does what you did.

Toula: What the...

Gus: You married a kseno.

Toula: My husband!

Gus: He's a nice boy, very nice, but not Greek, a kseno.

Toula: How can you say that?

Paris: Please stop!

Toula: Do I speak for all mothers of teens when I ask, "Does it ever get better?"

Nick: Hey, hey, hey. Ela, Costa!

Gus: Nicko.

Nick: Hey, Dad, pop the trunk. I'm freezing my nads off.

Costa: Too much makeup.

Maria: We're gonna have a nice day. And we'll paint, and we'll do nice things. Gus, I put your pills by your coffee.

Gus: Yeah, yeah, yeah. Costa, did you finish drawing Alexander the Great?

Costa: Uh-huh. And I sculpted a Parthenon out of soap.

Gus: Very good, very good. Oh, no. Spell check corrected "spanakopita" to "spina bifida."

Nick: Kisses. Ela.

Toula: Aw, kisses from your child. That's over. My sister did it right. When her sons became possessed by the *Teen Wolf* hormones, she popped out another one. And another one.

Anna: Let's go!

Angelo: Put on your hat.

Anna: Paris, you should come and help at the restaurant sometime.

Aristotle: You should butter the garlic bread.

Paris: Can't wait.

Anna: Come here, darling. Toula, you and Ian seen these eyes? You better fix this.

Gus: Okay, bye, bye.

Anna: After school you have hockey. Your brothers are coming, so you make sure you score.

Gus: You will score. The Greeks invented hockey.

Costa: Yes, because what do you play hockey on? Ice.

Aristotle: What is the Greek word for ice? Pago.

Costa: Pago, puck. There you go.

Aristotle: There you go.

Gus: There you go. Now, give me a word, any word... and I will show you how the root of that word is Greek.

Costa: Uh, Facebook.

Gus: Huh. The Greeks invented Facebook. We called it the telephone.

Aristotle and Costa: Bye-bye! Bye, Pappou!

Gus: Paris. Keep your eyeballs open now for a nice Greek boy so one day you can make babies. Don't waste your eggs.

Paris: Outstanding.

Toula: Paris! Pappou didn't mean to say anything hurtful. You're beautiful, so beautiful. Of course you don't look old. He just says stuff like that. To me, too. You don't need a boyfriend, you don't need to get married and make babies!

Girl 1: Oh, my God.

Guy 1: The lady's back again.

Paris: Mother. When did my name change from... Mommy! to... Mother!

Tommy: Drama.

Paris: Shut up, Tommy.

Toula: I guess when my daughter started to pull away, I should have retreated. But I stayed too close. I kept volunteering at her school. I wanted her to think I was cool again.

Guy 2: Loser!

Toula: Then I remembered I've never been cool.

Tommy: Here comes the principal.

Toula: My husband has always been cool. He just has it. And he always knows the perfect thing to say.

Ian: You okay, babe?

Toula: Okay, so just when my daughter doesn't want me around anymore, my parents need me more than ever. So I go with them to get groceries, to their doctors, and to physical therapy.

Woman 1: The old guys suck the chocolate off those nuts.

Toula: I loved being a travel agent, but in a tight economy, the first things to go are luxuries like travel and dry cleaning. Well, luckily, people still eat. Hold up, Dad.

Toula: My sister and brother have young children so I help at the restaurant. It's what we do. Because families that are close like mine, we make it through bad economies and sickness and even wars because we stick together. But some of us just get stuck.

Ian: Hey, Paris. Hey.

Paris: Dad, do not talk to me. People think I'm a narc!

Ian: Well, shouldn't you be in class right now?

Paris: You track me all day. Mom's needy, Pappou wants to marry me off, Yiayia constantly tells me to never ever let a boy touch my poulaki because "once he feels it, he wants it"! This family.

Tommy: Hey! Save it for the shrink.

Paris: Shut up, Tommy.

Ian: Honey, your mom felt the same way about being Greek.

Paris: Dad, that's obtuse. Why would I have an issue being Greek? I can't take that everyone is always in my business. Give me some air. I'm not a kid. I can be late to a class. There won't be a spasmodic catastrophic ripple in the space-time continuum. And, yes, four of those words are Greek.

****

Toula: Hi.

Woman 2: Hi.

Parent Volunteer 1: Where were you when we set up?

Toula: I'm so sorry. My pipes froze.

Parent Volunteer 2: And decorated the gym.

Toula: So I had to plunge my sink.

Parent Volunteer 1: You're on clean-up.

Toula: Thank you.

Ian: Hi.

Toula: Hi.

Ian: You can say no to them.

Toula: Oh, yeah, sure.

Ian: Been a long time since those two made fun of your lunch.

Toula: They called it moose-caca.

Ian: Eh, come on, don't let them boss you around.

Toula: There's Paris.

Ian: If she goes to Northwestern, she'll stay in Chicago.

Toula: Please, oh, please. Let's go over there.

Ian: No.

Toula: Right.

Maria: There she is!

Ian: Did you invite the family?

Gus: Paris!

Toula: I told my ma.

Toula: Hold on. Hey! Hey!

Taki: We're just in time. We're here!

Maria: I want you to be a dental hygienist. A mother working two days a week, perfect!

Cousin Nikki: Paris, be a hairdresser. Like me!

Gus: Ian, look. Everybody has boys. You vegetarian. One girl. Slow sperm.

Maria: That's Theia Voula on the FaceTimes.

Aunt Voula: Maria, I'm on my way. I was at Zumba.

Maria: Who is Zumba?

Toula: Sorry.

Gus: We need to find a boyfriend for Paris.

Taki: How about Ariana Skoufis' boy, huh?

Gus: Everybody on that island has six toes.

Taki: Let's wait until summer. We check his feet.

Aunt Voula: I see you. I don't see you. I see you. I don't see you. I see you. I don't see you. I
see you!

Ian: I see her.

Aunt Voula: Look at this app. Ten thousand steps, I met my goal. Where's Taki? He never
answers the phone.

Maria: Why stand when you can sit?

Gus: Look tired so they leave us alone.

Nick: Hey, Angelo. You get my flat-screen TV?

Angelo: Yeah, I got it right here.

Nick: You can't breathe. You can't breathe.

Ian: Guys!

Mike: All right, break it up. Break it up. You're coming with me.

Ian: Hey, Mike?

Mike: Hey, buddy.

Ian: You miss working here?

Mike: No. Way too scary for me. Hey, sorry we're late.

Mrs. White: Yeah, we had to stop and pick up Mana-Yiayia. Wait, where is she?

Family Members: Mana-Yiayia? Mana-Yiayia?

Mike: Look low, everybody.

Mana-Yiayia: Spanakopita!

Family Members: Let me in there! I want a piece. Easy. Guys. Easy.

Aunt Voula: Take a picture.

Family Members: Ooh, that's good.

Aunt Voula: Hey, come.

Toula: No, no, honey. You don't have to do that. Why don't you just...

Admission Officer: It's okay.

Cousin Nikki: Pull my neck back.

Family Member: Oh, yeah. And you do mine. Okay?

Mrs. White: Okay.

Cousin Nikki: One, two, three, pull!

Admission Officer: Okay.

Guy 3: Hey, Bennett.

Aunt Voula: Good?

Maria: Let me. I'll be the judge.

Cousin Nikki: Not bad.

Family Member: Oh, that looks good.

Toula: We should go.

Cousin Nikki: Why?

Toula: So Paris can speak with this gentleman and go to Northwestern.

Admission Officer: Well, if she gets in.

Nick: Come here. My niece wants to come to your school, you're gonna say, "Welcome." You got it?

Angelo: Come here, pal. And a tuition discount means a box of steaks for ya.

Admission Officer: Northwestern is very selective.

Gus: She's only coming there if you teach Greek history.

Admission Officer: Of course. We have an outstanding classics program. Greek, Italian.

Gus: The Greeks invented Italian.

Admission Officer: Actually, no.

Gus: Yes.

Admission Officer: Nope.

Gus: You Greek?

Admission Officer: No, sir. I'm a Sephardic Jew.

Gus: Then you Greek.

Admission Officer: No, my family is Spanish.

Gus: Alexander the Great went through Spain spreading his seed. You Greek.

Maria: This is not the time.

Admission Officer: And it's ridiculous.

Toula: Let's go!

Gus: The man doesn't know history. "Spreading his seed?"

Paris: Hey! Alabama, Florida, Texas, New York. These are the colleges I'm applying to, far, far away from here.

Toula: Why do you want to leave me?

Gus: Didn't I say, get your daughter a Greek boyfriend?

Toula: Dad!

Gus: And you, educate yourself. We are all descendants of Alexander the Great. I am for sure!

Maria: No, you're not.

Gus: Maria...

Maria: No, you're not.

Toula: It's okay.

Ian: He knows, he knows.

Toula: It's okay.

Admission Officer: Gracias.

****

Costa: Okay, give me a word. Any word.

Aristotle: Chimichanga.

Costa: Sure. "Chimi" comes from the Greek word "kima," which means "spicy beef." And "changa" comes from the Greek word "tsanda," which means "purse." So meat that is shaped like a purse. Chimichanga. There you go.

Gus: There you go.

Angelo: Quit setting me up.

Nick: Hey, just meet her. She's from Holland.

Angelo: Nah. I don't speak Hollandaise.

Family Member: Yeah, in the city.

Cousin Nikki: Exactly. It's ready.

Toula: Hey.

Paris: Hi.

Toula: Just because you don't want to be working here when you're my age doesn't mean you have to run off to college in another city. I just hope you applied to some local colleges, too.

Paris: Why do parents always say "dream big" when they really mean "not too big?" Like, "Fly, little birdy. Wait, no, let me hold your wings."

Gus: Payback.

Toula: What?

Gus: Office.

New Words

suffocation ['sʌfə'keɪʃən] *n.* the condition of being deprived of oxygen (as by having breathing stopped) 窒息

nads [nædz] *n.* (slang, rarely used in the singular) the testicles 睾丸

Parthenon ['pɑrθə,nɑn] *n.* a former temple on the Athenian Acropolis, Greece, dedicated to the goddess Athena, who the people of Athens considered their patron 帕特农神庙

hockey ['hɑki] *n.* a game resembling ice hockey that is played on an open field; two opposing teams use curved sticks trying to drive a ball into the opponents' net 曲棍球

therapy ['θerəpi] *n.* (medicine) the act of caring for someone (as by medication or remedial training etc.) 治疗

narc [nɑːk] *n.* a lawman concerned with narcotics violations 缉毒侦探

obtuse [əb'tuːs] *adj.* having difficulty in understanding things or making no effort to understand them 迟钝的

spasmodic [spæz'mɑːdɪk] *adj.* happening suddenly, for short periods of time, and at irregular intervals 间歇的

catastrophic [ˌkætə'strɑːfɪk] *adj.* extremely harmful; bringing physical or financial ruin 灾难的，毁灭性的

ripple ['rɪpl] *n.* a small wave on the surface of a liquid 波纹，涟漪

hygienist [haɪ'dʒiːnɪst] *n.* a person who is trained to clean people's teeth and to give them advice on how to take care of their teeth and gums 口腔保健员；牙科保洁员

sperm [spɜːm] n. the male reproductive cell; the male gamete 精子

Sephardic [si'fɑːdɪk] *adj.* （来自西班牙或葡萄牙的）赛法迪犹太人

Hollandaise [ˌhɔlən'deiz] *n.* eggs and butter with lemon juice 荷兰酱；荷兰汁

Phrases and Expressions

pop the trunk: to open the trunk 打开后备箱

pop out: to appear suddenly 蹦出来

boss sb around: to be bossy towards sb 对某人颐指气使

Notes

Alexander the Great: Alexander III was the King of the ancient kingdom of Macedonia, and creator of an empire that included Greece, Persia, Egypt, and many regions beyond them, commonly known as Alexander the Great. 亚历山大大帝，即亚历山大三世，马其顿王国国王，世界古代史上著名的军事家和政治家

IV. Exercises for Understanding

1. Answer the following questions according to the video clip you have just watched.

(1) What does Toula mean when she says that in her family there is no difference between hugging and suffocation?

(2) According to Gus, who invented the Facebook?

(3) Why does Toula have to give up her dream as a travel agent?

(4) How does Paris comment on his parents?

(5) What kind of university does the family want Paris to apply to? Why?

2. Decide whether the following statements are true or false according to the video clip you have just watched. Write a "T" for true or an "F" for false.

_____(1) Gus urges Paris to get a Greek boyfriend and have babies soon.

_____(2) Toula now spends more time with her parents than with her daughter Paris as the daughter is now a grown-up.

_____(3) Gus is very satisfied that his daughter Toula gets married with a non-Greek man.

_____(4) The admission officer finally admits that he is kind of Greek as the descendant of Alexander the Great.

_____(5) It seems that Gus is able to trace every English word to its Greek origin.

Section B　**Reading**

Norms of social interaction are beliefs about what is acceptable in a social context. They are socially accepted rules of behavior and conduct that are prescribed by society and expected of an individual by that society. Social norms are based on traditions, beliefs and values of a society and they may change from one society to another. These rules may be explicit or implicit. Human behavior is influenced by a perceived group norm. Individuals who do not conform to these rules are said to have deviated from social norms.

Goodbyes

Norms of social interaction, like many other social phenomena, are the unplanned, unexpected results of individuals' interactions. It has been argued that social norms ought to be understood as a kind of grammar of social interactions. Like grammar, a system of norms specifies what is acceptable and what is not in a society or group. For this reason, adherence to social norms

Greetings

means obeying the old proverb: "When in Rome, do as the Romans do."

Gratitude

Much of the world's business is done while enjoying social events rather than in a bland office environment. How can we act properly and gracefully at the dining table, especially under the circumstances of the Belt and Road Initiative? The following tips are hoped to be helpful.

Dining Practice

The dining protocol includes what to eat, how to eat, when to eat, and where to eat, etc. Dining protocol in different cultures reflects different cultures' underlying values. The purpose of dining with business associates is not merely to eat or drink, but to extend the business meeting through the mealtime. It is an opportunity for an enjoyable interchange in association with the pleasure of eating or drinking.

Time and place of dining also vary in different cultures. In some parts of the world, the main meal is at noon while in others the main meal is in the evening. Lunchtime in many cultures is from noon to 2 p.m., but in Mexico, lunchtime is 2 p.m. to 4 p.m. and is the main meal of the day. In some cultures, business meals are eaten in private homes while in other cultures usually eaten at restaurants.

The manner of eating is widely diverse. You will have your own plate of food on a Western dinner table, while in China the dishes are placed on the table and everyone shares. Tahitian food is eaten with the fingers. In the Middle East, be prepared to eat with your fingers if your host does, but use the right hand only.

In Bolivia, you are expected to clean your plate; Egyptians, however, consider it impolite to eat everything on your plate. Dining in Japan, especially in Japanese homes, requires sitting in a kneeling position on a tatami mat. Men keep their knees 3 or 4 inches apart; women keep their knees together. Being able to lower yourself to a position and rise from it gracefully requires practice.

Strict Muslims do not consume pork or alcohol. Orthodox Jews eat neither pork nor shellfish. Hindus do not eat any beef because the cow is considered sacred. People from countries such as India are often vegetarians because of personal or religious beliefs.

Drinking Protocol

Drinking is always involved in many social entertainments. Different cultures have various attitudes towards alcohol drinking. For example, Muslims have a complete shunning of alcohol, while alcohol is a part of Chinese folklore and has a long history. In modern China, alcohol maintains its important role, despite many social changes. It still appears at almost all social activities, the most common occasions being business dinner, birthday parties, wedding feasts and sacrifice ceremonies in which liquor must be the main drink to show respect and express happiness. In Japan or Korea, it is traditional for the host and the guest to take turns filling the cups of each other and encouraging each other to gulp it down. Do as Romans do when you are in Rome.

Perhaps the best-known drinking culture in the world is in Russia. No Russia meal is complete without vodka, which is a big business in the country. People in many countries drink beer quite often, but with different preference. In the US beer drinkers prefer their brew cold, while in the UK and much of Europe, beer is served at room temperature.

Seating Arrangement

As for the seating arrangements, in business dining or negotiation, the primary principle is to achieve your goal: honor your important business guest with a seat next to the host or as close as possible so that the host can communicate with him/her.

Still, different cultures have different seating forms. Sitting at a long table, the most important people sit at the center of each long side, facing each other. The most important guest sits to the right. Men and women alternate in this way, with the least important guests seated farthest from the hosts. Remember right-hand side is always the preferred side.

In Asia, tables are usually either circular or square. The honored guest is seated facing the door. Someone's left-hand side is preferred side.

In Middle Eastern cultures, seating is usually circular, but not necessarily around a table. Guests might sit on the floor. Someone's right-hand side is the preferred side. Women usually sit separately.

Tipping

Tipping is acceptable in some countries and not necessary or even not allowed in others. Therefore, there are tipping cultures and non-tipping cultures. In a tipping culture, a tip of 15% of the bill is considered to be a generous tip in numerous situations like fine restaurants. In many European restaurants, 10% to 15% has been already added to the bill, but you can leave extra if the service was especially good. Most services should be tipped in a tipping culture. If the service is very bad, you are not expected to leave a tip but should report the situation to the manager. Leaving a few coins—insult tipping—shows a lack of respect and is inappropriate regardless of how poor the service is.

However, in a non-tipping culture, tipping can offend or insult the people of that culture. In Australia and New Zealand, tipping is frowned upon—virtually non-existent. People in

China and Japan, too, consider helping you with your luggage as a gesture of hospitality and would "lose face" if you tip them. Observing cultural differences in tipping can be helpful for you to communicate in a proper and graceful way.

Exercises for Understanding

1. Answer the following questions according to the passage you have just read.

(1) When is the main meal of the day for Mexicans?

(2) Is it polite for Westerners to eat all the food on their own plates?

(3) Are there any food taboos for certain cultures? What are they?

(4) What countries consider alcohol as an important role in their banquets?

(5) What is the way of seating arrangement in Middle Eastern cultures?

(6) What is considered as a rude behavior in a tipping culture?

2. Click (√) your preferable items in the table below and discuss with your partner the reason for your choices.

How to Communicate with North Americans	
(1) Read much into North Americans' words (Be oversensitive to nonverbal nuances).	
○ Almost never	○ Rarely
○ Sometimes	○ Quite often
○ Most of the time	
(2) Self-affirmation and individuality are important to North Americans.	
○ Absolutely correct	○ Perhaps
○ Not really	○ Absolutely wrong
(3) One should use polite speech with family members and intimate friends, and also with strangers.	
○ Absolutely correct	○ Perhaps
○ Not really	○ Absolutely wrong
(4) Consider it good to speak directly and that requests are often stated directly and explicitly.	
○ Almost never	○ Rarely
○ Sometimes	○ Quite often
○ Most of the time	
(5) Recognize that being assertive is valued in North American culture.	

○ Almost never	○ Rarely
○ Sometimes	○ Quite often
○ Most of the time	

(6) What Chinese consider modesty may be viewed by North Americans as low self-confidence.

○ Absolutely correct	○ Perhaps
○ Not really	○ Absolutely wrong

(7) Be cautious about asking personal questions.

○ Almost never	○ Rarely
○ Sometimes	○ Quite often
○ Most of the time	

(8) North Americans like to express their opinions openly.

○ Absolutely correct	○ Perhaps
○ Not really	○ Absolutely wrong

(9) What Chinese consider a delicacy may be considered inedible by some Westerners.

○ Absolutely correct	○ Perhaps
○ Not really	○ Absolutely wrong

3. Small group task: getting along with the Chinese.

Imagine that you are living in the West. A Western acquaintance tells you she is about to live in China for several years, and she wants you to give her some advice on how to get along well with Chinese people.

Make a list of tips for her. State each as a piece of advice. Be prepared to share your list with the class.

Section C Case

The Scenario

Scan and Listen

What's True Friendship?

Yang Ruifang worked as a secretary in an Australian company in Melbourne. She became friendly with one of the Australian secretaries, a woman named Cathy Lane. The two usually ate lunch together and Yang Ruifang often asked Cathy for advice on problems she faced when adjusting to Australian society. Cathy gave her a lot of advice and helped her move from one apartment to another. Cathy went with Yang Ruifang to the Immigration Bureau several times to help sort out some problems. Yang Ruifang visted Cathy several times at home but did not invite Cathy to her apartment because she shared it with four other people. If they did not see each other over the weekend, they usually talked on the telephone. As Yang Ruifang was also preparing to take an English test, she was able to get a lot of help with English in this way.

However, sth seemed to be going wrong. Cathy seemed to be getting impatient, even a little cold. She started going out by herself at lunchtime instead of eating with Yang and seemed reluctant to answer questions. Yang Ruifang was puzzled. She couldn't imagine what the problem was.

Exercise

Listen to the case above and answer the following questions.

(1) What was the friendship between Yang Ruifang and Cathy like in the very beginning?

(2) What was Yang Ruifang doing that made Cathy decide that the relationship was not a true friendship?

(3) Why did Yang Ruifang think the relationship was developing well?

(4) From this case, what do you think Australians and other Westerners expect from their friends?

(5) Would you give advice to Cathy and Yang Ruifang to help them restore their friendship?

Module 4
Nonverbal Communication

Unit 8　Body Language

Video Clip Appreciation

I. Introduction to the TV Series *Lie to Me*

Lie to Me is an American crime drama television series. It originally ran on the Fox network from January 21, 2009 to January 31, 2011. In the show, Dr. Cal Lightman and his colleagues in The Lightman Group accept assignments from third parties and assist in investigations, reaching the truth through applied psychology: interpreting microexpressions and body language.

The show is inspired by the work of Paul Ekman, the world's foremost expert on facial expressions and a professor emeritus of Psychology at the University of California San Francisco School of Medicine. Dr. Ekman has served as an advisor to police departments and anti-terrorism groups and acted as a scientific consultant in the production of the series. He is also the author of 15 books, including *Telling Lies* and *Emotions Revealed*.

Season one opens with Cal and Gillian hiring a new associate: TSA officer Ria Torres, who scored extraordinarily high on Cal's deception-detection diagnostic, and is in turn labeled a "natural" at deception detection. Her innate talent in the field clashes with Cal's academic approach, and he often shows off by rapidly analyzing her every facial expression. She counters by reading Lightman and, when he least expects it, peppers conversations with quotes from his books.

It was gradually revealed that Dr. Lightman was driven to study micro-expressions as a result of guilt over his mother's suicide. She claimed to have been fine in order to obtain a weekend pass from a psychiatric ward, when she was actually experiencing agony.

For a small number of the early episodes, Lightman would team up with Torres to work on a case, while Foster and Loker would team up on a separate case. Occasionally, their work would intertwine, or Foster and/or Lightman would provide assistance on each other's cases. As the first season progressed, the cases became more involved, and all four of the main characters would work together on one case for each episode.

In addition to detecting deception in subjects they interview, Lightman and his team also use various interviewing and interrogation tactics to elicit useful information. Rather than by force, they use careful lines of questioning, provocative statements, theatrics and healthy doses of deception on their own part. In the show's pilot episode, Lightman is speaking to a man who is refusing to speak at all, and is able to discern vital information by talking to him and gauging his reaction to each statement.

II. Introduction to the Video Clip

What you have here is Dr. Cal Lightman, looking at human behavior, facial tics and body gestures which will ultimately be used for investigative purposes. He is known for looking at his subjects quite intensively which makes them feel uncomfortable. In this scene, a woman named Jane is being questioned on the topic of her relation with John Stafford and the group S. R. P. Dr. Cal Lightman clearly sees the evasiveness in her answers and tells her that he knows she is lying about everything. A few associates also watch each and every sign of hesitation and nervousness by analyzing her eye contact and the coherence of her answers in the next door. Dr. Cal Lightman uses his power of unconventional mentalist to get the facts right and the ultimate truth.

Video Clip

III. Script of the Video Clip

Jane: Whatever people may feel personally about John Stafford and S. R. P., it's been a great help in my life, and in a lot of people's lives. And John would never hurt anyone.

Gillian: But you left S. R. P. Why?

Jane: You can leave whenever you want. When your course work is finished, it's time to move on.

Ria: Broken eye contact, hesitation.

Dr. Lightman: That's a straight up lie, Jane.

Jane: No, it's not. I still embrace the precepts, but I choose to live my own life now.

Dr. Lightman: Precepts?

Ria: Defensive.

Terres: She feels attacked.

Dr. Lightman: I'm not trying to attack you, but from the look in your eye, you got a story to tell.

Ria: He's in.

Jane: I knew John... in the beginning. S. R. P. started off as... a beautiful thing, just a few of us exchanging ideas on how we could change our lives. People got interested and more people came. We were doing sth special. We were helping them.

Gillian: And then what happened?

Dr. Lightman: Money. And more money, eh? You hate the money, don't ya? Ruined everything.

Jane: It changed John. He appointed himself our leader. My boyfriend at the time, Martin, he was the first one to leave.

Gillian: So, where's Martin now?

Jane: There was a fire. The police said it was an accident. John said it was Martin's own negativity that lit the fire that killed him.

Gillian: You blame stafford.

Dr. Lightman: You blame mine.

Jane: Blame is a very negative term.

Gillian: You blame yourself.

Jane: I blame no one.

Dr. Lightman: You blame everyone.

Ria: Head down, eyes down, blocking the eyes with the hand.

Terres: Shame.

Gillian: Were you what they call an initiate?

Jane: What are you suggesting?

Dr. Lightman: You're the one who's doing that, darling. You still love him.

Jane: I will always love Martin.

Dr. Lightman: I'm not talking about Martin and you know that. Stafford's done with you though, right? He's through. How old are you?

Jane: I'm 37.

Dr. Lightman: You're outraged at the fact that you're being replaced by younger women, right? You ever thought of suicide?

Ria: Shame again.

Dr. Lightman: Send this one on to Florida before she goes running back to Stafford.

Gillian: Stafford's a narcissist. He's his own weak spot and we just have to wait and he'll trip himself up.

Dr. Lightman: There's no time for that. He had his thugs break into my house.

Gillian: I called him a narcissist and you make this about you?

Dr. Lightman: Oh, that reminds me. I want a big wanky picture of myself to put up in my office.

Gillian: Can you just wait until I get my purse?

****

John: You know, it's easy to be negative. Everything around us is designed to make us think negatively. But guess what? We ain't buying it. We ain't buying it. Go on, say it.

Crowd: We ain't buying it.

John: We ain't buying because we know the truth that can't be bought or sold. Young lady, would you come up here? Welcome.

Dr. Lightman: Mind your back. That's it.

John: How long have you been with us?

Girl: 11 months.

John: 11 months. And how's that going?

Dr. Lightman: Thank you.

Girl: I'm on the fourth transition.

Dr. Lightman: Where's Carol?

Ria: I don't know. No one's seen her.

Dr. Lightman: Right. Excuse me.

Girl: S. R. P. is the best thing I've ever done.

John: Come on, you can say it. It's OK, you're with family now.

Girl: S. R. P.'s the best thing I've ever done.

Gillian: She's disappeared?

Dr. Lightman: Yeah, you noticed it?

****

Gillian: Dr. John.

Dr. Lightman: Carol Ashland? Any news?

John: Would you excuse me? Um... I don't know where Carol Ashland is. That's the truth and you know it.

Dr. Lightman: You want to know why you get on my nerves? I'm going to tell you anyway. Although I don't see any lies on your face, also, I can't see any truth.

John: Look, I'm sure you thought you were helping Carol by coming here, Dr. Lightman.

Dr. Lightman: Any fear for her safety? I can't even see that, can you?

John: Maybe Danielle knows sth.

Gillian: Carol's daughter, Danielle? It's just the way you said Danielle's name just now, you seem more familiar with her than her own mother does.

Dr. Lightman: See, you know, even though I don't get sweet F. A. from your face... huh? That's a classic, that is.

****

Gilliana: Were you ever a member of S. R. P.?

Dr. Lightman: Not really a question, that one, love. So... on you go.

Danielle: How did you find out?

Dr. Lightman: Stafford.

Danielle: He told you?

Dr. Lightman: In a manner of speaking, yeah.

Danielle: I was in S. R. P. until a few months ago. It just wasn't for me.

Dr. Lightman: What did he do to you?

Danielle: I was in the core group, an initiate. We had sex every day for nearly a year. I'd be in the middle of something and someone would say John wanted to see me, so I'd go.

Anytime, night or day. Sometimes you wouldn't even know where you were going. They'd send a jet and fly you back in the morning. At first I liked it. I was proud of myself. I felt like I was better than the rest of the women. But then I saw myself... what I was really doing. It got bad... really bad. Some nights... I would just... scratch myself. My face. I wanted to be ugly. I didn't want him to touch me.

Dr. Lightman: But you didn't leave.

Gillian: You couldn't.

Danielle: It feels like there's no world outside S. R. P.

Dr. Lightman: So, you come to see us about your mum? But it's not just her.

Danielle: I want to kill him.

Dr. Lightman: Well, it could cost you a little extra. What are you so excited about?

Ria: John Stafford loves a close-up. Everything's right here. He's just hard to pin down, all these stored microexpression. So I isolated the most obvious examples.

Dr. Lightman: Stop. Pan on the left. Go back. All right, there. Subcutaneous muscle damage. No wonder we couldn't get a read on him. Do you care to take a guess?

Ria: Surgery. I was already there.

Dr. Lightman: All right, well, calm down, because this is the first time I've seen these.

Ria: Do you want to see what he looked like before?

Dr. Lightman: Yeah, fire away.

Dr. Lightman: Blimey, no wonder we couldn't get a read on him.

Ria: Meet Carl Weatherly from Ontario. Wanted by the R. C. M. P. since 1989 for vehicular manslaughter. Leaving a wife and a kid.

Dr. Lightman: John Stafford is not John Stafford.

New Words

precept ['priːsept] *n.* a general rule that helps you to decide how you should behave in particular circumstances 准则，规范

ruin ['ruːɪn] *v.* to severely harm, damage, or spoil sth 毁坏，糟蹋

initiate [ɪ'nɪʃieɪt] *n.* beginning, threshold, opening and conception 开始；新加入者，接受初步知识者

outraged ['aʊtreɪdʒɪd] *adj.* extremely angry 震怒的

suicide ['suːɪsaɪd] *n.* the act of deliberately killing oneself 自杀

narcissist ['nɑːrsɪsɪst] *n.* someone in love with themselves 自我陶醉者

thug [θʌɡ] *n.* a violent person or criminal 暴徒；恶棍；刺客

wanky ['wæŋkɪ] *adj.* very stupid or very poor quality 蠢的；劣质的

subcutaneous [ˌsʌbkju'teɪnɪəs] *adj.* sth that is situated, used, or put under your skin 皮下的

close-up ['kləuzʌp] *n.* a photograph or a picture in a film that shows a lot of details because it is taken very near to the subject 特写镜头

vehicular [viː'hɪkjələ] *adj.* sth that relates to vehicles and traffic 车辆的；交通的

blimey ['blaɪmi] *interj.* an exclamation of surprise or annoyance 天哪，表示吃惊或恼怒

manslaughter ['mænslɔːtə] *n.* the crime of killing sb. illegally but not deliberately 过失杀人

Phrases and Expressions

trip up: to cause sb to make a mistake （使）犯错；（使）失误

get on one's nerves: to make sb continually worried and anxious about the situation 使人不安

pin down: to try to discover exactly what, where, or when it is 确定

IV. Exercises for Understanding

1. Answer the following questions according to the video clip you have just watched.

(1) Why did Jane leave S. R. P. finally?

(2) How does Ria tell that Jane feels ashamed of her words?

(3) Why was Jane once outraged during her stay in S. R. P.?

(4) What kind of changes did Danielle undergo when she stayed with John Stafford as a member of S. R. P.?

(5) Why did Dr. Lightman say in the end of the movie clip that John Stafford is not John Stafford?

2. Decide whether the following statements are true or false according to the video clip you have just watched. Write a "T" for true or an "F" for false.

_____(1) Broken eye contact is a sign of shame according to Ria and Terres in the video.

_____(2) The relationship between John Stafford and Jane broke up because they didn't love each other anymore.

_____(3) The police said that it was Martin's own negativity that caused him to light fire that killed him.

_____(4) John Stafford loves a close-up to show that he is a narcissist to a great extent.

_____(5) John Stafford received a surgery in his face so that Dr. Lightman could not read his microexpressions easily.

3. Match the lines on the left with their speakers on the right.

(1) Blame is a very negative term.　　　　　　　　A. Dr. Lightman

(2) That's a straight up lie, Jane.　　　　　　　　B. John

(3) It feels like there's no world outside S. R. P.　　C. Jane

(4) Broken eye contact, hesitation.　　　　　　　　D. Danielle

(5) Maybe Danielle knows something.　　　　　　　E. Ria

Section B　Reading

The study of body language is known as Kinesics. Kinesic behaviors include gestures, head movements, facial expressions, eye behaviors, and other physical movements that can be used to communicate. No single type of behavior exists in isolation. Specific body movements can be understood only by taking the person's total behavior into account.

Your Body Language May Shape Who You Are

William Shakespear emphasized the significance of body language by saying that "There is language in her eye, her cheek, her lip." E. M. Forster in *A Passage to India* wrote: A pause in the wrong place, an intonation misunderstood, and a whole conversation went awry.

According to a survey conducted by Grayson and Stein in 1981—First they filmed people walking in the streets of New York, then showed the films to prisoners, who indicated which walkers appeared vulnerable to attack—people who walked confidently with swinging foot movements were less likely to be selected as victims.

Consciously or unconsciously, intentionally or unintentionally, we make important judgments and decisions concerning the internal states of others—states they often express without words. Nonverbal communication is so subtle that a shifting of body zones can also send a message. Nonverbal communication is important because we use the actions of others to learn their affective or emotional states. If we see someone with a clenched fist and a grim expression, we do not need words to tell us that this person is not happy. Nonverbal communication is also significant in human interaction because it is usually responsible for first impressions. Think for a moment how often your first judgments are based on the color of a person's skin or the manner in which he or she is dressed. More important, those initial messages usually influence the perception of everything else that follows. Nonverbal communication has value in human interaction because many of our nonverbal actions are not easily controlled consciously. This means that they are relatively free of distortions and deception.

In 1969, Paul Ekman and Wallace Friesen suggested that there are five categories of kinesic behaviors. They are emblems, illustrators, affect displays, regulators, and adaptors.

Emblems are nonverbal behaviors that have a direct verbal translation. They are direct replacements for words (e.g. the peace sign).

Illustrators are nonverbal behaviors directly tied to or accompanying the verbal message (e.g. a circular hand movement to describe a circle).

Affect displays are facial and body movements that show feelings and emotions (e.g. hugging to express love, and smiling to express happiness).

Regulators are nonverbal behaviors that maintain or regulate turn-taking conversations. They are used by speakers to indicate whether others should take a turn and by listeners to indicate whether they wish to speak or would prefer to continue listening (e.g. raising your hand when you want to speak).

Adaptors are personal body movements that occur as a reaction to an individual's physical and psychological state (e.g. chewing your fingernails or twirling your hair).

Body languages are very important in that it is estimated that less 10% of the whole message understood by an audience is the actual content, some 30% is attributed to the pitch and tenor or a person's voice, and 60% to other forms of nonverbal communication from body language to facial expressions to hand gestures. Body language says more than what words can say.

Arab men often greet by kissing on both cheeks. In Japan, men greet by bowing, and in the United States, people shake hands. In Thailand, to signal another person to come near, one moves the finger back and forth with the palm down. In the United States, people beckon someone to come near by holding the palm up and moving the fingers toward their body. The Tongans sit down in the presence of superiors; in the West, we stand up. Crossing one's legs in the United States is often a sign of being relaxed; in Korea, it is a social taboo. In Japan, gifts are usually exchanged with both hands. Muslims consider the left hand unclean and do not eat or pass objects with it. Buddha maintained that great wisdom arrived during moments of silence. In the United States, people talk to arrive at the truth.

Overall, nonverbal behavior functions as a culturally rule-governed communication system. The rules are governed by culture, and the rules and nonverbal behavior differ among cultures. However, what we need to recognize is that not all people engage in the same actions we have

Body Language

illustrated. We might, for example, note that many native American children avoid direct eye contact as a sign of respect; yet because of individual differences, there may well be some exceptions to this assertion. We should note that we are more than our culture. Besides, we should not forget that nonverbal behaviors seldom occur in isolation. Individual messages, in reality, are but part of the total communication context. We usually send many nonverbal cues simultaneously and these cues are normally linked to both our verbal messages and the setting in which we find ourselves.

Exercises for Understanding

1. Answer the following questions according to the passage you have just read.

(1) What do kinesic behaviors generally include? What are the categories?

(2) Who are less likely to be attacked, according to the survey conducted by Grayson and Stein?

(3) How do you understand that nonverbal communication is valuable in social interaction?

(4) What is the difference between emblems and illustrators?

(5) How do Thais behave differently from Americans in beckoning people to come here?

(6) Can nonverbal messages be judged in isolation? Why or why not?

2. Small group task: gestures around the world.

One person's positive gesture may be another person's insult. The world is full of nonverbal gestures that can mean the exact opposite in different cultures. First describe the following gestures and then discuss their meanings in different cultures.

3. Role-play the following demonstrations concerning handshakes.

The handshake is the most common and most meaningful physical contact you will have with people. Analyzing people's handshake may provide some clues into their characters and intentions. The following are some handshake basics:

■ A handshake in which an individual grips firmly but not too firmly, pumps your hand once or twice and looks you straight in the eye can signify an individual who is confident, sees you as an equal and intends an honest, up-front negotiation or discussion. If a person continues to hold onto your hand for longer than expected, he or she may be attempting to show sincerity.

■ If while shaking your hand, an individual tries to guide you into a room or toward a seat, it may indicate that that individual likes to be in control and insists on having his or her way. It can signal difficult talks if things do not go their way. In many Asian nations, however, such an action should be seen as a sign of respect and friendship, not a power play.

■ If someone grips your hand and then twists his/her hand so it is on the top, the signal is that of a competitive person who is saying that, although you may be starting out as equals, he or she will win in the end.

■ Most people have been the victim of a handshake where an individual attempts to crush your hand in a vice-like grip. This is an indication of a person who is competitive and plans to win at all costs but associates physical strength with acuity. Their bark (or, in this case, their handshake) is often much worse than their bite.

■ When offered by a Westerner, the limp handshake that resembles grabbing hold of a dead fish usually indicates someone with low energy and lack of enthusiasm and confidence. In Asia, such a handshake is common and is an indicator of equality, not deference. Some Southeast Asian societies will actually use their other hand to support their handshaking wrist. This is a sign of respect, not weakness.

4. Guess the meanings of the following typical gestures from American movies and TV series.

5. Matching.

Different gestures may serve the same function and the same gesture can have a number of unexpected consequences in different cultures. Think over the following items, then surf the Internet and make a proper match between cultures and gestures or the meanings they express.

(1) How to beckon somebody to come over?

1) in the US   A. waving the hand with the palm down

2) in the Middle East   B. just waving the index finger

3) in Portugal   C. downward waving of the arm

4) in Tonga   D. waving the hand with the palm up

(2) How to point something or somebody out?

1) in the US   A. pointing with the lips

2) in Mongolia   B. pointing with the tongue

3) in India   C. extending the index finger

4) in Guinea-Bissau   D. pointing with the chins

(3) How to show approval?

1) in France   A. raising one's eyebrows

2) in Greece   B. having the thumbs up

3) in Tonga   C. having one thumb up

4) in Kenya   D. tilting one's head

(4) What may the "OK" sign mean?

1) in Brazil   A. rudeness

2) in Russia   B. money

3) in France   C. something vulgar

4) in Japan   D. something worthless

(5) What may the folded arms suggest?

1) in the US   A. no special meaning

2) in Russia   B. impatience

3) in Finland   C. being rude

4) in Wales   D. arrogance

(6) What's the appropriate type of handshake?

1) in the US   A. soft handshake

2) in France   B. handshake and free hand placed on the forearm of the other

3) in Japan   C. firm handshake

4) in the Middle East   D. handshake with the arm firmly extended

(7) What may a widening of eyes mean?

1) in the US and the UK   A. persuasion (I'm innocent!)

2) in Latin America   B. surprise, wonder (Really?)

3) in France   C. challenge (I don't believe you!)

4) in Africa   D. call for help (I don't understand!)

(8) What may the tug on one's earlobe suggest?

1) in Greece   A. you are a sponger

2) in Spain   B. something wonderful

3) in Portugal   C. a warning

4) in Scotland   D. doubt about what you are saying

6. Self-testing.

(1) Surf the website (https://testyourself.psychtests.com/testid/3764) to test your ability to read other people's body language.

(2) Surf the website (https://www.kent.ac.uk/careers/interviews/nvc.htm) for body language in interview.

Section C Case

The Scenario

Scan and Listen

Whose Car Is It?

A joint venture in Beijing involved Chinese and American partners. American-recruited specialists were working together with Chinese specialists in establishing a factory. The American side of this project had provided most of the material and equipment necessary to start the plant, including a car. The use of this car became the focus of an on-going battle that was regularly raised at each semi-annual management meeting.

The Americans claimed that the car had been provided for project use during working hours and for private use for American project members outside office hours. They claimed that this implied that the American team members should be able to drive it. The Chinese felt that the car should only be driven by authorized Chinese drivers, which effectively limited its use by Americans but increased its use by senior Chinese project members.

The conflict centered on the registration. The car first has a registration that prevented its being driven by the Americans. Their aim was to change this registration. The Chinese were apologetic—it could not legally be done. The Americans cited the Memorandum of the Understanding that formed the legal basis of the project; they cited the Chinese law and precedents. All agreed that it was possible. The Chinese authorities answered with a number of practical difficulties, but conceded that the Americans had the right to drive the car and promised to look into this matter.

Six months later, nothing had changed. The matter was again raised at the semi-annual management meeting. The right of the Americans to drive the car was again acknowledged, difficulties mentioned and the action promised.

Exercise

Listen to the case above and answer the following questions.

(1) What does having the car mean to the Chinese group and to the American group?

(2) What strategies are the Americans using to get the car?

(3) What strategies are the Chinese using to keep the car?

(4) How would you explain the situation to the Americans? What more effective strategies can they use to achieve their goal?

Unit 9　Time

Section A　**Video Clip Appreciation**

I. Introduction to the Movie *In Time*

In 2169, the physical aging of the human body stops when people turn to 25, after which the "watch" on everyone's forearm starts to click. A person dies when the countdown of the "watch," originally set for one year, reaches zero. No cash, credit cards, or any other kind of payment method is used at that time. Instead, people do their job to earn themselves more time, the only currency in circulation. The world is divided into different Time Zones according to the amount of time owned by the people in each district. Day after day, the rich are bored to death in the leisure brownstone area New Greenwich, while the poor struggle to survive in

Dayton, where people rarely have over 24 hours left and what's worse, Minutemen murder for watches with more time. Will Salas, a poor young man living in Dayton, is accused of larceny and murder after he saves Henry Hamilton, who comes from New Greenwich and owns more than a decade in his watch, from a group of Minutemen led by Fortis. In his escape from the Timekeepers, Will meets Sylvia Weis, the daughter of a millionaire named Philippe Weis. They then start making their efforts to challenge or even destroy the existing time system.

II. Introduction to the Video Clip

Will Salas is a 25-year-old factory worker living in Dayton with his mother, Rachel Salas. It is Rachel's 50th birthday, so Will spends the time he earned last night buying his mother a bottle of decent champagne as a birthday present. Both of them decide to celebrate Rachel's birthday after she comes back home from work two days later. After a day's work in the time capsule factory, Will goes to the pub to meet his best friend Borel. Borel tells Will that there is a madman who has been buying drinks all night. The madman's name is Henry. Will notices that there is over a century in Henry's watch, so he tries to warn him of the dangers of flaunting his wealth in Dayton. Unfortunately, the time robbers, or Minutemen, come soon after they receive the message of Henry's visit to the pub and are about to clean his watch, leaving him to die alone. At this crucial moment, Will rescues Henry from being robbed and they escape from the Minutemen.

III. Script of the Video Clip

Will: [*Monologue*] I don't have time. I don't have time to worry about how it happened. It is what it is. We're genetically engineered to stop aging at 25. The trouble is, we live only one more year unless we can get more time. Time is now the currency. We earn it and spend it. The rich can live forever. And the rest of us? I just want to wake up with more time on my hand than hours in the day.

Video Clip

Will: Hey, Mom.

Rachel: You got in late last night.

Will: I put in some overtime.

Rachel: Where'd it go?

Will: On you. They drink it in New Greenwich. Happy 50th!

Rachel: Fifty?

Will: That's right. Twenty-five for the 25th time.

Rachel: I was sure I'd have a grandchild by now.

Will: Here we go.

Rachel: Bela's daughter is always asking about you.

Will: Who has time for a girlfriend? Besides, what's the hurry? What do you got?

Rachel: Three days. Not even. We owe half that in rent. Eight for the electric and we're still late on that loan.

Will: I can make extra on the side, you know. I could...

Rachel: What, start fighting? Nobody wins.

Will: Yeah…

Rachel: Remember, I'm not here tonight. I got two days' work in the garment district.

Will: I know.

Rachel: Meet me at the bus stop tomorrow. After I pay off the loan, I won't have long.

Will: I'll be there.

Rachel: Will... I just wouldn't know what to do if I lost you.

Will: I'm late.

Rachel: Let me give you 30 minutes so you can have a decent lunch.

Will: I love you. Happy birthday, Mom. When you get back, we're going to celebrate.

Mya: Will! Will! You got a minute?

Will: What are you talking about, Mya? You have a whole year.

Mya: Not a year I can use yet. Come on, Will. I've got bills to pay.

Will: Here, take five minutes. Get out of here.

****

Will: Four minutes for a cup of coffee?

Borel: Yesterday, it was three.

Seller: You want coffee or you want to reminisce?

Will: Two coffees. How many shifts you got today, Borel?

Borel: Just the two. Really excited about it. If you had any of your father in you, we could make a fortune.

Will: I don't fight.

Borel: There's another one. Broad daylight.

Will: Whoa, what is this? Where's the rest?

Officer: Never met the quota.

Will: My units are up from last week.

Officer: So's the quota. Next.

Will: That's a joke, right?

Officer: Next.

Workers: Move it. You're taking forever.

Gambler: You in, Will?

Will: I don't have time to gamble anymore.

Gambler: Thank God. Because ever since you stopped playing, I started winning.

Will: You still owe me an hour. You seen Borel?

Borel: Will!

Will: Hey, man. Your wife's looking for you.

Borel: You're not gonna believe it. This madman's been buying drinks all night. He's got a
century!

Will: Come on, let me get you home.

Borel: Soon as I finish this drink.

Henry: Hey! You! You! More everything!

Will: Excuse me. You need to get out of here. Somebody's gonna clean that clock.

Henry: Yes!

Will: I mean, they aren't going to rob you. They are going to kill you. They can't take that
much time and let you live to tell about it.

Henry: Yes.

Will: I don't think you understand. You should not be here!

Borel: Will! Will! Minutemen! Minutemen! Walk away, Will. Those gangsters aren't playing
around.

Will: Wait, wait.

Borel: He's asking for it. Let's go. He's not one of us. You think he'd help us?

Will: Don't worry. I won't do anything stupid. Go.

Fortis: The name's Fortis. And that, sir, is a very nice watch. Do you mind if I try it on? I
think it would suit me.

Will: Let's get you out of here.

Fortis: Get him!

Henry: Stop. What are you doing? I can take care of myself.

Will: Yeah, it looked like it.

Henry: I know what I'm doing.

Will: Run. Run!

New Words

genetically [dʒə'netɪkli] *adv.* by genetic mechanisms 从遗传学角度；基因方面

currency ['kʌr(ə)nsɪ] *n.* the money used in a particular country 货币，通货

overtime ['əʊvətaɪm] *n.* time spent doing job in addition to normal working hours 加班时间

loan [ləʊn] *n.* a sum of money that you borrow 贷款，借款

garment ['gɑːm(ə)nt] *n.* a piece of clothing; used especially in the manufacture or sale of clothes 衣服（尤指服装加工和销售）

decent ['diːs(ə)nt] *adj.* to be of an acceptable standard or quality 得体的，像样的

reminisce [ˌremɪ'nɪs] *v.* to write or talk about sth in the past, often with pleasure 缅怀往事；叙旧，回忆

shift [ʃɪft] *n.* each of two or more recurring periods in which different groups of workers do the same jobs in relay 轮班

quota ['kwəʊtə] *n.* a fixed share of sth that a person or group is entitled to receive or is bound to contribute 配额，份额

gamble ['gæmb(ə)l] *v.* to play games of chance for money; to bet 赌博

gangster ['gæŋstə] *n.* a member of an organized group of violent criminals（结成团伙的）匪徒

Phrases and Expressions

make a fortune: to acquire great wealth by one's own efforts 发财，赚大钱

play around: to behave in a silly way to amuse oneself or other people 胡闹；轻率对待

Notes

Greenwich: The term "Greenwich" is a place-name first used by the Anglo-Saxons. Today it mainly refers to the area in southeast London, on the south bank of the Thames River with a population around 210,000. It is where the Royal Greenwich Observatory located between 1675 and 1948 and the area itself is located within the larger Royal Borough of Greenwich. At the 1884 International Longitude Conference, the meridian crossing Greenwich was defined as the Prime Meridian, the staring point for the division of time zones and geographical longitude. In this movie, Greenwich is a brownstone district in which the residents own so much time that they are almost immortal. 格林尼治，是英国伦敦的一个区，位于伦敦东南部、泰晤士河

南岸。1675—1948 年设皇家格林尼治天文台。1884 年在华盛顿召开的国际经度会议决定以经过格林尼治的经线为本初子午线，也是世界计算时间和地理经度的起点。在电影中，"格林尼治"是所谓的"富人区"，这里的人们拥有无穷的"时间"，因此他们是永生的。

Minutemen: Minutemen were the civilian soldiers from armed militias during the American Revolutionary War. They were renowned for their extremely rapid response to the external threats. It is said that they were able to get ready in a minute after receiving the notice for battles. They were thus called the minutemen. Today, the US military will also use this term as a code in some circumstances to recall the glory and patriotism of their country. In the movie, however, the Minutemen are a group of gangsters who come very soon to rob others' time whenever a rich man steps into Dayton. "一分钟人"是美国独立战争时期马萨诸塞殖民州的特殊民兵组织，成员从美国各地民兵中挑选，以具有高机动性、快速部署的能力而著称。在电影中，"一分钟人"则是指掠夺他人"时间"的恶棍。

Exercises for Understanding

1. Answer the following questions according to the video clip you have just watched.

(1) What is the difference between the time in the movie and that in the real world?

(2) How old is Will's mother?

(3) Why does Will's mother look as young as him?

(4) Why does Will complain to the officer?

(5) Who is Fortis? What does he come to the bar for?

2. Decide whether the following statements are true or false according to the video clip you have just watched. Write a "T" for true or an "F" for false.

_____(1) Will worked overnight yesterday to buy her mother a birthday present.

_____(2) Will's mother will work for two days in the clothes factory.

_____(3) Borel gets only one shift today.

_____(4) The "madman" in the bar has over a decade in his clock.

_____(5) Henry thanks Will for saving his life.

3. Fill in the blanks according to the video clip you have just watched.

Mya: Will! Will! You got a minute?

Will: What are you talking about, Mya? You have a (1) _____ year.

Mya: Not a year I can use yet. Come on, Will. I've got (2) _____ to pay.

Will: Here, take five minutes. Get out of here.

Will: Four minutes for (3) _____?

Borel: Yesterday, it was three.

Seller: You want coffee or you want to reminisce?

Will: Two coffees. How many (4) _____ you got today, Borel?

Borel: Just the two. Really (5) _____ it. If you had any of your father in you, we could make

a (6) _____.

Will: I don't fight.

Borel: There's another one. Broad daylight.

Will: Whoa, what is this? Where's (7) _____?

Officer: Never met the quota.

Will: My (8) _____ are up from last week.

Officer: So's the quota. Next.

Will: That's a (9) _____, right?

Officer: Next.

Workers: Move it. You're (10) _____.

The Concept
of Time

Section B   Reading

Time & Chronemics

Time is the manifestation of motion, the continuity of variation and the succession of events and existences. People usually use time as a parameter to describe the process of material motion or event occurrence. Chronemics, the study of time, not only focuses on the study of people's understanding and use of time, but also covers contents within the study of human tempo "as it relates to interdependent and integrated levels of time-experiencing. (Thomas, 1980)" Different cultures perceive time differently, some considering it monochronic whereas some others regarding it polychronic.

Monochronic Time

In the monochronic time system, people usually have a long-term plan but only make short-term arrangements. The low-involving monochronic people will only do one thing at a time and they barely tolerate any change in their time schedules. Besides, they put special emphasis on efficiency and personal privacy. A typical example of this time system existed in the United States during the Industrial Revolution, when time was considered to be so precious a resource that a minute or even a second was not allowed to be wasted. People at that time, basically working in factories, always lived a scheduled life, in which everything would start and end at certain times, not only when they were working but also when they were doing daily routines such as watching TV shows. Under such time system, the accomplishment of missions or tasks can be guaranteed, but those things, which need some extra time or efforts, are very possibly going to fail on the verge of success.

Polychronic Time

Different from the monochronic people, polychronic people are so involved with each other that they prefer to "keep several operations going at once." (Hall, 1966) People with this kind of culture usually treasure human relationship and feelings more than results. They tend to believe that success will come when conditions are ripe. Flexibility is the character of their way of doing things. This leads to the comparatively lower-efficiency in everything but on the other hand, a person will feel respected and cared when working or living in the country with such a culture. Taking the dining experience as an example, when having a dinner in a restaurant of the polychronic countries, it is possible for you to be served first even if you are the last to enter as long as you are really running out of time. Moreover, polychronic people often understand time as a fluid and adjustable concept, which is why "cultures that use the polychronic time system often schedule multiple appointments simultaneously" and for them "keeping on schedule is an impossibility." (Lewis and Nick, 2003)

Time Orientations

Time orientation refers to the sense of time held by the members of a particular culture. How people value and attach significance to time varies in cultures with different time orientations. Basically speaking, there are four types of time orientations, namely, past-oriented, time-line oriented, present-oriented and future-oriented.

Hurry up
Culture in ROK

Past-oriented cultures are more likely to revere the success and glory in the past and respect previous experiences, which are thought to have important reference value to present and future activities. A typical example of this kind of culture is China. The Chinese people have long been appreciating the long Chinese history, whereas pay less attention to what are probably going to happen very soon, because they regard future as something unpredictable. Filial piety, which means the elderly are to be respected and maintained properly, is considered one of the most essential virtues in Chinese culture. Countless time-honored brands, some of which may have enjoyed a history of over hundreds of years, still own great popularity in the modern society. In such cultures, history and former experiences play a vital role in the measuring of the value of both people and things.

Cultures with time-line orientation always uphold a linear way of thinking. People in these cultures often focus on the details rather than the outline, thus making it hard for them to attend to several ongoing events at the same time. For them, the procedures of solving a problem or the unfinished things in their schedule are preferably arranged one after another.

Present-oriented cultures are mainly rooted in the Central and South American countries, such as Brazil, Argentina and Mexico. Various carnivals and celebrations are one of the most outstanding features of these cultures. Present-oriented people won't get themselves entangled in the existing troublesome facts or unpredictable potential annoyances. Instead, all they care about is the present living experiences. Brazil owns the world's largest carnival, the Brazil Carnival, which is held 47 days before Easter. During the three-day celebration, the passionate Brazilians, both man and women, rich and poor, will join into the parading procession, venting whatever kind of feelings they have at the moment. With the lissome Samba steps, you might find yourself totally lost and immersed in the festive atmosphere. The Latin word "carpe diem" best displays the spirit of present-oriented culture, namely enjoying the pleasures of the moment, without concern for the upcoming future.

People in a future-oriented culture always put their focus on the possible outcomes in the future, while barely caring about the happened or ongoing events. They will set an achievable and realistic goal before taking actions and take advantage of all the available resources to reach this goal. They observe the world in a broad picture, in which former experience may not definitely be a valuable reference and the current gains and losses are never in their concern. Immigrant countries like the US, Australia and New Zealand well present the characteristics of future-oriented culture. Compared with the four cradles of civilization, the history of the US is neither long nor consecutive, but full of struggles on the way to get itself independent and prosperous. The American people are thus a little indifferent to what took place in the past. Nevertheless, their concern lies in the development trend of the country, which in their opinion should be a place of freedom and democracy. This is also why the famous notion "American Dream" would have been so inspiring for the youngsters in that particular era.

Exercises for Understanding

1. Answer the following questions according to the passage you have just read.

(1) Is time monochronic or polychronic for you? Explain the reasons.

(2) Give some more examples to illustrate why China owns a past-oriented culture.

(3) Suppose you are going to emigrate to a foreign country, what is your most preferred destination? Elaborate the reasons for your choice by comparing the features of the four time orientations.

2. Small group task: presentation.

Step 1: Form groups, each of 4 to 5.

Step 2: Each group chooses one type of time orientation as the topic.

Step 3: All the groups will be allowed 5 minutes to get prepared for a speech.

Step 4: The speakers from each group will make a 3-minute speech on the chosen topic, illustrating their views on questions like "What exactly is the time orientation you choose?" or "Why would you think this kind of time orientation is comparatively better than the rest three?", etc.

Section C **Case**

The Scenario   Scan and Listen

An "Urgent" Call

Tim, a 45-year-old American, had been working in the fashion industry for over 20 years and was the supervisor of a clothing factory on an island somewhere in the Caribbean Sea. He was in charge of the recruitment affairs, thus trying his best to find low-cost labors for his factory. With more and more workers coming by to apply for positions in the factory, things seemed to go in the right direction. However, something unexpected and tough was just around the corner.

The problem lay in the number of people who were hired. In fact, the natives of the island had long been living under a certain status system, which helped to keep the existing balance of power. To get more job opportunities, some of the natives lowered their expected salary. Their successful recruitment broke the balance, arousing great dissatisfactions among the natives of all parts, so the leaders of each party decided to meet each other and have a discussion on the current situation, looking for a proper solution.

The discussion last for quite a long time and when they finally reached an agreement about the reallocation of jobs, it was already 2 o'clock in the morning. They were so excited about their decision that an immediate phone call was made to Tim, who they thought might feel as pleased as their supporters to hear about the reached agreement. Whereas it turned out that after picking up the phone Tim got very anxious as he did not understand the local language and, what's worse, this phone call was made at a time which shows a sign of extreme urgency, so he turned to the US Marines for help. Due to the huge language gap, it took hours before the locals finally managed to make the Americans believe that they were not meant to cause any trouble.

On the second day, with the help of an interpreter, the natives finally were able to have a discussion with Tim about their concern and the solution on the recruitment problem. Tim was very confused about the reason why the natives cared about the recruiting so much that they couldn't wait until the next morning, because he believed that such recruitment bias seemed meaningless compared to the overall picture. While on the other hand, the natives insisted that they could only fully devote to their work when the current situation was properly dealt with. A mutual consensus was eventually built, but the production was far behind schedule.

Exercise

Listen to the case above and answer the following questions.

(1) What did Tim do on the island?

(2) What was the "unexpected and tough" thing mentioned in Paragraph 1?

(3) What did the natives think of the recruitment of Tim's factory?

(4) Why did the leaders decide to call Tim immediately?

(5) Why did Tim call the US Marines for help?

Unit 10   Space

Section A   Video Clip Appreciation

I. Introduction to the Movie *Wonder*

Auggie is a 10-year-old boy born with rare facial deformity. He has been home-schooled but it does not conceal his cleverness and fondness for astronomy. At his fifth grade, his parents decide to enroll him into a local school. He is initially isolated by many classmates because of his different appearance. Supported by his family, teachers and some friends, Auggie struggles to fit into the larger community. Inspired by this extraordinary boy, people around Auggie also learn to discover their compassions and respect.

II. Introduction to the Video Clip

Before Auggie starts school, the principal arranges a tour for him with three other students: Jack, Julian, and Charlotte. When school starts, Auggie is teased by Julian and some unfriendly classmates. He sits alone in the classroom and eats alone. He feels upset and his family helps to comfort and encourage him. Then Auggie starts to show his smartness in science class and develops a close relationship with Jack.

III. Script of the Video Clip

Photographer: Guys, can you please... [*Chattering*] Okay. You... you guys, skooch. Sit. Just be closer.

Mr. Browne: Ladies and Gentlemen.

Video Clip

Photographer: Stay. Stay, good. Hey, hey. What's your name?

Mr. Browne: Auggie. Nice boots.

Photographer: Great. Thanks. Okay, everybody, here we go. We're skooching and say "Cheese."

All: Cheese!

Auggie: School became... Well, I got used to it. Except for dodgeball. What evil man invented dodgeball? But my least favorite zone at school is courtyard. Because the whole school's there. No one does anything mean. Or says anything. Or laughs. They all just look, then look away, then look back. They're just being normal kids. I kinda wanna tell them, "Hey, I know I look weird, but it's okay." I mean, if Chewbacca started going to school here one day, I'd probably stare at him a bit, too.

[*Chewbacca grunting*]

Auggie: I'm sorry if my staring made you feel weird.

[*Grunting*]

Ms. Petosa: In order for any of us to see, we need light. So right now, light is bouncing off this card traveling through the air, through the glass, to your eye. But what if we added water?

All: Whoa!

[*Chuckles*]

Ms. Petosa: Whoa, indeed. Any time light passes from one material or medium to another, it bends. This bending of light is also known as...

Auggie: Refraction.

Ms. Petosa: Very good, Auggie. Jack, you okay?

Jack: Yeah, yeah, refraction.

Ms. Petosa: Good. Clear your desks. Pop quiz.

[*All groaning*]

Auggie: [*Whispers*] Hurry.

[*Kids chattering*]

Julian: Hey, Jack, come sit here.

Jack: In a sec.

Miles: Where's he going?

Jack: Hey. Thanks for your help today.

Auggie: No problem.

Jack: And don't worry, I got a couple wrong so Ms. Petosa wouldn't know.

Auggie: I'm not worried. The worst they can do is kick me out.

Jack: Not loving school either, huh?

Auggie: Oh, it's great.

Jack: [*Chuckles*] I wanted to go to Wayne Middle. The one with the great sports teams.

Auggie: Then why'd you come here?

Jack: They gave me the scholarship.

Auggie: Well, if you need help in science, you can come to my house after school. You know, if you want.

Jack: Great. Thanks! What's wrong?

Auggie: I just don't like eating in front of people.

Jack: What do you mean?

Auggie: It's a long story, but when I eat, I think I chew like some prehistoric swamp turtle.

Jack: No joke? Me too!

[*Both laughing*]

Auggie: Now there's tuna on your face.

Jack: Yeah! Tuna, man!

Auggie: No, no, no, let me show you how it's done.

[*Chuckles*]

[*Mimics chomping*]

[*Both chuckling*]

Jack: Dude, that's even more gross.

Auggie: I'm going as Boba Fett this year.

Jack: I like Halloween, but Christmas is still the best holiday.

Auggie: No way. Halloween is the best.

Jack: A pillowcase of candy versus two weeks off school. You're nuts.

[*Barks*]

Jack: You see? Even your dog agrees.

Auggie: Hey, Mom, is it okay if Jack comes over? Yes!

Jack: Thanks, Mrs. P. I mean, you get snow on Christmas.

Auggie: But you can get snow on Halloween.

Jack: How?

Auggie: If you live in Alaska or there's a blizzard.

Isabel: [*Exhales*] I've got to be cool.

[*Both grunting*]

Jack: You ever thought about having plastic surgery?

Auggie: No, I've never thought about it. Why?

[*Chuckles*]

Auggie: Dude, this is after plastic surgery! It takes a lotta work to look this good.

[*Both laughing*]

Auggie & Jack: Oh my God! Oh my God. 1, 2, 3, 4, I declare a thumb war. Bow, kiss, begin.

Isabel: Nate. Fire.

[*Inaudible*]

New Words

deformity [dɪˈfɔːmɪti] *n.* a part of someone's body which is not the normal shape because of injury or illness, or because they were born this way 畸形

skooch [skuːtʃ] *v.* to move a short distance 挪位子

dodgeball [ˈdɒdʒbɔːl] *n.* a game in which players, in teams, form a circle and try to hit opponents with a large ball 躲避球游戏

refraction [rɪˈfrækʃən] *n.* the fact or phenomenon of light, radio waves, etc. being deflected in passing obliquely through the interface between one medium and another or through a medium of varying density 折射

swamp [swɒmp] *n.* an area of low-lying, uncultivated ground where water collects; a bog or marsh 沼泽

blizzard [ˈblɪzəd] *n.* a very bad snowstorm with strong winds 暴风雪

Notes

Chewbacca: a fictional character in the *Star Wars* movie series. He is tall and covered with long hair, looking like a gorilla. He is loyal and the co-pilot of the spaceship. 楚巴卡，《星球大战》系列电影中的人物

Boba Fett: a bounty hunter in the *Star Wars* movie series. 波巴·费特，《星球大战》系列电影中的人物

Exercises for Understanding

1. Fill in the blanks according to the video clip you have just watched.

Auggie: School became…Well, I got used to it. Except for dodgeball. What (1) _____ man invented dodgeball? But my least favorite (2) _____ at school is courtyard. Because the whole school's there. No one does anything (3) _____. Or says anything. Or laughs.

They all just look, then look away, then look back. They're just being (4) _____ kids. I kinda wanna tell them, "Hey, I know I look (5) _____, but it's okay." I mean, if Chewbacca started going to school here one day, I'd probably stare at him a bit, too.

Auggie: I'm sorry if my staring made you feel weird.

Ms. Petosa: In order for any of us to see, we need light. So right now, light is (6) _____ off this card traveling through the air, through the glass, to your eye. But what if we added water?

All: Whoa!

Ms. Petosa: Whoa, indeed. Any time light passes from one (7) _____ or (8) _____ to another, it bends. This (9) _____ of light is also known as...

Auggie: Refraction.

Ms. Petosa: Very good, Auggie. Jack, you okay?

Jack: Yeah, yeah, refraction.

Ms. Petosa: Good. Clear your desks. (10) _____.

2. Decide whether the following statements are true or falses according to the video clip you have just watched. Write a "T" for true or an "F" for false.

_____(1) Dodgeball is one of Auggie's favorite games at school.

_____(2) The words on the paper changes from now to won because of reflection.

_____(3) Jack has difficulties in science and asks Auggie to help him in the test.

_____(4) Jack is the first student to eat with Auggie.

_____(5) Isabel calls Nate because the house is on fire.

3. Answer the following questions according to the video clip you have just watched.

(1) What does Auggie do during the group photographing? Why?

(2) Why does Auggie sit by himself alone in the science class?

(3) Why does Jack choose this school instead of Wayne Middle?

(4) How does Auggie's mother Isabel, react when she sees Auggie walking with Jack?

Section B   Reading

When you are having lunch by yourself in the school cafeteria, would you mind someone coming over and asking to sit with you? Or would you mind asking to sit with someone you do not know? How you answer this request largely depends on your concept of comfortable space between you and

Space Concept in Russia

strangers. We have around ourselves a certain boundary that encompasses a personal territory, analogized as a "bubble" of space. Compared with general national boundaries, this invisible boundary between people is more complex and largely dependent on the living environment.

Edward T. Hall coined the study of personal space and its effect on human communication as proxemics. Within this concept, interpersonal distance is divided into four zones. The closest is the intimate distance (0–50cm) reserved for close friends, family members and lovers in embracing, touching and whispering. The second is the personal distance (>50–120cm) among ordinary friends and relatives in daily conversations. The third is the social distance (>120–270cm) for newly formed groups and new acquaintances. The farthest is the public distance (>270cm) for public speeches and lectures which involve a larger group pf audience.

People are usually sensitive about the space within their intimate and personal distance. Allowing other people to enter personal space indicates the recognition of mutual relationship. If unfamiliar people enter the personal "bubble," for example, touching or talking within the distance of close friends, people may feel violated, discomforted or anxious. By contrast, if close friends suddenly keep a distance, it may also reveal something unpleasant.

Most people implicitly agree to the rule of protecting their own bubbles while preventing themselves from invading other bubbles. However, this does not seem like an easy job as the size of the "bubble" is highly variable. What appears to be natural for us may be offensive for others, due to different cultural backgrounds or individual preferences. People living in the overcrowding capital, for example, may discover their spatial attitudes different from those in other parts of the region.

Northern Europeans, Scandinavians for example, have quite large space bubbles where people tend to guard their privacy. Finnish, for instance, perform a distinctive queuing habit. Instead of standing closely one after another, they tend to keep a long distance from the person in front of them. In Germany, it is common to maintain an arm's length during conversations. Any further approaching may be considered as an encroachment of personal space. The German dwellings are organized accordingly. Fences and hedges separate houses and gardens. Gate and room doors are often locked. During conversations, Scandinavians or British people traditionally do not touch or hug whereas they reserve such intimate actions to closer friends or family members.

However, the case is much different in Southern Europe, such as France, Italy, Greece and Spain. Usually, the newcomers will find the natives extremely amiable when they are greeted with a kiss or a hug. Daily conversations take place in closer distance. Many places in these countries also face the problem of overcrowding. If a Northern European comes to the south, he or she may find the pushing or shoving in crowded train stations very awkward or anxious, which in the eyes of the Southern European is quite common.

Japan is another example of land scarcity. Small houses and narrow roads create a cramped living environment. Nonetheless, Japanese pay large attention to the protection of their personal bubble. They set up strict borderline between personal space and public space. Family members love to cling together in private. Yet in the public, they keep a certain distance. Unlike some broader countries, it is hard for the Japanese to guarantee their personal distance physically. They think of other ways to make up for it. For instance, in the urban area such as Tokyo, many people like to wear hygiene masks. Except for sickness precaution, masks are used to create anonymity and a mental interpersonal distance.

Middle Eastern cultures also distinguish personal and public space rigidly. Houses have few or no windows facing towards the streets. Families separate themselves from each other as a unit. Inside the house, however, individual space is limited. Family members emphasize close relationship together. Gender is also an important factor especially in many Islamic backgrounds. Men and women keep a longer distance than the same sex. Physical touching between two women such as walking hand in hand is acceptable, yet the opposite sex is not.

Cultures over the world have their own spatial customs and interpretation. These concepts and behaviors are changeable due to socioeconomic development. Before visiting a country or meeting with foreigners, it is always important to familiarize ourselves with the appropriate space in that culture in order to make sure we do not come across as too aggressive or too remote.

Exercises for Understanding

1. Decide whether the following statements are true or false according to the reading. Write a "T" for true or an "F" for false.

_____(1) Proxemics studies the effect of personal space on communication.

_____(2) The social distance is reserved for good friends.

_____(3) In Finland, it is common for people to stay close in conversations.

_____(4) The French do not expect others to greet with a hug.

_____(5) Middle Eastern people pay attention to individual privacy at home.

2. Multiple choice.

(1) According to Edward T. Hall, what kind of distance do couples keep from each other?

A. intimate distance   B. personal distance   C. social distance   D. public distance

(2) Which of the following emotions does NOT occur when you keep a distance too close to a friend?

A. offended   B. uncomfortable   C. flattered   D. anxious

(3) Which country is expected to have the smallest personal space?

A. Germany   B. Finland   C. Spain   D. the UK

(4) What is a common phenomenon in Japan?

A. House windows are facing the inside garden instead of the streets.

B. People stand far away from another while lining in a queue.

C. Women usually greet with a hug in the public.

D. People like to wear hygiene masks in the underground.

(5) Which of the following statement is correct according to the passage?

A. Spatial attitudes and behaviors are unchanging in a cultural across time.

B. Keeping an inappropriate distance is interpreted as aggressive or remote.

C. Protecting the "bubble" of oneself is more important than keeping away from others.

D. People of different nationalities keep the same distance in crowded cities.

3. Case study the following chart and have a discussion about it.

International Students Handbook

Gestures and movements

- Direct eye contact is given and expected in return by Americans talking with other people.

- A smile is the universal sign of greeting and Americans give it freely.

- People who have good posture usually appear more self-confident.

- Some Americans tell stories or talk in a dramatic manner, using a lot of hand and body gestures. These people are considered popular, attractive, and of high social status.

- Men take up more space than women in their use of gestures, body posture and movements.

- Legs spread apart when standing;

- Wide use of arms when speaking;

- And legs crossed at the ankles when sitting.

- Imitating the posture of the person with whom you are communicating shows you are probably agreeing with him/her.

- Some people use a lot of nodding and smiling as they listen.

- Others choose to communicate by leaning forward, touching, or use of a conversational style.

To touch or not to touch

- Researchers classify Americans as low touchers in relation to other people of the world. However, touch in a multicultural society is very individual.

- You will meet some people who will never touch you, even though they highly prize your friendship. And you will meet others who will touch you often, usually on the shoulders and arms, but such touches will not really express a meaning.

- Because US society is very aware of the potential for people to use negative touch to intimidate or threaten, people are careful in how they touch.

- In the US, touch is used mainly as a greeting or to say goodbye.

- Americans can give the feeling of touch (without touching) by allowing others to moving in close when talking.

- Good friends may exchange hugs, friendly punches, kisses, and may touch frequently when talking to each other.

- For acquaintances and superiors, like professors or interviewers, a simple handshake is all that is expected.

- Some people are high touchers and give friendly arm, back and shoulder touches even to new acquaintances.

- You will find that some students feel free to show in public what might be considered "private" expressions of affection in your culture. An example might be kissing outside classroom.

Space is jealously guarded

- Privacy is the key to understanding the use of space and territory in the US.

- The Americans claim, use, and will defend what is their chair, their television, their stereo, or their kitchen.

- Most interpersonal disagreements between roommates focus around the use of space and the idea of ownership. For instance:
  - "He drank my milk from my side of refrigerator."
  - "She used my stapler and kept it on her desk."
  - "They just walked in and turned on my stereo without asking."
  - "He took five drawers for his clothes and left me just two!"

- US students feel free to decorate their environments if they have "paid" for them through rent or dorm fees.

- In general, Americans are generous people who will lend and give freely their possessions, but only to those who ask first.

- Even in public places (library or large dorm lounge), people often "mark" their space by putting down a piece of clothing (coat), books or food to show that, "This place is mine and I'll be right back. Don't come here."

- Doors send messages. In almost all cases, the open door says "I'm friendly," and the closed door suggests "I'd rather be alone." You might shut your door only because you want to study, but you should be aware that others may see that shut door and, fairly or not, assume it represents your whole attitude or personality.

- 68 to 72 degrees Fahrenheit is considered a comfortable room temperature.

- The Americans are very aware of scents and smells, judging others and their dwellings by the type and intensity of scents detected. Windows and doors are usually kept wide open to let in "the fresh air."

Section C Case

Scan and Listen

The Scenario

Too Close for Comfort

Bill had just arrived from the United States to study engineering at a Chinese university. He studied Chinese back at his home university and was confident that doing his graduate study at a Chinese university would give him an edge in taking advantage of future opportunities in the growing economy.

In the first few days, he met and moved in with his roommate Zemin and met several of the students who lived in nearby dormitory rooms. Most of them were also studying engineering but had little experience with Americans. He usually went to the student cafeteria with them and they were very helpful in showing him around and in gently correcting his classroom Chinese.

One evening, he settled in for his study session in his room. After some time, Zemin left to visit another room where friends were listening to a radio broadcast. Bill said he would join later. When Bill decided to take a break and see what the "guys" were up to, he found Zemin and two other boys huddled over the radio. Bill found it quite odd, however, that Zemin was draped over the back of the boy seated in front of the radio. Moreover, that boy had his feet propped up on his roommate who was seated nearby. It seemed to Bill that he had startled them, since they jumped up and welcomed him and even offered him tea. After Bill had a cup of tea and a chair to sit in, the group returned to the radio.

　　Bill shrugged the incident off, but over the next few days he noticed that female students on campus frequently walked arm-in-arm or even holding hands. He noticed, too, that students of both sexes, but especially the boys would huddle around newspaper displays in a fashion of close contact similar to Zemin and others around the radio. Bill felt rather uncomfortable and wondered how he would respond if one of his classmates were to put his arms around him.

Exercise

Listen to the case above and answer the following questions.

(1) Why did Bill come to China to study?

(2) Did Bill get along well with his Chinese roomates?

(3) What did some Chinese guys do one evening over a radio?

(4) What did Bill feel about Chinese boys and girls' close body contact with each other? And why?

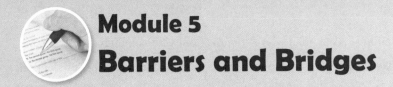

Module 5
Barriers and Bridges

Unit 11 Ethnocentrism and Stereotypes

Section A Video Clip Appreciation

I. Introduction to the Movie *Crash*

Over a thirty-six-hour period in Los Angeles, a handful of disparate people's lives intertwine as they deal with the tense race relations that belie life in the city. Among the players are: the Caucasian district attorney, who uses race as a political card; his Caucasian wife, who has recently been carjacked by two black men, believes that her stereotypical views of non-whites is justified and cannot be considered racism; the two black carjackers who use their race to their advantage and as an excuse; partnered Caucasian police constables— one who is a racist and uses his authority to harass non-whites, and the other who hates his partner because of his racist views, but who may have the same underlying values;

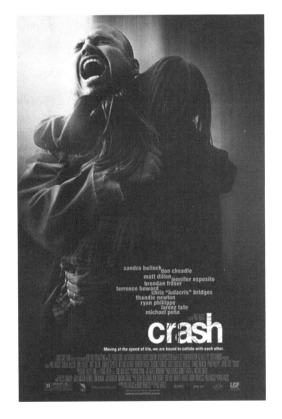

a black film director and his black wife, who believes her husband doesn't support their black background enough, especially in light of an incident with the racist white cop; partnered police detectives and sometimes lovers—one Hispanic female and the other black male, the latter who is dealing with a drugged out mother that feels he isn't concerned enough about taking care of the family; an East Asian man who is run over but who is hiding some valuable cargo in the back of his van; a Persian store owner, who feels he isn't getting satisfaction from American society after his store has been robbed time and time again; and a Hispanic locksmith who just wants to keep his family, especially his young daughter, safe in a seemingly unsafe world.

II. Introduction to the Video Clip

A black man, Detective Graham Waters, speaks dazedly about the nature of Los Angeles and the need for people to crash into each other. A Latino woman in the driver's seat of the car, Ria, mentions they were hit from behind and spun around. She gets out of the car and goes to the cop and the other driver, an Asian woman. The two women blame each other for the mishap and make racial jibes. The Latina identifies herself as a detective.

Waters gets out walks toward more police cars and a crime scene. Another cop mentions they have a body. An intense stare crosses Waters' face as he looks at something.

The scene flashes back to "Yesterday."

At a gun shop a Persian man Farhad and his daughter Dorri are buying a handgun. The shop owner gets upset with the Persians speaking Farsi and the two men quickly begin exchanging angry insults. Farhad leaves fuming and Dorri tells the shop owner that she'll either take the gun or take their money back, stating that she hopes she gets the money back. She also selects a red box of free bullets as she takes the gun, despite the owner making a cryptic remark about the type of bullets she's chosen.

Two young black men, Anthony and Peter, leave a restaurant. Anthony claims they were victims of racism and poor service, and Peter laughs it off. Jean and Rick Cabot, a white couple, walk down the sidewalk. Jean notices the two black men, averts her gaze and clutches Rick's arm. Anthony takes it as a racial slight, but then the two young men suddenly draw handguns and carjack the Cabots' black Lincoln Navigator. Peter places a St. Christopher statue on the dashboard over Anthony's objections.

Detective Waters and his partner Ria arrive at a crime scene. A uniformed cop tells them there was shooting between two drivers. The surviving white man is identified as an undercover cop named Conklin. The dead driver in a Mercedes is also a cop, a black man named Lewis. The investigators are unsure who started the shooting in the road rage incident.

At the Cabots' house Jean is still upset, and even though a locksmith is already changing the door locks. Seeing that the smith has several tattoos and is Latino, she angrily tells her husband she wants the job done again the next day. Jean loudly claims the locksmith will sell the keys and they will be robbed again. The locksmith, Daniel, overhears and leaves two sets of keys on the kitchen counter as he leaves. Rick is running for District Attorney re-election and wonders how to use the carjacking to an electoral advantage while talking to his assistants.

III. Script of the Video Clip

Movie Clip

Detective Graham Waters: It's the sense of touch.

Ria: What?

Detective Graham Waters: Any real city, you walk, you know? You brush past people. People bump into you. In L.A., nobody touches you. We're always behind this metal and glass. I think we miss that touch so much... that we crash into each other just so we can feel something.

Lt. Dixon: You guys okay?

Ria: I think he hit his head.

Detective Graham Waters: You don't think that's true?

Lt. Dixon: Stay in your car.

Ria: Graham, I think we got rear-ended. I think we spun around twice. And somewhere in there, one of us lost our frame of reference. And I'm gonna go look for it.

Lt. Dixon: Calm down, ma'am.

Kim Lee: I am calm!

Lt. Dixon: I need to see your registration and insurance.

Kim Lee: Why? It's not my fault! It's her fault! She do this!

Ria: My fault?

Lt. Dixon: Ma'am, you really need to wait in your vehicle.

Ria: My fault?

Kim Lee: Stop in middle of street! Mexicans no know how to drive. She "blake" too fast.

Ria: I "blake" too fast? I "blake" too fast. I'm sorry you no see my "blake" lights.

Lt. Dixon: Ma'am.

Ria: See, I stop when I see a long line of cars stopped in front of me. Maybe you see over steering wheel, you "blake" too!

Lt. Dixon: Ma'am!

Kim Lee: I call immigration. Look what you do my car.

Ria: Officer, can you please write in your report how shocked I am to be hit by an Asian driver!

Lt. Dixon: Ma'am!

Ria: Ma'am, no. See, Detective...

Lt. Dixon: All right. You've got to calm down.

Police Officer: Hey, Detective! Nice entrance.

Detective Graham Waters: Fuck you.

Police Detective: Hey, you okay?

Detective Graham Waters: I'm freezin'.

Police Detective: Shit. I heard it might snow.

Detective Graham Waters: Get outta here.

Police Detective: That's what I heard.

Detective Graham Waters: You got a smoke?

Police Detective: Nah. I quit.

Detective Graham Waters: Yeah, me too. What do you got?

Police Detective: Dead kid.

Detective Graham Waters: Hey, Bob.

****

[*Yesterday*]

Gun Store Owner: You get one free box of ammunition. What kind do you want?

[*Farhad and Dorri talking in Spanish*]

Gun Store Owner: Yo, Osama! Plan a jihad on your own time. What do you want?

Farhad: Are you making insult at me?

Gun Store Owner: Am I making insult "at" you? Is that the closest you can come to English?

Farhad: Yes, I speak English! I am American citizen.

Gun Store Owner: Oh, God, here we go.

Farhad: I have right like you. I have right to buy gun.

Gun Store Owner: Not in my store, you don't! Andy, get him outta here now!

Dorri: Go wait in the car.

Gun Store Owner: Now. Get out!

Farhad: You're an ignorant man!

Gun Store Owner: I'm ignorant? You're liberating my country and I'm flying 747s into your mud huts and incinerating your friends? Get the fuck out!

Farhad: No, you get the fuck out! No, don't touch me! He cheat me!

Gun Store Owner: Andy, now!

Security Guard: Let's go.

Dorri: Okay. You can give me the gun or give me back the money. And I am really hoping for the money.

Gun Store Owner: What kind of ammunition do you want?

Dorri: Whatever fits.

Gun Store Owner: We got a lot of kinds. We got long colts, short colts, bull heads, flat nose, hollowpoints, wide cutters, and a dozen more that'll fit any size hole. Just depends upon how much bang you can handle.

Dorri: I'll take the ones in the red box.

Gun Store Owner: You know what those are?

Dorri: Can I have them?

****

Anthony: Did you see any white people waiting... an hour and 32 minutes for a plate of spaghetti? And how many cups of coffee did we get?

Peter Waters: You don't drink coffee! And I didn't want any.

Anthony: Man, that woman poured cup after cup to every single white person around us. But did she even ask you if you wanted any?

Peter Waters: We didn't get any coffee that you didn't want and I didn't order, and that's evidence of racial discrimination? Did you notice that our waitress was black?

Anthony: And black women don't think in stereotypes? You tell me. When was the last time you met one…who didn't think she knew everything about your lazy ass... before you even opened your mouth, huh? That waitress sized us up in two seconds. We're black, and black people don't tip. So she wasn't gonna waste her time. Somebody like that? Nothing you can do to change their mind.

Peter Waters: How much did you leave?

Anthony: You expect me to pay for that kind of service? What? What the fuck is you laughin' at, man?

D. A. Rick Cabot: I'm seriously starting to think that you're jealous of Karen.

Jean Cabot: Hardly. I'd just like to see you get through a meal without calling her or anyone else.

D. A. Rick Cabot: Okay, no more phone calls. As a matter of fact, you can hold the battery. Okay?

Jean Cabot: Ten bucks says she calls you in the car.

Anthony: Wait, wait, wait. See what that woman just did? You see that?

Peter Waters: She's cold.

Anthony: She got colder as soon as she saw us.

Peter Waters: Ah, come on, don't start.

Anthony: Man, look around you, man. You couldn't find a whiter, safer or better-lit part of this city right now. But yet this white woman sees two black guys... who look like UCLA students strolling down the sidewalk, and her reaction is blind fear? I mean look at us, dog. Are we dressed like gangbangers? Huh? No. Do we look threatening? No. Fact. If anybody should be scared around here, it's us! We're the only two black faces surrounded by a sea of over-caffeinated white people... patrolled by the trigger-happy L. A. P. D. So you tell me. Why aren't we scared?

Peter Waters: 'Cause we got guns?

Anthony: You could be right.

Peter Waters: Get the fuck outta the car!

Anthony: Gimme the keys!

Peter Waters: Hurry up! Get down!

Jean Cabot: Okay, okay, okay, okay.

D.A. Rick Cabot: No, no! Please!

Peter Waters: Don't look at me! Turn around!

D.A. Rick Cabot: Come on! Go! We're fine! Just keep moving!

Anthony: No, no, no! Take that voodoo-assed thing off of there right now.

Peter Waters: I know you just didn't call Saint Christopher voodoo. Man's the patron saint of travelers, dog.

Anthony: You had a conversation with God, huh? What did God say? "Go forth, my son, and leave big slobbery suction rings on every dashboard you find"? Why the hell do you do that?

Peter Waters: Look at the way your crazy ass drive, then ask me again.

Officer Johnson: Chevy pickup and Mercedes driving north on Balboa. Pickup cuts in front. Driver of the Mercedes gets pissed, pulls a gun. Doesn't realize the guy in the pickup is a cop coming off shift.

Detective Graham Waters: This Barry Gibb dude is a cop?

Officer Johnson: Yeah. Name's Conklin. He's a narc out of Wilshire.

Ria: I got the Mercedes.

Officer Johnson: Mercedes takes a shot at him. Detective Conklin returns fire. One shot. Mercedes rolls to a stop. Driver opens the door, falls out dead.

Detective Graham Waters: He looks very relaxed for just having shot somebody.

Officer Johnson: He says he kept tryin' to drive away. The Mercedes kept pulling up next to him, screaming, waving a gun. Shot back in self-defense.

Detective Graham Waters: Anybody actually see who shot first?

Officer Johnson: They just heard two bangs.

Detective Graham Waters: Find me a witness. That is a nice gun.

Ria: The car's registered to a Cindy Bradley. And that's not Cindy. That is a William Lewis. Found under the front seat. Hollywood Division.

Detective Graham Waters: Looks like Detective Conklin shot himself the wrong nigger.

****

Jean Cabot: How much longer are you gonna be?

Daniel Ruiz: This is the last one.

Jean Cabot: Thank you.

D. A. Rick Cabot: You don't think reporters listen to police calls?

Jean Cabot: I need to talk to you for a second.

D. A. Rick Cabot: You just give me a minute, all right? Find Flanagan, will you? Now.

Bruce: Yes, sir.

D. A. Rick Cabot: Yes, honey?

Jean Cabot: I want the locks changed again in the morning.

D. A. Rick Cabot: You want... Why don't you just go lie down? Have you checked on James?

Jean Cabot: Of course. I've checked on him every five minutes since we've been home. Do not patronize me. I want the locks changed again in the morning.

D. A. Rick Cabot: It's okay. Just go to bed.

Jean Cabot: You know, didn't I just ask you not to treat me like a child?

Maria: I'm sorry, Miss Jean. It's okay I go home now?

D. A. Rick Cabot: It's fine. Thank you very much for staying.

Maria: You're welcome, no problem. Good night.

Jean Cabot: Good night.

D. A. Rick Cabot: We'll see you tomorrow.

Jean Cabot: I would like the locks changed again in the morning. And you might mention that we'd appreciate it if next time they didn't send a gang member.

D. A. Rick Cabot: A gang member? You mean that kid in there?

Jean Cabot: Yes. The guy with the shaved head, the pants around his ass, the prison tattoo.

D. A. Rick Cabot: Those are not prison tattoos.

Jean Cabot: Oh, really? And he's not gonna sell our key... to one of his gangbanger friends the moment he is out our door?

D. A. Rick Cabot: We've had a tough night. It'd be best if you went...

Jean Cabot: And wait for them to break in? I just had a gun pointed in my face.

D. A. Rick Cabot: You lower your voice!

Jean Cabot: And it was my fault because I knew it was gonna happen. But if a white person sees two black men walking towards her, and she turns and walks in the other direction, she's a racist, right? Well, I got scared and I didn't say anything. And ten seconds later I had a gun in my face! I am telling you. Your amigo in there is gonna sell our key to one of his homies. And this time it'd be really fucking great if you acted like you actually gave a shit!

New Words

ammunition [ˌæmjuˈnɪʃən] *n.* bullets and rockets that are made to be fired from weapons 弹药

insult [ɪnˈsʌlt] *n.* a rude remark, or sth a person says or does which insults you 侮辱；辱骂；冒犯

incinerate [ɪnˈsɪnəreɪt] *v.* to burn sth completely in a special container 把……烧成灰烬

racial [ˈreɪʃl] *adj.* relating to people's race 种族的

discrimination [dɪˌskrɪmɪˈneɪʃən] *n.* the practice of treating one person or group of people less fairly or less well than other people or groups 歧视

pickup [ˈpɪkʌp] *n.* a light truck with an open body and low sides and a tailboard 小卡车

patrol [pəˈtroʊl] *v.* to move around in order to make sure that there is no trouble there 在……巡逻

gimme [ˈgɪmi] *v.* used in written English to represent the words "give me" when they are pronounced informally 给我（等于 give me）

voodoo [ˈvuːduː] *n.* 伏都教（一种西非原始宗教）；伏都教徒

slobbery [ˈslɑbəri] *adj.* 潮湿的；流口水的；过于伤感的；懒散的

suction ['sʌkʃn] *n.* the process by which liquids, gases, or other substances are drawn out of somewhere 抽吸（液体、汽体等）

dashboard ['dæʃbɔːrd] *n.* the panel facing the driver's seat where most of the instruments and switches are （机动车辆的）仪表板

narc [nɑːrk] *n.* a police officer whose job is to stop people selling or using drugs illegally 缉查毒品的刑警

nigger ['nɪgər] *n.* an extremely offensive word for calling a black person 黑人（对黑人的一种极具侮辱性的称呼）

patronize ['peɪtrənaɪz] *v.* to treat someone in a way that seems friendly, but which shows that you think that they are not very intelligent, experienced, etc. 以高人一等的态度对待

amigo [ə'miːgəʊ] *n.* friend 朋友（源于西班牙语 amigo）

Phrases and Expressions

brush past: to glance off 擦肩而过

rear-ended: colliding with the rear end 追尾的

steering wheel: the wheel which the driver holds when he or she is driving 驾驶盘

flat nose: a kind of bullet for military use 平头弹

size up: to carefully look at the person or think about the situation, so that you can decide how to act 估计；品评

stroll down: to walk leisurely 漫步，闲逛

patron saint: a saint who is believed to give people special help and protection 守护神

cut in front of: to drive in front of another vehicle leaving too little space for that vehicle to maneuver comfortably 突然插到别的车前

off shift: to go off work 下班

Notes

UCLA: University of California at Los Angeles 加州大学洛杉矶分校，位于美国洛杉矶市，是世界著名的公立研究型大学。

L. A. P. D. : Los Angeles Police Department 洛杉矶警察局

Chevy: Referred to as Chevy and formally the Chevrolet Division of General Motors Company, an automobile division of the American manufacturer General Motors 雪佛兰，美国通用汽车公司旗下的一个汽车品牌，1918 年被通用汽车收购，现为通用汽车旗下最为国际化和大众化的品牌之一。

Mercedes: The post-1926 German brand of automobiles, engines, and trucks 梅赛德斯－奔驰是世界闻名的豪华汽车品牌，以高质量、高性能的汽车产品著称。

Exercises for Understanding

1. Answer the following questions according to the video clip you have just watched.

(1) Why does Detective Graham Waters say in the very beginning "We crash into each other just so we can feel something"?

(2) Why doesn't the gun store owner sell ammunition to Farhad?

(3) According to Anthony, why doesn't the black waitress ask what kind of drinks he wants?

(4) Do you think that the robbery of car of Jean Cabot by Anthony and Peter Waters is an intended one? Why or why not?

(5) What does Jean Cabot complain to Rick Cabot? Do you think it is a stereotype?

2. Put the following sentences in the right order according to the video clip you have just watched.

_____(1) Anthony and Peter Waters robbed a car.

_____(2) Detective Graham Waters arrived on the spot investigating a gun murder incident.

_____(3) Ria and a Korean argued about whose fault it was in a rear-ended car accident.

_____(4) Jean Cabot complained to Rick Cabot about the black locksmith.

_____(5) Ria bought a one free box of ammunition in a gun shop.

Section B   Reading

"Ethnocentrism" is the tendency to think of one's own culture as being at the center of the world; in other words, to assume that your own culture's way of thinking and acting is more natural, normal, and correct than the way people from other cultures think and act. ("Ethno-" means "race" or "people.")

People are almost always ethnocentric to some degree; in fact, it is almost impossible not to be ethnocentric. As we grow up and learn what is right and wrong, true and false, normal and abnormal, and so forth, we naturally learn to view the world as our culture views it. For example, children who grow up in cultures where men usually greet each other by kissing naturally assume that this is the normal way for men to greet; in contrast, children who grow up in cultures where men never kiss each other will probably find it strange and even offensive if they see men greet each other by kissing. The process of learning about our world and the process of learning our own culture are so thoroughly mixed together that most people grow up without being able to clearly distinguish one from the other. (This is especially true if we grow up in places where we have little contact with people from other cultures.)

Because our ideas about the world are formed in childhood, they are so deeply rooted in our minds and hearts that often we are not even aware of them. We also tend to feel quite strongly about many of them, and it is not easy for us to change them. For example, even if Chinese men go to live in a country where men greet each other by kissing, they will probably always feel at least a little uncomfortable kissing other men, no matter how hard they try to adapt to local customs, and they may not be willing to adapt to such a custom at all.

While ethnocentrism is very natural, it is also the root of many problems in intercultural communication. Because we naturally feel that the ways and ideas of our culture are more natural and correct than those of other cultures, we tend to use the norms of our own culture—our ideas of what is good/bad, right/wrong, normal/abnormal—as standards when we judge the behavior of people from other cultures. Chinese tend to judge Westerners according to the standards of Chinese culture, Westerners tend to judge Chinese according to Western standards, and so on. So when we encounter foreigners who behave or think in ways that differ from our cultural norms, we too quickly tend to judge these other ways as strange, wrong, or bad.

Few of us believe that our own culture is perfect, but deep in our hearts most of us feel that our own culture is generally superior to other cultures, especially with regard to the issue of right and wrong. Ethnocentrism is one major reason why people are prone to judge the behavior of foreigners negatively.

Effective intercultural communicators must learn to be careful about using their own cultural norms to judge people from other cultures. One of the best ways to learn this is to cultivate the habit of learning about other cultural perspectives, and of trying to understand the world from other cultural perspectives. The norms of our own culture are not necessarily wrong—often they are very good—but we should learn not to judge other cultures' ways of acting and thinking as bad only because they differ from our own.

Another obstacle in the process of effective intercultural communication is stereotype. As more and more people from different backgrounds, countries, cultures and religions immigrate to foreign lands, those countries become an intercultural melting pot. In order for the native people and the immigrant population to blend and create a thriving and successful atmosphere, both sides need to develop some sort of intercultural tolerance and understanding of the differences that may exist between them.

Stereotypes in Canada

Stereotypes are at their most basic level a set of assumed characteristics about a certain group of people whose actual beliefs, habits and realities more often than not disagree with the imposed assumptions. Stereotypes are usually based on factors such as exaggeration, distortion, ignorance, racism, cultural factors or even historical experiences. Stereotyping is therefore rightly seen as a negative way of seeing people. This is even true of what are called "positive stereotype."

Stereotypes in Northern Island

A positive stereotype is where we use a blanket expression for a whole people, i. e. all the Chinese are great at math, all Germans are well organized or all English people are well mannered. Although the intent behind the statement is positive, it still does not reflect the truth.

Cultural competency is a term used to describe the ability to work, communicate and live across cultures and cultural boundaries. One achieves this through an instilled understanding of cultures on a general level as well as an informed one about specific cultures on a more detailed level. As well as knowledge it has to work in tandem with behavioral and attitudinal changes.

Cultural competency is important in this day and age for exactly the reasons cited in this article. We, as citizens of planet earth, are no longer confined to our national and cultural borders. We mix with people from different cultures, ethnicities, religions and colors on a daily basis. In order to make this intercultural experience work on all levels from education to business to government, people have to develop basic skills in intercultural communication and understanding.

Exercises for Understanding

1. Answer the following questions according to the passage you have just read.

(1) What is "ethnocentrism"? Why are people ethnocentric?

(2) Why does ethnocentrism cause difficulty in intercultural communication?

(3) How should you deal with ethnocentrism?

(4) What does the term "stereotype" mean? What kind of impact can stereotypes have on individuals?

(5) How can we break negative stereotypes?

2. Small group task.

Heaven is where the police are English, the cooks are French, the mechanics are German, the lovers are Italian and everything is organized by the Swiss. Hell is where the police are German, the cooks are English, the mechanics are French, the lovers are Swiss, and everything is organized by the Italians.

First, read the above old joke about national stereotypes, and then in groups, please discuss the reasons implied and what other examples or proofs are related with ethnocentrism or stereotypes in daily life.

Section C Case

Scan and Listen

The Scenario

Sharing the Wealth

Anna Bilow has been working for a Chinese-owned and operated company in Nanjing for about six months. The division she is working in has a small collection of Chinese-English dictionaries, English language reference books, and some videos in English including a couple of training films and several feature films that Anna brought at her new employer's request when she came from Europe. Anna knows that some of the other sections have similar collections. She has sometimes used her friendship with one of the women in another department, Gu Ming, to borrow English novels and reference books and in return has let Gu Ming borrow books from her section's collection. On other occasions, she has seen friendly, noisy exchanges, where one of the other workers in her division has lent a book or video to a colleague from another section.

Anna thought it was a great idea when a memo was circulated saying that the company's leaders had decided to collect all the English language materials together into a single collection. The plan was to put them in a small room that was currently being used for storage so that all employees could have equal access to them. Now she would no longer have to go from department to department trying to find the materials she needed.

Anna was surprised to hear her co-workers complaining about the new policy. When the young man in charge came to the department to collect their English language materials, she was astounded to see them hiding most of the books and all but one of the videos in their desks. When she checked out the new so-called collection, she found that the few items were all outdated or somehow damaged. She also noticed that none of the materials she had borrowed from Gu Ming were in the collection. She asked her friend why the Chinese were unwilling to share their English language materials with all their co-workers, when they seemed willing to share them within their departments.

Exercise

Listen to the case above and answer the following questions.

(1) How did Anna find English language materials when she first worked in the Chinese-owned and operated company?

(2) What was the memo about?

(3) What explanations do you think Gu Ming gave Anna?

(4) What problems do you expect to encounter if you are asked to share resources with people who are not part of your group?

Unit 12　Culture Shock and Adaptation

Section A　Video Clip Appreciation

I. Introduction to the Movie *English Vinglish*

Shashi Godbole is a homemaker, who makes and sells laddoos as a home-run business. Her husband Satish and daughter Sapna take her for granted, mock her poor English skills, and generally treat her with disrespect, making Shashi feel negative and insecure. However, her young son, Sagar loves her as she is, and her mother-in-law offers her words of sympathy.

Shashi's older sister Manu, who lives in New York, invites Shashi's family to her daughter Meera's wedding to Kevin. It is decided that Shashi will go to New York alone five weeks before the wedding to help Manu organize. Her husband and children will join her as the wedding approaches. During her flight to New York, Shashi is given inspirational advice by a fellow passenger. While Shashi is in New York, she has a traumatic experience at a cafe due to her inability to communicate in English. She is comforted by a French chef Laurent, who happened to be queuing up behind her at the cafe.

Using the money she made from selling laddoos, Shashi secretly enrolls in a conversational English class that offers to teach the language in four weeks, showing her resourcefulness at navigating an unfamiliar city alone. The class comprises David Fischer, the instructor; Eva, a Mexican nanny; Salman Khan, a Pakistani cab driver; Yu Son, a Chinese hairstylist; Ramamurthy, a Tamil software engineer; Udumbke, a closeted African-Caribbean man; and Laurent. Shashi quickly becomes a promising and committed student, earns everyone's respect with her charming behavior and her cuisine, and gains self-confidence. Laurent becomes attracted to Shashi. When he tries to kiss her at the rooftop of a building, Shashi rejects him and runs off, but fails to explain that she is married.

Meanwhile, Shashi's niece Radha, who is Meera's younger sister, finds out about her secret English classes and is supportive of her pursuit. Shashi starts watching English films at night and does her homework assiduously. To complete the English-speaking course and get a certificate, each student must write and deliver a five-minute speech. Shashi's family joins her in New York earlier than planned, to surprise her. Shashi tries to continue attending class but decides to quit because of scheduling conflicts; she asks Radha to inform Fischer. The test date coincides with that of the wedding, forcing Shashi to miss the test.

Radha invites Fischer and the entire class to the wedding, where Satish is taken aback at being introduced to a diverse group of people by his wife. Shashi gives a touching and enlightening toast to the married couple in English, surprising everyone who knew her as a typical, conservative, Indian homemaker. In her speech, Shashi extols the virtues of being married and having a family, describing the family as a safe space of love and respect where weaknesses are not mocked. Satish and Sapna regret treating her with disrespect. Fischer declares that she has passed the course with distinction and issues her the certificate. Shashi thanks Laurent for making her feel better about herself. Shashi's family returns to India; during their flight home, Shashi asks the flight attendant in fluent English whether she has any Hindi newspapers.

II. Introduction to the Video Clips

Clip 1

We are learning about the experiences of an Indian woman in New York. Some of these experiences might be similar to what some of you have had, or will have when traveling overseas. The main character, Shashi, is in New York to help with a family wedding. Nevertheless, she comes across an embarrassing situation at a coffee shop simply because she was not able to communicate clearly in English. In other words, she felt humiliated because her English was not understood. The clerk at that coffee shop quickly became quite impatient with her, and as a result, Shashi became very upset. She dropped someone's meal and ran out of the shop as fast as she could while crying desperately. Soon after, a kind Frenchman cheered her up and gave her a coffee from that same coffee shop while letting her know that the clerk over there isn't a nice person. From now on, let's see what Shashi decides to do to overcome her linguistic handicap and make better use of her time in New York. Will she withdraw into a shell by only speaking with others who speak Hindi or will she take the bull by the horn and try to improve her English?

Clip 2

The end of the movie *English Vinglish* leaves a lump in your throat. Every word and every expression of Shashi's speech in the last scene is so balanced. Her transformation from a conscious housewife to a confident entrepreneur becomes clearly evident. Her husband and children have arrived for the occasion, not knowing her secret English lessons. In front of all the guests, Shashi is asked to make a speech to the newlyweds. Shashi stands up and uses her new-found voice to urge the bride and groom to value equality and treat each other with respect. This is one of the most moving and heartfelt wedding speeches in films that brings tears of remorse to her daughter.

III. Script of the Video Clips

Clip 1

[*Lyrics of the song*]

Manhattan.

Touching heaven, oh my god!

Manhattan.

New avenues of joy.

Shops full of dreams.

A new surprise, at every stop.

To your left is Prada.

To your right is Zara.

Giorgio Armani.

Thank God it's Friday!

Gucci and Versace.

Jimmy Choo, Givenchy.

Diesel, Dior, Hokey Pokey, Gap and Bloomingdale's.

Louis Vuitton.

Video Clip 1

Moschino.

Valentino...

So much to say yet speechless.

All together, still alone.

What a city! Touch wood.

5, 6, 7, 8 avenues.

Million billion legs and shoes.

Lots of colors, dollars dollars.

Sense of pidlee poo.

Breakfast is for all day.

Straight and gay they all sway.

Lexington, and Madison, it's all so ooh!

Frappuccino.

Mochaccino.

Cappuccino...

****

Meera: You gotto say balle balle while you do that...

Kevin: Balle balle balle balle!

Meera: Aunty, you're not eating food's not good?

Shashi: This parantha is really good.

Line: It's Mexican food, Quesadilla.

Shashi: Whatever it is. It's good!

Kevin: What's that? What did she say?

Line: She just abused you.

Kevin: So tell me about the dowry. What are you giving me?

Line: What am I giving you? We are not buying you. That's not how it works.

Crowd: The boy gives the girl's family the dowry. And lots and lots of gifts.

Kevin: So I'm going to go broke?

Shashi: I don't know why but I'm really sleepy.

Manu: Go sleep, my dear.

Shashi: Is that alright?

Manu: Yes of course.

Background: I feel so bad... she must be so tired. Must be the jet lag.

Shashi: Hello Satish... how are the kids? Have they gone to school? Have they taken their lunch boxes? Please do try to get home early... I'm feeling a bit strange here... without all of you...

Satish: Shashi... just enjoy yourself... I'm getting into an elevator... will talk later.

Manu: Slept well? Sorry... got to go to office for a bit. I'll try to be back as soon as possible... we'll start on the wedding plans.

Shashi: Drive carefully.

Manu: Bye darling, see you!

Meera: Good morning Aunty!

Shashi: Good morning. Should I make you some breakfast?

Meera: No. I have cereal. What are you going to do by yourself? We do have Zee TV Hindi but... I have an idea, why don't you come with me to college!

Shashi: What will I do there?

Meera: I have class for 2 hours... and you can hang out at a cafe... and I'll come join you.

Meera: You got cash... change?

Shashi: Yes.

Meera: And don't worry. In case you get lost... if you do get lost just call me.

Shashi: Don't worry, go now. The parks here are so beautiful.

Meera: Washington Square Park.

Shashi: Washington... Square... Park...

Meera: Good!

Passenger: Wow... that's a beautiful dress you're wearing!

****

Customer 1: Can I get a regular coffee and a blueberry muffin.

Waitress: Here's your receipt... please pick up your food over there.

Customer 1: Okay... have a nice day.

Waitress: Next! How are you doing today ma'am?

Shashi: I want...

Waitress: I asked how you were doing today.

Shashi: Doing... I'm doing... I'm doing...

Waitress: You can't take all that time. I got a long line here.

Shashi: Sorry... what to eat?

Waitress: Are you kidding me right now? Please hurry up, lady.

Shashi: Vegetarian.

Waitress: Vegetarian is fine. What do you want to eat?

Shashi: Only vegetarian.

Waitress: A bagel, a wrap, a sandwich?

Shashi: Sandwich.

Waitress: Okay. And what kind of filling do you want inside? Do you want cheese, tomatoes, lettuce?

Shashi: Ah?

Waitress: Lady, you're holding up my line. This is not rocket science. Cheese?

Shashi: Yes. Cheese.

Waitress: Yes to cheese! Anything to drink? Water, still or sparkling?

Shashi: Only water.

Waitress: Still or sparkling?

Shashi: Coffee... ?

Waitress: Americano? Cappuccino? Latte?

Customer 2: Lady, I ain't got all day.

Waitress: Americano? Cappuccino? Latte?

Shashi: Nescoffee.

Waitress: What?

Shashi: Nescoffee.

Waitress: Yes we have nice coffee. We have the best coffee in Manhattan. You know... I'll just give you an Americano. Small or medium?

Shashi: Small.

Waitress: Small. Is that it? $10.20.

Shashi: 10 dollars. Sorry. Thank you.

Waitress: Hello. The least you could do is say thank you!

Shashi: Sorry. Thank you.

Customer 3: Stupid idiot!

Shashi: Sorry...

Waitress: I am not cleaning that up!

Customer 4: Don't bother.

Customer 5: What a stupid woman.

Laurent: Madam. Your coffee, from the coffee shop. Cafe not good. Woman... not nice! Okay.

Shashi: Thank you.

Laurent: Bye.

Clip 2

Video Clip 2

Manu: Shashi, it's time for the ceremony.

Manu: To my darling daughter Meera and my dear son Kevin. How I wish Anil was here. When Meera was going through her troubled teens, she was 14. She was only 14 years old when she came in fuming and asked us: Why did you give birth to me? She was so angry with life that she was furious that we gave birth to her without asking for her permission! I will answer that today Meera. You were born so your dad and I could share complete happiness. You were born so you could bring happiness into our lives. I am so sorry I didn't take your permission. Love you both sweethearts! God bless both of you always.

Kevins's Father: Son, you just got lucky! But fortune smiles on those who embrace its offerings. So love each other. And son, leave me and your mother alone! It's time for us to focus on each other.

Meera: Shashi Aunty, your turn.

Crowd: Yes. Come on.

Satish: Sorry, my wife's English is not very good so…

Shashi: May I? Meera, Kevin. This marriage is a... Oops sorry... I started in Hindi. This marriage is a beautiful thing. It is the most special friendship... friendship of two people who are equal. Life is a long journey. Meera, sometimes you will feel you are less. Kevin, sometimes you will also feel you are less than Meera. Try to help each other to feel equal. It will be nice. Sometimes married couple don't even know how the other is feeling. So how they will help the other? It means marriage is finished? No. That is the time you have to help yourself. Nobody can help you better than you if you do that. You will return back feeling equal. Your friendship will return back. Your life will be beautiful. Meera, Kevin, maybe you'll very busy, but have family, son, daughter in this big world, your small little world. It will make you feel so good. Family, family can never be… never be judgemental! Family will never put you down, will never make you feel small. Family is the only one who will never laugh at your weaknesses. Family is the only place where you will always get love and respect.

That's all. Meera and Kevin, I wish you all the best. Thank you.

[*Applause*]

David: Well Shashi. You don't "return back," you just return, and you missed a few "a" s and "the" s. else you passed with distinction!

Meera: Shashi Aunty you were amazing! Yes. I'm so proud of you. Do you want me to help?

Shashi: Bring the other tray.

Shashi's Son: Next time you speak in English in front of mama, please think she can talk better than you!

Shashi: David Sir... ladoo!

David: Thank you. I have something for you!

Laurent: Shashi...

Shashi: When you don't like yourself, you tend to dislike everything connected to you. When you learn to love yourself, then the same old life starts looking new, starts looking nice. Thank you for teaching me how to love myself! Thank you for making me feel good about myself. Thank you so much! Ladoo.

Meera: Broke the French heart, didn't you?

Satish: Shashi. Do you still love me?

Shashi: If I didn't, why would I give you two ladoos? And, good choice!

[*Music and dance*]

****

Flight Attendant: What newspaper would you like sir?

Satish: *New York Times* please.

Flight Attendant: And you, ma'am?

Shashi: *The New York*. Sorry, do you have any Hindi newspaper?

Flight Attendant: No, sorry.

Shashi: It's OK. Thank you.

New Words

avenue ['ævənuː] *n.* a wide, straight road, especially one with trees on either side 林荫大道

dowry ['daʊri] *n.* the money and goods which, in some cultures, her family gives to the man that she marries 嫁妆

cereal ['sɪriəl] *n.* food made from grain, often eaten for breakfast with milk 麦片

blueberry ['bluːberi] *n.* a small dark blue fruit that grows on bushes in North America 蓝莓

muffin ['mʌfɪn] *n.* a small, round, sweet cake, usually with fruit or bran inside, often eaten for breakfast 小松饼

vegetarian [ˌvedʒə'teriən] *n.* someone who never eats meat or fish 素食主义者

bagel ['beɪgl] *n.* a ring-shaped bread roll 百吉饼

lettuce ['letɪs] *n.* a plant with large green leaves that is the basic ingredient of many salads 生菜

still [stɪl] *adj.* not sparkling 不起泡的

sparkling ['spɑːrklɪŋ] *adj.* slightly carbonated (饮料) 起泡的

furious ['fjʊriəs] *adj.* marked by extreme anger 狂怒的

tease [tiːz] *v.* to mock or make fun of playfully 取笑

sneak [sniːk] *v.* to go stealthily or furtively 溜进

blushing ['blʌʃɪŋ] *adj.* having a red face from embarrassment, shame, agitation or emotional upset 脸红的

kohl [koʊl] *n.* a cosmetic preparation used to darken the edges of the eyelids 眼影粉

cappuccino [ˌkæpu'tʃiːnoʊ] *n.* equal parts of espresso and hot milk topped with cinnamon and nutmeg and usually whipped cream 卡布奇诺咖啡

latte ['lɑːteɪ] *n.* strong espresso coffee with a topping of frothed steamed milk 拿铁咖啡

Phrases and Expressions

go broke: to become penniless or bankrupt 破产

jet lag: fatigue and sleep disturbance resulting from disruption of the body's normal circadian rhythm as a result of jet travel 时差感，飞行时差反应

hang out: to go and stay in a place for no particular reason, or spend a lot of time there 闲逛

Notes

parantha: A kind of rusk which is popular in India. 一种平底锅烹制的小面包干，是最受印度德里旁遮普人欢迎的早餐。

Prada: An Italian luxury fashion house, specializing in leather handbags, travel accessories, shoes, ready-to-wear, perfumes and other fashion accessories, founded in 1913 by Mario Prada. 普拉达，意大利奢侈品品牌，于 1913 年在米兰创建。

Zara: A Spanish clothing and accessories retailer based in Arteixo, Galicia. The company was founded in 1975 by Amancio Ortega and Rosalía Mera. It is the main brand of the Inditex Group, the world's largest apparel retailer. 西班牙服装零售连锁品牌，创建于 1975 年，隶属于印地纺集团（Inditex Group）。该品牌在 87 个国家和地区设有超过两千家连锁店。

Armani: A high-end label specializing in ready-to-wear, accessories, glasses, cosmetics, and perfumes. It is available only in Giorgio Armani boutiques, specialty clothiers and select high-end department stores. The logo is a curved "G" completing a curved "A," forming a circle. 阿玛尼，世界知名奢侈品品牌，1975 年由时尚设计大师乔治·阿玛尼（Giorgio Armani）创立于意大利米兰。该品牌以使用新型面料及制作精良而闻名。

Gucci: An Italian luxury brand of fashion and leather goods, part of the Gucci Group, which is owned by the French holding company Kering. Gucci was founded by Guccio Gucci in Florence in 1921. 古驰，意大利时装品牌，由古驰奥·古驰在 1921 年创办于意大利佛罗伦萨。古驰的产品包括时装、皮具、手表、领带、丝巾、香水、家居用品及宠物用品等。

Versace: An Italian luxury fashion company and trade name founded by Gianni Versace in 1978. The Versace logo is the head of Medusa, a Greek mythological figure. Gianni Versace chose Medusa as the logo because she made people fall in love with her and they had no way back. He hoped his company would have the same effect on people. The Versace brand is known for having flashy prints and bright colors. 范思哲创立于1978 年，品牌标志是希腊神话中的蛇发女妖美杜莎（Medusa），代表着致命的吸引力。该品牌产品以鲜明的设计风格、独特的美感和极强的先锋艺术表征风靡全球。

Givenchy: A French luxury fashion and perfume house. It hosts the brand of haute couture clothing, accessories, perfumes and cosmetics. 纪梵希，法国的时装品牌，以优美、简洁、典雅的风格著称。最初以香水为其主要产品，后开始涉足护肤及彩妆事业。

Dior: A French luxury goods company founded in 1946 and chaired by French businessman Bernard Arnault, who also heads LVMH—the world's largest luxury group. 迪奥，法国著名时尚品牌，总部设在巴黎。主要经营服装、首饰、香水、化妆品等高档消费品。

Bloomingdale's: A luxury department store owned by Macy's. It was founded in 1861. 布鲁明戴尔百货店是美国著名的百货商店，成立于 1861 年，是美国梅西百货（Macy's）旗下的连锁商店。该商店气氛与品牌既有年轻化和摩登的一面，也有务实的一面。

Louis Vuitton: A French fashion house founded in 1854 by Louis Vuitton. The label's LV monogram appears on most of its products, ranging from luxury trunks and leather goods to ready-to-wear, shoes, watches, jewelry, accessories, sunglasses, and books. 自1854 年以来，路易·威登以卓越品质、杰出创意和精湛工艺成为时尚旅行艺术的象征。其产品包括手提包、旅行用品、小型皮具、配饰、鞋履、成衣、腕表、高级珠宝及个性化订制服务等。

Exercises for Understanding

1. Answer the following questions according to the video clips you have just watched.

(1) How many brands of luxuries are mentioned in Clip 1?

(2) What is the first impression of Shashi about Manhattan?

(3) What can we learn from Clip 1 about Shashi when she made a phone call home?

(4) Why was Shashi laughed at when she was in the cafeteria?

(5) In the eyes of Shashi, what is the real meaning of family?

2. Decide whether the following statements are true or false according to the video clips you have just watched. Write a "T" for true or an "F" for false.

_____(1) In Indian culture, it is usually the men who prepare dowry for weddings.

_____(2) Shashi could not make her well understood by the waitress in the cafeteria because of her poor English.

_____(3) From Clip 2, we can infer that Anil was the father of Meera.

_____(4) According to Shashi, men are superior to women in a family.

_____(5) Shashi doesn't love her husband any more.

3. Fill in the blanks according to the video clips you have just watched.

Manhattan.

(1) _____, oh my god!

Manhattan.

New avenues of joy.

Shops (2) _____.

A new surprise, at every stop.

To your left is Prada.

To your right is Zara.

Giorgio Armani.

Thank God it's Friday!

Gucci and Versace.

Jimmy Choo, Givenchy.

Diesel, Dior, Hokey Pokey, Gap and Bloomingdale's.

Louis Vuitton.

Moschino.

Valentino...

So much to say yet (3) _____.

All together, still alone.

What a city! Touch wood.

5, 6, 7, 8 avenues.

Million billion (4) _____.

Lots of colors, dollars dollars.

Sense of pidlee poo.

Breakfast is for all day.

(5) _____ they all sway.

Lexington, and Madison, it's all so ooh!

Frappuccino.

Mochaccino.

Cappuccino...

4. Match the lines with the characters.

(1) You passed with distinction.   A. Shashi

(2) So I'm going to go broke?   B. David

(3) This is not rocket science.   C. Manu

(4) You were born so you could bring happiness into our lives. D. Waitress

(5) Try to help each other to feel equal. It will be nice.   E. Kevin

Section B Reading

Culture shock is troublesome feelings such as depression, loneliness, confusion, inadequacy, hostility, frustration and tension caused by the loss of familiar cues from the home culture. It is a common experience of people who have been suddenly transplanted abroad.

Then why do people suffer from culture shock? Many reasons bring about culture shock. Some factors including the characteristics of the communicating participants and others are related to the situation to which the participants are trying to adapt. The traditional explanation for the onset of culture shock is somewhat lined with the sorrow people feel after losing their beloved ones. Today, culture shock is mainly due to three reasons: the theory of negative events, the theory of decrease in social support and the theory of different values.

Culture shock results from the anxiety of losing all our familiar signs and symbols of social contact. Those cues or signs include various ways in which we adapt ourselves to the situation of daily life: when to shake hands and what to say when we meet people, when and how to give tips, how to buy things, when to accept and when to refuse invitations, when to take statements seriously and when not. These cues, which may be words, gestures, facial expressions, or customs, are acquired by all of us in the course of growing up and are as much a part of our culture as the languages we speak or the beliefs we accept. All of us defend for peace of mind and our efficiency on hundreds of cues, most of which we do not carry on the level of conscious awareness.

People experiencing culture shock may undergo a series of uncomfortable changes both physically and mentally. When you have culture shock, you may first have mental discomfort: loneliness, helplessness, anxiety, unease and withdrawal. Then physical discomforts like insomnia, inattentiveness, loss of appetite and headaches may occur. Finally, people may have social stress such as disruption, fragility, indulgence in smoking and drinking, loss of self-confidence, and even overindulgence on others. It is like a fish out of water.

Realizing what you are going through is normal. Remember that the unpleasant feelings are temporary, natural and common to any transition that a person makes during their life. Be patient and give yourself time to work through the process. Keep in touch with your home country. Read newspaper from home, international magazines, etc. Watch international television channels or surf the Internet. Call home regularly. Have familiar things around you that have personal meaning, such as photographs or ornaments. Find a supplier of familiar foods or visit restaurants that are similar to your home cuisine. Take care of yourself. Eat well, exercise, and get enough sleep. Talk to someone. Find friends who are going through a similar process, call your family back home, or see a counselor. Have fun and relax! Join student groups. Get out and volunteer to help others. Take up a sport. Participate in activities, clubs and student organizations of interest to you. Make a point to join activities that give you the opportunity to share in conversation and express your identity.

Culture shock is not that scaring because most people can go through the process of intercultural adaptation. Adaptation is a process with identifiable stages. Learning about the process will not prevent culture shock, but it will help you understand what is happening to you.

There are four steps in the process of intercultural adaptation. In Stage 1, which is called honeymoon period, you have excitement about the new situation. You have a sense of pleasure and self-satisfaction. Except for refugees and others who are being pushed to leave home against their will, most people who go abroad to live temporarily or permanently in a new culture do so willingly. They have some specific purpose in mind such as furthering their education, pursuing economic or professional opportunities, or simply experiencing something new. During this period, nearly everything appears wonderful. The food is exciting; the people seem friendly. Although you may experience some of the symptoms mentioned earlier, such as sleeplessness and mild anxiety, your enthusiasm and curiosity quickly overcome these minor discomforts. The sense of euphoria is so great that some writers call this stage the honeymoon stage. In Stage 2, the culture shock period, honeymoon is over. Things have gone sour. After a while, you begin to feel anxious, restless, impatient, and disappointed. You are meeting more people who do not speak your language, and yet your foreign language knowledge has not improved dramatically. You are confused when faced with the hidden aspects of culture. You suffer from frustration when old ways of dealing with situations fail to work. This period of adaptation is marked by a loss of social cues and a time of inconvenience that you had not experienced earlier. The confusion heightens with the unfamiliar smells, sounds, food, and cultural customs. You are angry and homesick. Instead of blaming or doubting yourself, you start to put the blame for the difficulties on the new culture and its people.

Now things begin to get better, and you enter the period of initial adjustment. After several months in the new culture, you may find that you view both the negative and positive in a balanced manner. You finally have learned a lot more about the culture and while you still do not like some things, you now like more than a few months ago. Now everyone is a crook, you think to yourself, and in fact, there are some good folks along with some bad. By now, you have become more accustomed to the food, sights, sounds, smells, and nonverbal behaviors of the new culture. Also, you have few headaches and upset stomach problems and less confusion, uncertainty and loneliness. Your physical health and mental health have improved. Normal contacts with host nationals are increasing, and you do not feel that you must defend yourself. You can accept yourself and others around you. Congratulations! You have just made it through the worst of culture shock.

The fourth stage is the period of acceptance and integration. You pick up a sense of effectiveness as new skills are acquired and are fully ready to have more challenging intercultural experiences. Your efforts pay off. You may improve your language skills and equally important you have growing ability to communicate nonverbally. You know what facial expressions and body movements are called for in most situations. You know what you can say or should say. You are able to make more accurate assessments about what the behavior of the host country people means and you can choose your responses deliberately rather than being overwhelmed by feelings of doubt or anger. Further, you can move beyond effectiveness in the new culture to an attitude of appreciation. You are able to live a full life, experiencing the full range of human feelings in the new culture. You can love, trust, laugh and solve problems, just about everything you can do at home. You are becoming more creative, expressive and able to take initiative and responsibility. A more positive way of moving through this state is to become a culture interpreter who helps others bridge the gap between cultures.

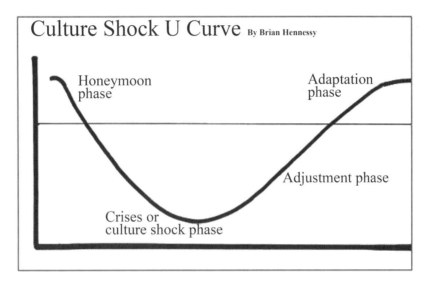

People who have spent considerable time outside their home cultures may experience a similar process when they return to their native countries, although the stages are often shorter and less intense. No one wants to admit that he or she is having difficulty readjusting to the home culture, so the reentry process has often involved people suffering quietly with stress.

In order to adapt to a new culture successfully, we need to develop competence in intercultural communication. The competence of intercultural communication is often evaluated from the cognitive, affective and behavioral perspectives. Related to these three dimensions, knowledge, a willing motivation and a mastery of skills are required to better understand a new culture and effectively adapt to it. Developing empathy is also important. That is being able to see things from the point of view of others so that we can better know and adjust to other people. Doing this, you are suggested that you resist the tendency to others' verbal and nonverbal actions from our culture's orientation. Learn to suspend, or at least keep in check, the cultural perspectives that are unique to your experience. Knowing how the frame of reference of other cultures differs from your own will assist you in accurately reading what meaning lies behind words and actions.

Exercises for Understanding

1. Answer the following questions according to the passage you have just read.

(1) What are the reasons for culture shock in today's society?

(2) What are the physical and mental symptoms of culture shock?

(3) According to the passage, how to deal with culture shock properly?

(4) How do people feel in the second period of intercultural adaptation?

(5) How to develop empathy in cultivating intercultural communication competence?

2. Small group task.

Imagine that you are going to a large urban American university for study. To evaluate your adaptation potential, rate yourself on the Adaptation Checklist below. Give yourself a score for each item according to the following scale.

1—Poor

2—Not as good as most people

3—Average

4—Better than most people

5—Excellent

Adaptation Checklist	
Score	**Adaptation Factors**
	Background and preparation
	Age—youth is an advantage
	Education—the higher the better
	Urban background—city dwellers do better than rural residents
	High level of professional skills
	General knowledge of the new culture: its history, customs, arts, etc.
	Special knowledge of the new situation: company, city, university, etc.
	Oral and written fluency in the language of the new culture
	Previous out-of-culture experiences
	Similarities of home culture to the new culture
	Personality Factors
	Tends to be accepting of different ways of doing things
	Likes to meet new people and do new things
	Stays calm in difficult situations
	Pays attention to people and not just tasks

	Can tolerate ambiguous or uncertain situations
	Has a sense of humor
	Strong but flexible in character
	Willing to take risks; not too concerned about social and psychological security
	Attitudes and Motivation
	Voluntarily chooses to be in contact with the new culture
	Attracted to the new situation rather than escaping problems at home
	Has admission and respect for the new culture
	Does not think that one culture is superior or inferior to another
	Has few stereotypes (inaccurate broad generalizations) about the new culture
	Health
	Has robust good health
	Has good health habits
	Has high energy level
	Total Score

After you have completed the checklist, discuss it with your classmates.

(1) What are your advantages and disadvantages in adapting to a new culture?

(2) What can you do to increase your adaptation potential?

3. Knowledge application.

Talk with a foreigner living in your country about his or her adaptation, the greatest difficulties he or she has met and the strategies he or she uses to overcome difficulties. The following is a chart about Strategies for Coping with Adaptation Stress for your reference.

Strategies for Coping with Adaptation Stress
(1) Do what you can to increase your score on the above cultural adaptation checklist.
• You can't change your age, but you can learn more about your company or city and you can adjust your thinking.
(2) Be alert for signs of adaptation stress.
• Health problems
• Loss of self-confidence
• Loneliness, sense of loss, severe homesickness
• Withdrawal from social contacts
• Negative feelings

• Behaving more aggressively than usual
(3) Tell people at home what kind of support you really need from them.
• You may need freedom to make new decisions and their understanding of the difficulties you face more than their advice.
(4) Use your "retreats" from the new culture constructively.
• Find home culture time and friends to refresh yourself and restore your positive feelings (speak your language, eat familiar food, etc.).
• Look for people from your home country with positive attitudes.
• Don't spend time with people from home who reinforce negative feelings.
(5) Pay attention to differences within the new culture.
• Avoid making broad generalizations about everybody in the host culture.
• Notice differences in background, motivation, personality; some people will be more like you than others.
• Just as you are not like anyone from your culture, so not anyone from the new culture is alike.
• People from the host culture may also be experiencing adaptation stress. When you are sensitive to their adaptation stress, you won't take their responses to you too personally.
(6) Try to find two mentors (experienced helpers).
• Look for someone from your home culture who has more experience in the new culture than you do.
• Look for someone from the new culture with much experience with your culture.
• Consult your mentors to check your interpretations of intercultural events.
• Use your mentors to learn about hidden aspects of the new culture.
(7) Seek out positive experiences within the new culture.
• If you like to watch football, watch football with the people from the new culture.
• If you enjoy music, enjoy it with people from the new culture.
• That is, take your pleasures and relaxing activities into the new culture.
(8) Be tolerant of yourself and others.
• Keep your sense of humor; misunderstandings can turn into funny stories.
• Assume that new culture associates have reasons for their actions even if you don't understand them.
• Recognize that you are leaning cultures as you go through difficult experiences.
• If necessary, adjust your goals and time frame to make them more realistic.
(9) Use your intercultural experiences to increase your skills.
• Notice and imitate the communication styles of the people from the new culture.
• Use concepts from intercultural communication study to interpret your experience and adjust your behavior.

4. Eastern and Western cultures comparing.

The following are observations of the differences in emphasis between Eastern and

Western cultures made by an Asian Christian cleric. Do you agree with them? Why or why not?

Eastern Cultures	Western Cultures
Live in "time"	Live in "space"
Value rest and relaxation	Value activity
Passive, accepting	Assertive, confronting
Contemplative	Diligent
Accept what it is	Seek change
Live in nature (part of nature itself)	Live with nature (co-existing with nature)
Want to know meaning	Want to know how it works
Freedom of silence	Freedom of speech
Lapse into meditation	Strive for articulation
Marry first, then love	Love first, then marry
Love is silent	Love is vocal
Focus on considerations of others' feelings	Focus on self-assuredness and own needs
Learn to do with less material assets	Attempt to get more of everything
Ideal: love of life	Ideal: being successful
Honor austerity	Honor achievement
Wealth or poverty: results of fortune	Wealth or poverty: results of enterprise
Cherish wisdom of years	Cherish vitality of youth
Retire to enjoy the gift of one's family	Retire to the rewards of one's work

5. Brainstorming: brain the ways to know if he or she is an American by referring to the following case.

Jim is an American who has lived in China for many years. He has shared his insights into Chinese culture. Believe it or not, if you find your behaviors or manners coincide with some of the following, you are 90% Chinese.

20 Ways to Know If You Are Chinese

If you are a Chinese…

(1) You like to eat chicken feet and suck on fish heads and fish fins.

(2) You prefer your shrimp with heads and legs still attached.

(3) You like congee with thousand-year-old eggs.

(4) You carry a stash your own food whenever you travel. These snacks are always dried and include dried plums, mango, ginger and squid.

(5) You wash your rice at 2–3 times before cooking it.

(6) You keep a thermos of hot water available very often.

(7) You sing karaoke and play mahjong in your spare time.

(8) You leave the plastic covers on your remote control.

(9) You use the dishwasher as a dish rack.

(10) You've seldom kissed or hugged your mom or dad.

(11) You take showers at night and your hair sticks up when you wake up.

(12) You usually stir eggs with chopsticks instead of whisk.

(13) When you are sick, your parents tell you not to eat fried food or baked goods due to yeet hay.

(14) You know someone who can get you a good deal on jewelry or electronics.

(15) You own your own meat cleaver and sharpen it.

(16) You bring oranges with you as a gift when you visit people's home.

(17) You flight over who pays the dinner bill.

(18) Your parents prefer you to live next door, or at least in the same neighborhood when you are married.

(19) You like the number of 8 or 6.

(20) You hold an umbrella even if it is a sunny day.

Section C Case

Scan and Listen

The Scenario

A Peruvian in the United States

Soon after arriving in the United States from Peru, I cried almost every day. I was so tense that I heard without hearing, and this made me feel foolish. I also escaped into sleeping more than twelve hours at a time and dreamed of my life, family, and friends in Lima. After three months of isolating myself in the house and speaking to no one, I ventured out. I then began to have severe headaches. Finally, I consulted a doctor, but she only gave me a lot of drugs to relieve the pain. Neither my doctor nor my teachers ever mentioned the two magic words that could have changed my life: culture shock! When I learned about this, I began to see things from a new point of view and was better able to accept myself and my feelings.

I now realize most of the Americans I met in Lima before I came to the US were also in one of the stages of culture shock. They demonstrated a somewhat hostile attitude toward Peru, which the Peruvians sensed and usually moved from an initally friendly attitude to a defensive, aggressive attitude or to avoidance. The Americans mostly stayed within the safe cultural familiarity of the embassy compound. Many seemed to feel that the difficulties they were experiencing in Peru were specially created by Peruvians to creat discomfort for foreigners. In other words, they displaced their problem of adjustment and blamed everything on Peru.

Exercise

Listen to the case above and answer the following questions.

(1) What's the living state of the Peruvian when he first arrived in the United States?

(2) Why did the man consult a doctor?

(3) How did he change his attitude after learning about culture shock?

(4) Why did Americans choose to stay in the embassy compound when they were in Peru?

(5) Whom did the Americans blame for their discomfort in Peru?

Module 6
Contexts of Intercultural Communication

Unit 13   Intercultural Communication in Business Context

Section A   Video Clip Appreciation

I. Introduction to the Movie *Shanghai Calling*

Imagine a steady stream of emigrants, traveling across a vast ocean to a foreign country, searching for new jobs and better lives. But the emigrants are Americans, and the country they are moving to is China. *Shanghai Calling* is a romantic comedy about modern-day American emigrants on an unfamiliar land.

When ambitious New York attorney Sam is sent to Shanghai on assignment, he immediately stumbles into a legal mess that could end his career. With the help of a beautiful relocation specialist, a well-connected old-timer, a clever journalist, and a street-smart legal assistant, Sam might just

save his job, find romance, and learn to appreciate the beauty and wonders of Shanghai.

II. Introduction to the Video Clip

Got-getting New York lawyer Sam Chao who's proud that he's "never been above 79th Avenue" and describes himself as only "technically" Chinese, is transferred to Shanghai for a three-month stint. Bracing himself for a hardship posting, he is almost peeved to be proven wrong by "relocation specialist" and eventual love-interest Amanda Wilson, who not only furnishes him with a six-star luxury apartment complete with a tiger mother housekeeper, but shows him Shanghai's glittering surfaces and can-do spirit, with a dash of shrewd insight into the current Sino-American relations.

III. Script of the Video Clip

Voice Over: We have a saying here in China. Shanghai… is like a beautiful woman. Seductive. Mysterious. And these days, very attractive to foreign businessmen. Executives, bankers, engineers, salesmen. Hundreds of thousands of Americans now live and work in Shanghai. This is a story of an American named Sam. A good man. Easy to get along with. Never arrogant or crocky. And because of this, he was loved by everyone he met in Shanghai. Or maybe not.

Video Clip

[*New York City, a short time ago*]

Voice Over: Sam just won the most important court case in his life. Sam Chao… is on his way to the top.

Powell & Davis: … and after poaching the client from a senior associate no less. Ballsy.

Sam: Thank you, sir. Thank you.

Powell & Davis: The reason we asked you here? Sam, we've got exciting news for you.

Imagined Crowd: Yeah, Sam! Way to go!

Powell & Davis: We are sending you to China.

Sam: I'm sorry?

Powell & Davis: Groff Technologies just moved its headquarters to Shanghai. Word is they're onto sth big. A game changer. And if our top client goes to Shanghai, that means we go, too. We've been in touch with Donald Cafferty from AmCham, the American Chamber of Commerce out there. He's found us an office and hired us a local staff. Now we need someone to head it up. You're the obvious choice. You're single, you're a go-getter. And you're even Chinese.

Sam: Technically, yes, I'm Chinese. Isn't there something else you guys wanted to say to me?

Powell & Davis: We're aware of the rumors. We're just not ready to name a new partner just yet. But we are ready to send you to China. This is a huge opportunity, Sam.

Sam: Well, it's an incredibly attempting offer, but I just feel I'm more of an asset here… in

New York. I know the ins and outs, I know everything. And my thirtieth birthday is coming. I've rented Thomas Keller's restaurant, I've got a DJ coming, I've got a lot of stuff going on.

Powell & Davis: You know what we like around here, Sam? A team player. Three months, that's all we ask. What do you say?

****

Sam: That's me.

Amanda: Welcome to China. Amanda Wilson, relocation specialist. It's my job to help you get adjusted.

Sam: Hi.

Amanda: I thought I missed you. I was running late. My Ayi was sick, and I have to find a babysitter and so… Everything OK?

Sam: Yeah… I was just expecting someone with… slightly darker hair.

Amanda: Here's your survival pack. Some Chinese yuan, money, in other words. A map of Shanghai, your business card, and your mobile phone. Your number is right on the back. Before going to your apartment, I want you to meet Donald from AmCham. He's kind of the "mayor of Americatown."

Sam: "Americatown"?

Amanda: Yeah, it's what we call our expat community over here. It's kind of like Chinatown in the US, but the other way around.

Sam: Ah.

Amanda: Here you go. (转身对出租车司机) 我们去浦西，淮海路。

Taxi driver 1: 好。

Sam: You speak Chinese?

Amanda: Of course, don't you?

Sam: …

Sam: What's going on here?

Amanda: Restaurant opening.

Sam: Oh yeah? I love a good restaurant. What kind of food do you have?

Amanda: Donald!

Donald: Amanda! Good morning! Well this must be Sam. Donald Cafferty, president of JFC China.

Sam: Sam Chao. Nice to meet you. Never see so much fanfare at a fast-food place before.

Donald: Our eight thousandth store opening called for a little celebration. The Chinese are crazy about fried chicken. Here, have a coupon for a free spicy chicken sandwich. Welcome to Shanghai. What are you doing Thursday night?

Sam: Um…

Donald: Great. Meet me for drinks out on the Bund. I'll introduce you to all of the top business execs in town. Microsoft, P&G, Ford… I'm gonna drive a lot of business your way. Ever been to China before?

Sam: I have never been above 79th street before. New York. It's a street. Joke.

Donald: He's gonna be a homesick one, I can tell. Lucky for you, I own an American bar out in Hongqiao. You ever get lonely, come on by.

Sam: OK. Sounds great.

Donald: Good man. Now if you'll excuse me, I'm late for my photo shoot.

Amanda: Modeling career finally taking off?

Donald: No, AmCham election's coming up.

Amanda: Hmn…

Donald: See you Thursday, Sam.

Sam: Yeah, Thursday.

Amanda: So, ready to see your new apartment?

Sam: As ready as I'll ever be.

Amanda: Sorry?

Sam: Look, I had a nice life back in New York, so whatever you found me… better not be too much of a letdown.

Amanda: OK. Here we are. Two bed, two bath, hardwood floor, recycled glass windows, hi-def TV, solar panels on the roof, and the entire building is brand new. What do you think?

Sam: That's awesome. I'll take it.

Amanda: OK, I'll get the papers ready. You've got to be kidding me.

Sam: What the hell was that?

Amanda: Construction. But they're supposed to be finished by now.

Sam: Are you telling me this building is still being built?

Amanda: Shanghai and construction go hand in hand. Sometimes these greener buildings take a little bit longer to get… OK, I have to get you out of here. I have a backup apartment down the street. It's not as nice as this one, but at least it's finished.

Sam: Is it a dump?

Amanda: No… I mean, umm… it's a tad smaller, and the amenities are less new. But it's a really nice place, in a good neighborhood.

Sam: It's a dump. I'm staying here, forget about it.

Amanda: Sam, I cannot let you stay here with all that noise going on upstairs.

Sam: I completely agree. So here is what you do: just tell them the future partner of a huge US law firm just moved in. They need to shut it down for three months, or I'll sue them. Here's my card.

Amanda: This may not work.

Sam: Amy?

Amanda: Amanda.

Sam: Your job was to find me a nice quiet place to live, and you failed. Are you going to resolve this issue, or do I need to replace you?

[*Phone rings*]

Amanda: It's you.

Sam: This is Sam.

Fang Fang: Hello, Mr Chao. This is Fang Fang, your new assistant. I hope you had a good flight. Are you planning to attend the Marcus Groff meeting today?

Sam: Today? No. I thought the meeting was tomorrow, the 17th.

Fang Fang: Yes. But today is the 17th.

Sam: That's impossible. I left New York on the 15th. I lost one day crossing the date line. That makes today the 16th.

Fang Fang: Actually, you lost two days. It became the 16th in the US while you were in the air. When you crossed the date line, it became the 17th. And Mr. Groff will be here in 30 minutes.

Sam: I'll be right there. Problem…

Amanda: I heard… you know what, you get to your office, and I will go upstairs and see what I can do about the constructions.

Sam: When did I do this… Oh jeez! Who the hell are you?

Nanny: 我都替你挂好了。你应该好好保管你的东西，它放在箱子里都弄皱了。

Sam: I got nothing. I don't speak Chinese. Who are you?

Nanny: 哦，你不会说中文，你是老外是不是啊？我是你的阿姨，阿姨。

Sam: "Ayi"?

Nanny: 阿姨。

Sam: Amanda said that word. Are you my nanny? You're like a housekeeper? You clean? Housekeeper?

Nanny: 哎哎，嗯。

Sam: Sleep? What? You live here, you live with me, you're my housekeeper, and you don't speak English. ¿Hablas español? That was really offensive on many, many levels. I am sorry about that, but I have to go. See you later.

Sam: OK… This is Yincheng Road. So that's gotta be… I have no idea. Which means…Screw it. Taxi! Can you take me to this address, please?

Taxi driver 2: 你要到的那个地方，就在那儿。

Sam: Just take me to the address.

Taxi driver 2: 你不需要坐出租车，走过去就行啦。

Sam: Why are we arguing?

Taxi driver 2: 看见了吗？前面的大楼就是你要去的地方。

Sam: Hohoho, all right. I get it. I'm from New York City. So don't think just because I'm from out of town, you can pad the fare by going the long way, or whatever it is you are trying to do. Just take me there!

Taxi driver 2: 到了。

Sam: Thank you.

New Words

seductive [sɪ'dʌktɪv] *adj*. very attractive 诱人的

arrogant ['ærəgənt] *adj*. behaving in a proud, unpleasant way toward other people because they believe that they are more important than others 傲慢的

crocky ['krɔki] *adj*. old and weak 老朽的，体弱的

poach [poʊtʃ] *v*. to secretly or dishonestly persuade people to join an organization or become its customers （通过不正当的手段或秘密）挖走（其他组织的成员或顾客）

ballsy ['bɔːlzi] *adj*. courageous, energetic and brave 有胆量的

fanfare ['fænfer] *n*. a short, loud tune played on trumpets or other similar instruments to announce a special event （特别仪式上的）嘹亮短曲

backup ['bækʌp] *n*. extra equipment, resources, or people that you can get help or support from if necessary 后备（设备、物资或人力）

dump [dʌmp] *n.* a place where rubbish and waste materials are left, for example, on open ground outside a town 垃圾场

sue [suː] *v.* to start a legal case against people, usually in order to claim money from them because they have harmed you in some way 诉讼，控告

Phrases and Expressions

go-getter: If someone is a go-getter, he or she is very energetic and eager to succeed. 干将；非常积极能干的人

hi-def: short term for high-definition 高清的

DJ: short term for disc jockey 流行音乐播音员，流行音乐节目主持人

Notes

Microsoft: An American multinational technology company headquartered in Redmond, Washington, which develops, manufactures, licenses, supports and sells computer software, consumer electronics and personal computers and services. 美国微软公司，由比尔·盖茨与保罗·艾伦始创于 1975 年，是一家美国跨国科技公司，也是世界个人电脑软件开发的先驱。公司总部设立在华盛顿州的雷德蒙德市，以研发、制造、授权和提供多种电脑软件为主要业务。

P&G: Procter & Gamble Co., also known as P&G, is an American multinational consumer goods company headquartered in downtown Cincinnati, Ohio, US, founded by William Procter and James Gamble, both from the UK. Its products include cleaning agents and personal care products. 宝洁公司，总部位于美国俄亥俄州的辛辛那提市。宝洁在日化品市场上知名度相当高，其产品包括洗护发用品、护肤用品、化妆品、婴儿护理用品、家居用品、个人清洁用品等。

Ford: The Ford Motor Company (commonly referred to simply as "Ford") is an American multinational automaker headquartered in Dearborn, Michigan, US. It was founded by Henry Ford and incorporated on June 16, 1903. 福特是世界著名的汽车品牌，为美国福特汽车公司旗下的众多品牌之一，公司及品牌名来源于创始人亨利·福特（Henry Ford）。福特汽车公司是世界上最大的汽车生产商之一，旗下拥有福特（Ford）和林肯（Lincoln）等汽车品牌，总部位于美国密歇根州的迪尔伯恩市。

Exercises for Understanding

1. Answer the following questions according to the video clip you have just watched.

(1) Why do Powell & Davis decide to send Sam to China?

(2) Why didn't Sam want to be sent to China?

(3) What was Amanda? Why was she late to receive Sam?

(4) Why did Amanda think that suing the construction company may not work out?

(5) What kind of culture shock did Sam encounter after he arrived in China?

2. Decide whether the following statements are true or false according to the video clip you have just watched. Write a "T" for true or an "F" for false.

_____(1) Sam was eager to go to work in China because he is a Chinese.

_____(2) Sam could speak Chinese fluently while Amanda was unable to understand Chinese at all.

_____(3) Sam was very satisfied with the apartment Amanda had chosen for him.

_____(4) Sam was confused about his arrival date in China.

_____(5) Sam insisted that he be taken to the company building by taxi.

3. Put the following sentences in the right order according to the video clip you have just watched.

_____(1) Sam complained about the noise in his apartment.

_____(2) Sam learned that he was going to be sent to China.

_____(3) Sam warned the taxi driver not to go a long way.

_____(4) Sam was arranged to meet Donald, nicknamed as the "mayor of Americatown" in China.

_____(5) Sam was told by his assistant Fangfang to go to a conference in 30 minutes.

Section B   Reading

As a professional in the modern business community, you need to be aware that the very concept of community is undergoing a fundamental transformation. A merchant supplied salt and sugar, and people made what they needed. The products the merchant sold were often produced locally because the cost of transportation was significant. A transcontinental railroad brought telegraph lines, shipping routes, and ports together from coast to coast.

Commerce—Comparing America and China

Shipping that once took months and years was now measured in days. A modern highway system and cheap oil products allowed for that measurement unit to be reduced to days and minutes. Just-in-time product delivery reduced storage costs from renting a warehouse at the port to spoilage in transit. Bar code and RDIF (radio frequency identification) tagged items instantly updated inventories and initiated orders at factories all over the world.

Communication, both oral and written, linked communities in ways that we failed to recognize. A system of trade and the circulation of capital and goods that once flowed relatively seamlessly have been challenged by change, misunderstanding, and conflict. Integrated markets and global networks bind us together in ways we are just now learning to appreciate, anticipate, and understand. Intercultural and international communication are critical areas of study with readily apparent, real-world consequences.

Agrarian, industrial, and information ages gave way to global business and brought the importance of communication across cultures to the forefront. The Pulitzer Prize-winning journalist Thomas Friedman calls this new world "flat," noting how the integration of markets and community had penetrated the daily lives of nearly everyone on the planet, regardless of language or culture. While the increasing ease of telecommunications and travel have transformed the nature of doing business. Friedman argues that "the dawning 'flat world' is a jungle pitting 'lions' and 'gazelles,' where 'economic stability is not going to be a feature' and 'the weak will fall farther behind.'" Half of the world's population that earn less than $2 (USD) a day felt the impact of a reduction in trade and fluctuations in commodity prices even though they may not have known any of the details. Rice, for example, became an even more valuable commodity than ever. To the individuals who could not find it, grow it, or earn enough to buy it, the hunger felt was personal and global. International trade took on a new level of importance.

Intercultural and international business communication has taken on a new role for students as well as career professionals. Knowing when the European and Asian markets open has become mandatory, so has the awareness of multiple time zones and their importance in relation to trade, shipping and the production cycle. Managing production in China from an office in Chicago has become common. Receiving technical assistance for your computer often means connecting with a well-educated English speaker in New Delhi. We compete with each other via Elance.com or Desk.com for contracts and projects, selecting the currency of choice for each bid as we can be located anywhere on the planet. Communities are no longer linked as simply "brother" and "sister" cities in symbolic partnerships. They are linked in the daily trade of goods and services.

We explore this dynamic aspect of communication. If the foundation of communication is important, its application in this context is critical. Just as Europe once formed intercontinental alliances for the trade of metals, leading

Gift Culture of ROK

to the development of a common currency, trade zone, and new concept of nation-state, now North and South America are following with increased integration. Major corporations are no longer affiliated with only one country or one country's interests but instead perceive the integrated market as team members across global trade. "Made in X," more of a relative statement as products from cars to appliances to garments, now comes with a list of where components were made and assembled and what percentage corresponds to each nation.

Global business is more than trade between companies located in distinct countries; indeed, that concept is already outdated. Intercultural and international business focuses less on the borders that separate people and more on the communication that brings them together. Business communication values clear, concise interaction that promotes efficiency and effectiveness. You may perceive your role as a business communicator within a specific city, business, or organization, but you need to be aware that your role crosses cultures, languages, value and legal systems, and borders.

We are not created absolutely equal. We are born light- or dark-skinned, to parents of education or parents without access to education, and we grow up short or tall, slender or stocky. Our life chances or options are in many ways determined by our birth. The Victorian *Rags to Riches* novels that Horatio Alger wrote promoted the ideal that individuals can overcome all obstacles, raising themselves up by their bootstraps. Some people do have amazing stories, but even if you are quick to point out that Microsoft founder Bill Gates became fabulously successful despite his lack of a college education, you must know that his example is exception, not the rule. We all may use the advantages of our circumstances to improve our lives, but the type and extent of those advantages vary greatly across the planet.

Cultures reflect this inequality, this diversity, and the divergent range of values, symbols, and meanings across communities. Can you tie a knot? Perhaps you can tie your shoes, but can you tie a knot to secure a line to a boat, to secure a heavy load on a cart or truck, or to bundle a bale of hay? You may not be able to. But if you were raised in a culture that place a high value on knot-tying for specific purposes, you would learn that which your community values.

People and their relationships to dominant and subordinate roles are a reflection of culture and cultural viewpoint. They are communicated through experience and create expectations for how and when managers interact with employees. The three most commonly discussed management theories are often called X, Y, and Z.

Gift-giving Etiquette in Russia

Theory X

In an influential book titled *The Human Side of Enterprise*, M. I. T. management professor Douglas McGregor, described two contrasting perceptions on how and why people work, formulating Theory X and Theory Y, which are both based on Maslow's hierarchy of needs. According to this Maslow, people are concerned first with physical needs (e.g. food, shelter) and second with safety. At the third level, people seek love, acceptance, and intimacy. Self-esteem, achievement, and respect are the fourth level. Finally, the fifth level embodies self-actualization.

McGregor's Theory X asserts that workers are motivated by their basic (low-level) needs and have a general disposition against labor. In this viewpoint, workers are considered lazy and predicted to avoid work if they can, giving rise to the perceived need for constant, direct supervision. A Theory X manager may be described as authoritarian or autocratic who does not seek input or feedback from employees. The view further holds that workers are motivated by personal interest. The Theory X manager uses control and incentive programs to provide punishment and rewards. Responsibility is the domain of the manager. Lack of training, inferior machines, or failure to provide the necessary tools are all reasons to stop working, and it is up to the manager to fix these issues.

Theory Y

In contrast to Theory X, Theory Y views employees as ambitious, self-directed, and capable of self-motivation. Employees have a choice, and they prefer to do a good job as a representation of self-actualization. The pursuit of pleasure and avoidance of pain are part of being human, but work is also a reward in itself and employees take pride in their efforts. Employees want to reach their fullest potential and define themselves by their profession. A job well done is reward in and of itself, and the employee may be a valuable source of feedback. Collaboration is viewed as normal, and the worker may need little supervision.

Theory Z

Theory X and Y may seem like two extremes across the range of management styles, but in fact they are often combined in actual work settings. William Ouchi's Theory Z combines elements of both and draws from American and Japanese management style. It promotes worker participation and emphasizes job rotation, skills development, and loyalty to the company. Workers are seen as having a high need for reinforcement, and belonging is emphasized. Theory Z workers are trusted to do their jobs with excellence and management is trusted to support them, looking out for their well-being.

Each of these theories of management features a viewpoint with assumptions about people and why they do what they do. While each has been the subject of debate, and variations on each have been introduced across organizational communication and business, they serve as a foundation for understanding management in an intercultural context.

Exercises for Understanding

1. Answer the following questions according to the passage you have just read.

(1) What kind of fundamental transformations have taken place in today's world?

(2) Why is intercultural and international communication of significance to the integrated markets today?

(3) How do you understand Thomas Friedman's interpretation of the world as "flat"?

(4) According to the passage, what is included in "Made in X" now?

(5) What does intercultural business communication value most?

(6) What does the author imply by the metaphor of "tying a knot"?

(7) How does Theory X differ from Theory Y in terms of employees' self-motivation in a company?

(8) How does Theory Z combine Theory X and Theory Y in management style?

2. Small group tasks.

(1) Imagine that you are a manager in charge of approximately a dozen workers. Would you prefer to rely primarily on Theory X, Y, or Z as your management style? Why? Write a short essay defending your preference, giving some concrete examples of management decisions you would make. Discuss your essay with your classmates.

(2) Describe your best boss and write a short analysis on what type of management style you perceive they used. Share and compare with classmates.

(3) Describe your worst boss and write a short analysis on what type of management style you perceive they used. Share and compare with classmates.

Section C Case

The Scenario

Scan and Listen

Cocktail Party

The cocktail party is perhaps a typical US symbol of entertainment, but an unfamiliar social phenomenon to many other cultures. Thus it may cause problems in intercultural communication.

An US manager may invite employees, clients, and customers so that they get to know one another. The goal at a cocktail party is to meet as many people as possible. Nobody expects to get into deep discussions. In fact, it would be rude to monopolize any one person. One makes small talk and walks the room, exchanging business cards and phone numbers so that one can get into contact later and establish future business relationships.

To Europeans, the cocktail party is a curious phenomenon. In Germany, for example, one invites only as many people as one has chairs for. To invite crowds and expect them to stand would not be polite and thus not acceptable. The art of small talk is not a forte of most Europeans either. They tend to view the US style of entertaining as superficial and lacking sincerity.

A US firm that hosts a cocktail party in Japan creates all sorts of problems because the cocktail party is based on the premise that one can walk up to anyone in the room and introduce oneself. In Japan, with its hierarchy and protocol for how to address others, it is almost impossible to introduce oneself without knowing the age and status of the other person. What it intends to do as a friendly gesture by the manager from the United States may cause discomfort and embarrassment for the Japanese guests.

People of different cultures may have different interpretations to the length of the cocktail party. For example, invitations in the United States may announce: "Cocktail party 5:00–7:00 p.m." Americans find this arrangement very considerate and efficient. The guests know that they don't have to reserve the entire evening for the event; they can make other plans for the rest of the evening. But it's unthinkable in cultures where hospitality is supposed to be unlimited, because to invite someone for a set time period is rude.

Exercise

Listen to the case above and answer the following questions.

(1) What's the goal of cocktail party in the United States?

(2) Do people have deep discussions at cocktail party in the United States?

(3) How would Europeans comment on the cocktail parties in the United States?

(4) Why may a US firm face problems when it holds cocktail party in Japan?

(5) What would cultures that emphasize hospitality think of Americans' set length of cocktail party?

Unit 14　Intercultural Communication in Tourism Context

Video Clip Appreciation

I. Introduction to the Movie *Little Miss Sunshine*

Sheryl Hoover is an overworked mother of two living in Albuquerque, New Mexico. Her brother, Frank, an unemployed scholar of Proust, is temporarily living at home with the family after having attempted suicide. Sheryl's husband Richard is a Type A personality striving to build a career as a motivational speaker and life coach. Dwayne, Sheryl's son from a previous marriage, is a Nietzsche-reading teenager who has taken a vow of silence until he can accomplish his dream of becoming a test pilot. Richard's foul-mouthed father, Edwin, recently evicted from a retirement home for snorting heroin, lives with the family. Olive, the daughter of Richard and Sheryl and the youngest of the Hoover family, is an aspiring beauty queen who is coached by Edwin.

Olive learns she is qualified for the "Little Miss Sunshine" beauty pageant that is being held in Redondo Beach, California in two days. Her parents and Edwin, who has been coaching her, want to support her, and Frank and Dwayne cannot be left alone, so the whole family goes. Because they have little money, they go on an 800-mile road trip in their yellow Volkswagen Type 2.

Family tensions play out on the highway and at stops along the way, amidst the aging VW van's mechanical problems. When the van breaks down early on, the family learns that they must push the van until it is moving at about 20 mph before it is put into gear, at which point they have to run up to the side door and jump in. Later on, the van's horn starts honking unceasingly by itself.

Throughout the road trip, the family suffers numerous personal setbacks and discovers their need for each other's support. Richard loses an important contract that would have jump-started his motivational business. Frank encounters the ex-boyfriend who, in leaving him for an academic rival, had prompted his suicide attempt. Edwin dies from a heroin overdose, resulting in the family smuggling the body out of a hospital and nearly having it discovered by the police. During the final leg of the trip, Dwayne discovers that he is color blind, which means he cannot become a pilot, a realization that prompts him to finally break his silence and shout his anger and disdain for his family. But he is then calmed down by Olive, and he immediately apologizes.

The climax takes place at the beauty pageant. After a frantic race against the clock, the family arrives at the hotel, and is curtly told by a pageant organizer that they are a few minutes past the deadline. A sympathetic hired hand instead offers to register Olive on his own time. As Olive prepares for the pageant, the family sees Olive's competition: slim, hypersexualized pre-teen girls with teased hair and capped teeth, performing highly elaborate dance numbers with great panache. It quickly becomes apparent that Olive is an amateur by comparison.

As Olive's turn to perform in the talent portion of the pageant draws near, Richard and Dwayne recognize that Olive is certain to be humiliated, and wanting to spare her feelings, run to the dressing room to talk her out of performing. Sheryl, however, insists that they "let Olive be Olive," and Olive goes on stage. Olive's hitherto-unrevealed dance that Edwin had choreographed for her is performed to Rick James's song *Super Freak*. Olive scandalizes and horrifies most of the audience and pageant judges with a burlesque performance that she joyfully performs while oblivious to their reactions. The pageant organizers are enraged and demand Sheryl and Richard remove Olive from the stage. Instead of removing her, one by one the members of the Hoover family join Olive on stage, dancing alongside her to show their support.

The family is next seen outside the hotel's security office where they are given their freedom in return for a promise never to enter a beauty pageant in the state of California again. Piling into the van with the horn still honking, they happily smash through the barrier of the hotel's toll booth and head back to their home in Albuquerque.

II. Introduction to the Video Clip

Little Miss Sunshine succeeds by making us all feel a little less weird and a little less alone. The film stands out from a moment of intense seriousness, such as the death of the grandfather, and from a comic scene where the family steals the body out of the hospital and puts it into the trunk of the car. A heartbreaking scene of despair will soon turn into a mission, which consists of stealing the body of Olive's heroine-addicted grandfather from the hospital where he died and eventually stick to the family's motto which is to never give up and keep moving forward no matter what happens. By hiding the body in the trunk of the car, the main characters once again defy the logic of common sense and bring together extreme emotions.

III. Script of the Video Clip

Video Clip

Olive: Mom? Dad?

Richard: What is it, hon?

Olive: Grandpa won't wake up.

Olive: Wanna take an eye test? Uncle Frank? An eye test?

Sheryl: Olive, come here. Put those away. We're gonna have a family meeting. Dwayne, family meeting. First of all, the doctors are doing everything they can to help Grandpa right now. He's had a long, eventful life, and l know he loves both of you very much. But if God wants to take him, we have to be ready to accept that, OK? Whatever happens, we're a family. And what's important is that we love each other. I love you guys so, so much.

Doctor: Are you the family of Edwin Hoover?

Richard: Yes.

Doctor: I'm sorry. We did everything we could. He was, uh... Well, it was too much. He probably just fell asleep and never woke up. I'll have someone come and talk to you about handling the remains.

Richard: Thank you.

Doctor: Linda!

Olive: Mom? Is Grandpa dead?

Sheryl: Yeah, honey. He passed away.

Linda: Hi. I'm your bereavement liaison, Linda. My consolations for your loss.

Richard: Thank you.

Linda: OK, these are the forms you need to fill out. A death certificate. A report of the death. An ME pink slip. Please try and be as detailed as possible. Um, this is a brochure for a grief recovery support group that meets on Tuesdays, and if you like, I can refer you to a funeral home so you can begin making arrangements.

Richard: Actually, prearrangements have already been made in Albuquerque.

Linda: Albuquerque?

Richard: We're actually on our way to California right now.

Linda: If the body is crossing state lines, you're gonna need a burial transit permit.

Richard: OK. But we're trying to get to Redondo Beach by three o'clock.

Linda: Three o'clock today? Hmm. Ain't gonna happen.

Richard: OK, um, can I just... I know that this, uh, might be a little unusual, but if maybe we could just go, and then we'll come back and take care of all the paperwork, and...

Linda: No. You can't just abandon the body.

Richard: No, no, no. Nobody's gonna abandon the body. We're just gonna go and...

Linda: Otherwise, the hospital becomes responsible.

Richard: We'll go, and come back.

Linda: Sir, there are ways we have of doing things.

Linda: You're not following me. Sir, you are not the only one that's had somebody die here today, okay?

Richard: Is there any way we might be able to view the remains?

Linda: We haven't had a chance to move him downstairs. So someone may come in a few minutes to take him to the basement. Tell them who you are, and they will wait.

Richard: Thank you.

Linda: And when you're done with the paperwork, I'll be at the nurses' station.

Richard: Great. Thank you, Linda.

Linda: Thank you.

Richard: God damn it, Dad. God damn it! Stupid...

Sheryl: We'll go to Little Miss Sunshine next year, okay, honey? Next year.

Richard: No. No. We've come 700 miles. I'll be damned if I'm not making that contest, Sheryl.

Sheryl: Well, Richard, we can't leave him here.

Richard: We're not gonna leave him.

Sheryl: Richard, what are you doing?

Richard: Fuck!

Richard: Dwayne, go around outside.

Sheryl: Richard, What are you thinking?

Richard: We're gonna take him with us.

Sheryl: No, no, that is not happening.

Richard: He's better off with us than these people. I want you to go round outside and underneath this window.

Sheryl: Dwayne, don't move. Honey, You stay here. We'll take Olive. Frank can drive.

Richard: No, Sheryl. We'll be there in two hours. Listen to me. I'll call a funeral home once we get there. One thing my father would have wanted is to see Olive perform in the Little Miss Sunshine Pageant. I believe we'd be doing a grave disservice to his memory if we were to just give up now. All right? There are two kinds of people in this world. There's winners, and there's losers. Okay? You know what the difference is? Winners don't give up. So what are we here? Are we winners, or are we losers? Huh?

Sheryl: OK. OK. Let's do it. You guys go. Olive, you watch the curtain.

Linda: I don't know. l have no reason to assume it's gonna be otherwise.

Richard: Watch. Get the back, get the back. Go, go, go.

Linda: Yeah, 1:00. Now?

Richard: He's very heavy. Be gentle. One, two... Okay. Three. Wait, wait, wait! Not yet, not yet. Okay. Go, go, go, go.

Sheryl: Richard, I can't do it.

Richard: I got him. I got him.

Sheryl: Come on.

Olive: Come on! Hurry up!

Richard: Okay, he's slipping. Hold on.

Frank: I got him, I got him, I got him.

Olive: Be careful.

Sheryl: Hurry up! Keep watch, Olive. Watch the curb, watch the curb. Watch his head! Watch it!

Frank: Keys.

Sheryl: Swing him around this way. Olive, get in. Okay, let's go.

Richard: Sheryl. Let's go, Frank. Did I mention that I am the preeminent Proust scholar in the US?

Richard: Here we go! Here we go!

Sheryl: Are you Okay?

Olive: Dad?

Richard: Yeah, honey?

Olive: What's gonna happen to Grandpa? Uncle Frank?

Frank: Yeah?

Olive: Do you think there's a heaven?

Frank: It's hard to say, Olive. I… I don't think anyone knows for sure.

Olive: I know, but what do you think?

Frank: Um, well...

Olive: I think there is one.

Frank: Do you think I'll get in?

Olive: Yes.

Frank: You promise?

Olive: Yes.

Richard: Whoa! Hey! Son of a bitch!

Frank: What happened?

Richard: He cut me off.

Richard: It's stuck.

Sheryl: Okay, just leave it.

Richard: It's stuck or sth.

Sheryl: Maybe try pulling it from here.

Richard: No, no. Just leave it. I'll fix it when we get there.

Sheryl: Okay, fine.

Richard: Shit! Oh, Jesus! God! I'm being pulled over. Here we go. Okay. Everybody just pretend to be normal, Okay? Like everything's normal here.

Policeman: How you folks doing?

Richard: Yeah, we're fine. Just...

Policeman: Little trouble with the horn?

Richard: What?

Policeman: Having a little trouble with your horn?

Richard: Yeah. A little trouble. Sorry. Uh. Sorry.

Policeman: Could you step outside the vehicle? Step this way, please.

Richard: No, no.

Policeman: What?

Richard: Don't.

Policeman: Don't what? Do you have sth in your trunk, sir?

Richard: It's nothing. I... Don't open it.

Policeman: Sir, you just gave me probable cause to search your trunk.

Richard: Just—I—I just...

Policeman: Sir, put your hands on the vehicle, now! Now! Don't move!

Richard: Okay. It's not illegal!

Policeman: I'd advise you to keep your mouth shut!

Sheryl: Oh, God. What is he doing?

Richard: It's not illegal. Goddamn!

Policeman: Sir, could you come back here? I love this stuff. I love it. God bless you, God bless you. Don't worry. I'm not gonna bust you.

Richard: Oh, thank you.

Policeman: How you doing? Cute. Cute family. That's nice.

Richard: Thank you.

Policeman: And this on the side. A little of this, a little of that. Sweet sweetness. That is sweet, yeah. Dirty. And this one is one of my favorites. Ah, good, yeah.

Richard: That's a little different choice. No?

Policeman: I'll leave that with you.

Richard: All right.

Policeman: You have a good day there.

Richard: Yeah.

Sheryl: What happened?

Richard: I'll tell you when I regain consciousness. Frank, Dwayne, get out and push.

Sheryl: Okay, there it is. Redondo Beach, 46.

Richard: It's 2:15. Might be a few minutes late.

Sheryl: They said three o'clock sharp. They were very explicit. We can't cross these people. Trust me.

Olive: Mom, Dwayne has 20/20 vision.

Sheryl: I bet he does.

Olive: Okay. Now I'm gonna check to see if you're color-blind.

Richard: Asshole!

Olive: What's the letter in the circle? No, no, no. Inside the circle. Right there. See? It's an "A." Can't you see it? Right there.

Frank: It's bright green. Oh, man. Dwayne, I think you might be color-blind. You can't fly jets if you're color-blind. We've got a little bit of... Okay, we've got an emergency back here.

Sheryl: What is it? What's the emergency?

Richard: Just pull over! It's all right, man. Dwayne, Dwayne. It's all right. Hold on.

Sheryl: Just pull over the car!

Richard: Okay. All right!

Sheryl: Get him to pull over, please?

Dwayne: Could you get him to pull over, please?

Sheryl: Richard, pull over! Pull over the car!

Richard: It's all right. We're pulling over. I'm pulling over. Please! No, no, no.

Frank: Dwayne! No. no. Dwayne! Sit down! God, this better be good!

Dwayne: Pull over.

Richard: I'm pulling over. All right!

Sheryl: Stop the car!

Richard: It's gonna be okay, Dwayne. All right. Do not open the door.

Sheryl: Dwyane? Oh, God.

Dwayne: Fuck!

Sheryl: What happened?

Frank: He's color-blind. He can't fly.

Sheryl: Oh, Jesus. Oh, no. Just give him a second. Dwayne? Dwayne, honey, I'm sorry. Dwayne, come on. We have to go.

Dwayne: I'm not going.

Sheryl: Dwayne...

Dwayne: I said I'm not. Okay? l don't care. I'm not getting on that bus again!

Sheryl: Dwayne, for better or worse, we're your family.

Dwayne: You're not my family! Okay? I don't wanna be your family! I hate you fucking people! I hate you! Divorce? Bankrupt? Suicide? You're fucking losers! You're losers! No. Please just leave me here, Mom. Okay? Plcasc, please, please. Please just leave me here.

Sheryl: Shit. I don't know what to do.

Richard: Well, it's getting late. Maybe... Can somebody stay here with him?

Frank: I'll stay.

Sheryl: That is not happening.

Richard: All right. Well... Just worried about the time. Olive, you wanna try talking to him?

Sheryl: Richard, no! There is nothing to say. We just have to wait. Honey...

Dwayne: Okay. Let's go. I apologize for the things l said. I was upset, and l didn't really mean them.

Sheryl: It's okay. Come on. Let's go.

New Words

eventful [ɪ'ventfl] *adj.* full of events or incidents 多事的

remains [rɪ'meɪnz] *n.* the dead body of a human being 遗骸

bereavement [bɪ'riːvmənt] *n.* state of sorrow over the death or departure of a loved one 丧亲之哀

liaison ['liːəzɑːn; li'eɪzɑːn] *n.* a channel for communication between groups 联络

consolation [ˌkɑːnsə'leɪʃən] *n.* the comfort one feels when consoled in times of disappointment 安慰，慰问

slip [slɪp] *n.* a small sheet of paper 纸片

brochure [brou'ʃʊr] *n.* a small book usually having a paper cover 手册，小册子

grief [griːf] *n.* intense sorrow caused by loss of a loved one (especially by death) 悲痛

pageant ['pædʒənt] *n.* a competition in which young women are judged to decide which one is the most beautiful 选美比赛

disservice [dɪs'sɜːvɪs] *n.* harm 伤害

preeminent [pri'emɪnənt] *adj.* greatest in importance or degree or significance or achievement 卓越的，超群的

horn [hɔːrn] *n.* the device on a vehicle such as a car that makes a loud noise as a signal or warning 喇叭

vehicle [viːəkəl] *n.* a conveyance that transports people or objects 车辆

trunk [trʌŋk] *n.* compartment in an automobile that carries luggage or tools 汽车车尾的行李箱

asshole ['æshoʊl] *n.* insulting terms of address for people who are stupid or irritating or ridiculous 令人讨厌的人

bankrupt [ˈbæŋkrʌpt] *n.* someone who has insufficient assets to cover their debts 破产者

Phrases and Expressions

funeral home: a mortuary where those who knew the deceased can come to pay their last respects 殡仪馆

pull over: to steer a vehicle to the side of the road 靠边停车

color-blind: unable to distinguish one or more chromatic colors 色盲的

Notes

Proust scholar: A Proust scholar is someone who focuses on studying the 20th century French author Marcel Proust. Proust's most renowned work was a seven-volume novel collectively entitled *Á la recherche du temps perdu*, which has been translated as both *In Search of Lost Time* and *Remembrance of Things Past*. A Proust scholar typically will focus his or her attention on this work but also will be interested in Proust's life and his other writings. 马塞尔·普鲁斯特（1871—1922，Marcel Proust）是 20 世纪法国最伟大的小说家之一，意识流文学的先驱与大师。他也是 20 世纪世界文学史上最伟大的小说家之一。

Exercises for Understanding

1. Answer the following questions according to the video clip you have just watched.

(1) What documents does Richard have to fill out for the death of his father Edwin Hoover?

(2) How did Richard manage to strike a balance between handling his father's death affairs and sending Olive to the pageant in California?

(3) Why did the policeman ask the Richards to pull over?

(4) How did Frank find that Dwayne was color-blind?

(5) What did Olive do to persuade Dwayne into continuing his journey to the pageant together with the family members?

2. Decide whether the following statements are true or false according to the video clip you have just watched. Write a "T" for true or an "F" for false.

_____(1) Sheryl first decided to take the remains of grandpa Edwin Hoover with them to the pageant in California.

_____(2) In the United States, it is okay to take the remains of a dead person across state lines with no burial transit permit.

_____(3) Linda, the bereavement liaison, said that the hospital would keep the remains of grandpa Edwin Hoover until the Richards came back from the California pageant.

_____(4) Richard and Sheryl knew in the very beginning that Dwayne was color-blind.

_____(5) Dwayne was in a rage when he knew that he was color-blind.

3. Match the Lines with the characters.

(1) Put those away. We'll have a family meeting.   A. Richard

(2) You can't just abandon the body.   B. Policeman

(3) Did I mention that I am the preeminent Proust scholar in the US? C. Dwayne

(4) Don't worry, I'm not gonna bust you.   D. Sheryl

(5) Dwayne has 20/20 vision.   E. Linda

(6) I hate you fucking people!   F. Olive

Section B   **Reading**

Collaborative Efforts a Must!

"We didn't all come over on the same ship, but we're all in the same boat."

—Bernard Baruch, American financier and statesman

It's no secret that today's workplace is rapidly becoming vast, as the traveling environment expands to include various geographic locations and span numerous cultures. What can be difficult, however, is understanding how to communicate effectively with individuals who speak another language, or who rely on different means of reaching a common goal.

Tourism is the most superficial way of an intercultural encounter and one of the biggest industrial sectors in the world. From time to time, people may spend two weeks in Turkey, Dubai, or on Bali. When going abroad people need to be aware of different behavioral rules and patterns. Both tourists and employees need to face their upcoming intercultural communication challenges. People with different cultural backgrounds not only speak different languages, they think and act differently.

Intercultural Communication—The New Norm

The Internet and modern technology have opened up new places that allow us to promote our traveling businesses to new geographic locations and cultures. And given that it can now be as easy to work with people remotely as it is to work face-to-face, intercultural communication is increasingly the new norm.

For those of us who are native English speakers, it is fortunate that English seems to be the language that people use if they want to reach the widest possible audience. However, even for native English speakers, intercultural communication can be an issue: just witness the mutual incomprehension that can sometimes arises between people from different English-speaking countries.

In this new world, good intercultural communication is a must.

Understand Cultural Diversity

Given different cultural contexts, this brings new communication challenges to the workplace. Even when employees located in different locations or offices speak the same language (for instance, correspondences between English speakers in the US and English speakers in the UK), there are some cultural differences that should be considered in an effort to optimize communications between the two parties.

Intercultural Encounters

In such cases, an effective communication strategy begins with the understanding that the sender of the message and the receiver of the message are from different cultures and backgrounds. Of course, this introduces a certain amount of uncertainty, making communications even more complex.

Without getting into cultures and sub-cultures, it is perhaps most important for people to realize that a basic understanding of cultural diversity is the key to effective intercultural communication. Without necessarily studying individual cultures and languages in detail, we must all learn how to better communicate with individuals and groups whose first language, or language of choice, does not match our own.

Develop Awareness of Individual Cultures

However, some learning of the basics about culture and at least sth about the language of communication in different countries is important. This is necessary even for the basic level of understanding required to engage in appropriate greetings and physical contact, which can be a tricky area interculturally. For instance, kissing a business associate is not considered an appropriate practice in the US, but in Paris, one peck on each cheek is an acceptable greeting. And, the firm handshake that is widely accepted in the US is not recognized in all other cultures.

While many companies now offer training in the different cultures where the company conducts business, it is important that employees communicating across cultures practice patience and work to increase their knowledge and understanding of these cultures. This requires the ability to see that a person's own behaviors and reactions are oftentimes culturally driven and that while they may not match our own, they are culturally appropriate.

If a leader or manager of a team that is working across cultures or incorporates individuals who speak different languages, practice different religions, or are members of a society that requires a new understanding, he or she needs to work to convey this.

Consider any special needs the individuals on your team may have. For instance, they may observe different holidays, or even have different hours of operation. Be mindful of time zone differences and work to keep everyone involved aware and respectful of such differences.

Generally speaking, patience, courtesy and a bit of curiosity go a long way. And, if you are unsure of any differences that may exist, simply ask team members. Again, this may best be done in a one-on-one setting so that no one feels "put on the spot" or self-conscious, perhaps even embarrassed, about discussing their own needs or differences of needs.

Demand Tolerance

Next, cultivate and demand understanding and tolerance. In doing this, a little education will usually do the trick. Explain to team members that the part of the team that works out of the Australia office, for example, will be working in a different time zone, so electronic communications and/or return phone calls will experience a delay. And, members of the India office will also observe different holidays such as Mahatma Gandhi's Birthday, observed on October 2nd.

Most people will appreciate the information and will work hard to understand different needs and different means used to reach common goals. However, when this is not the case, make it clear that you expect to be followed down a path of open-mindedness, acceptance and tolerance. Tolerance is essential. However, you need to maintain standards of acceptable behavior. The following "rules of thumb" seem universal:

Team members should contribute to and not hinder the team's mission or harm the delivery to the team's customer.

Team members should not damage the cohesion of the team or prevent it from becoming more effective.

Team members should not unnecessarily harm the interests of other team members.

Other factors (such as national law) are obviously important.

When dealing with people in a different culture, courtesy and goodwill can also go a long way in ensuring successful communication. Again, this should be insisted on.

Keep It Simple

When you communicate, keep in mind that even though English is considered the international language, it is a mistake to assume that every person speaks good English. In fact, only about half of the 800 million people who speak English learned it as a first language. And, those who speak it as a second language are often more limited than native speakers.

When you communicate interculturally, make particular efforts to keep your communication clear, simple and unambiguous.

And avoid humor until you know that the person you're communicating with "gets it" and isn't offended by it. Humor is notoriously culture-specific: many things that pass for humor in one culture can be seen as grossly offensive in another.

Exercises for Understanding

1. Answer the following questions according to the passage you have just read.

(1) How do you understand that tourism is the most superficial way of an intercultural encounter?

(2) According to the passage, what is the key to effective intercultural communication?

(3) According to the passage, what are the ways out when different needs and common goals cannot be met?

(4) According to the passage, what is the number of people who speak English as the first langauge? What should be kept in mind when speaking English in a foreign country?

(5) Why does the passage remind that people handle humor properly?

2. Small group task.

Read the following 3 pieces of Travel Tips (Dos and Don'ts) in China, Myanmar and the Middle East and discuss their common and different points culturally.

China Travel Tips: Dos and Don'ts

Many travelers from abroad are confused and frightened by Chinese customs. This handy reference tool makes it easy for newcomers to China to fit right in.

So come along, my alien friend! Welcome to China!

The order of Chinese names is family name first, then given name. Among some 440 family names, the 100 most common ones account for 90% of the total population. Brides in China do not adopt their husband's surnames.

Among Chinese, a popular way to address each other, regardless of gender, is to add an age-related term of honor before the family name. These include: lao (honorable old one), xiao (honorable young one) or occasionally da (honorable middle-aged one).

Unlike the Japanese, Chinese do not commonly bow as a form of greeting. Instead, a brief handshake is usual. While meeting elders or senior officials, your handshake should be even gentler and accompanied by a slight nod. Sometimes, as an expression of warmth, a Chinese will cover the normal handshake with his left hand. As a sign of respect, Chinese usually lower their eyes slightly when they meet others.

Moreover, embracing or kissing when greeting or saying good-bye is highly unusual. Generally, Chinese do not show their emotions and feelings in public. Consequently, it is better not to behave in too carefree a manner in public. Also, it is advisable to be fairly cautious in political discussions.

Chinese do not usually accept a gift, invitation or favor when it is first presented. Politely refusing two or three times is thought to reflect modesty and humility. Accepting sth in haste makes a person look aggressive and greedy, as does opening it in front of the giver. Traditionally the monetary value of a gift indicates the importance of a relationship, but due to increasing contact with foreigners in recent years, the symbolic nature of gifts has taken foot.

Present your gifts with both hands. And when wrapping, be aware that the Chinese ascribe much importance to color. Red is lucky, pink and yellow represent happiness and prosperity; white, grey and black are funeral colors.

The popular items including cigarette lighters, stamps (stamp collecting is a popular hobby), T-shits, and the exotic coins, make a good gift to the Chinese.

And the following gifts should be avoided:

(1) White or yellow flowers (especially chrysanthemums), which are used for funerals.

(2) Pears. The word for pear in Chinese sounds the same as "separation" and is considered bad luck.

(3) Clocks of any kind. The word clock in Chinese sounds like the expression—the end of life.

China is one of those wonderful countries where tipping is not practiced and almost no one asks for tips.

Traditionally speaking, there are many taboos at Chinese tables, but these days not many people pay attention to them. However, there are a few things to keep in mind, especially if you are a guest at a private home.

(1) Don't stick your chopsticks upright in the rice bowl. Instead, lay them on your dish. The reason for this is that when sb dies, the shrine to them contains a bowl of sand or rice with

two sticks of incense stuck upright in it. So if you stick your chopsticks in the rice bowl, it looks like a shrine and is equivalent to wishing death upon the people at the table!

(2) Make sure the spout of the teapot is not facing anyone. It is impolite to set the teapot down where the spout is facing towards sb. The spout should always be directed to where nobody is sitting, usually just outward from the table.

(3) Don't tap on your bowl with your chopsticks. Beggars tap on their bowls, so this is not polite. If you are in someone's home, it is like insulting the cook.

Myanmar Travel Tips: Dos and Don'ts

Myanmar is a Buddhism country and it is famous as the Golden Land. Otherwise, it is also called the Land of Pagodas. So when coming to Myanmar, tourists should know the behaviors both in public and religious monuments.

Dos

Say "Mingalarbar" when meeting each other.

Add "U" (for male) in front of the names for adult persons.

Add "Daw" (for female) in front of the names for adult persons.

Wear decent clothes to the pagodas or monasteries.

Let the oldest be served first.

Show respect to monks, novices and nuns.

Offer articles with both hands.

Keep the feet on the ground.

Bend a bit when crossing close in front of the elders.

Dress and act decent.

Speak slowly and clearly.

Seek permission on retrieving an article above a person's head.

Behave in a proper manner.

Don'ts

Don't wear shoes and shorts at pagodas and monasteries.

Don't sit with back against Buddha Image.

Don't offer to shake hands with a monk.

A woman should not touch a monk.

Avoid being a nuisance when taking photographs.

Don't handle Buddha Images or sacred object with disrespect.

Don't keep Buddha Images or sacred objects in inappropriate places.

Don't step on a monk's shadow.

Don't touch anybody on the head.

Don't touch a woman on any part of the body.

Don't point a finger straight in the face.

Don't step over any part of the person.

Don't gamble.

Don't go where you are advised not to go.

Travel Tips in the Middle East: Dos and Don'ts

The trafficking of drugs and pornography are not the only crimes to carry the death sentence in extreme case. Homosexuality is highly illegal in most of the Middle East and, although Christianity is tolerated in most countries, attempts to covert Muslims can also carry very serious consequences.

But it is not all doom and gloom—travelers who employ common sense and a large helping of respect and consideration for Islamic culture will enjoy a trouble-free trip. Below are some basic tips.

Appropriate Dress It's a myth that Western women have to wear headscarves; tourists are recognized as tourists and as such are generally exempt from any such obligations. Women should, however, dress conservatively at all times, especially when traveling alone.

The Sanctity of Marriage Unmarried women over the age of 25 tend to attract endless pity. If you prefer to avoid such attention, as well as excessive male attention, wear a wedding ring.

Leave the Girls Alone Guys, it's not a good idea to even contemplate relieving a girl of her honor, even careless long glance can be very risky.

A Bit of Decorum Try not to blaspheme, even in English—it tends to be dimly looked upon and considered disrespectful.

Wanna Haggle? Always haggle—that's the way of the Arab world—and never pay more than one third of the original asking price.

Calling Home Get a prepaid international sim card rather than using the expensive local telephone networks.

3. Case study.

People sometimes assume that learning about other cultures is unnecessary if we simply treat others as we would like to be treated. To test this assumption, try to answer the following questions.

(1) When receiving a gift from a friend, should you open it immediately, or wait to open it in private?

(2) When grocery shopping, should you touch fruits and vegetables to evaluate their freshness?

(3) In a conversation with your instructor or your supervisor at work, should you maintain direct eye contact?

4. Self-Test.

How Happy Are You?

Find out with this test designed by Dr. Raj Persaud, consultant psychiatrist at the Maudsley Hospital, London. Consider the following statements:

(1) My ability to concentrate is so good that I can forget how time has flown.

   Agree: A   Disagree: B

(2) There are many things about me that if others knew they would like me less.

   Agree: B   Disagree: A

(3) If people don't like me, it is usually because of their own problems.

   Agree: A   Disagree: B

(4) There are secrets about my past that I keep to myself and would not share.

   Agree: B   Disagree: A

(5) If I had my time over I would do practically everything I did again, the same way.

   Agree: A   Disagree: B

(6) There are many ways I could improve as a person.

   Agree: B   Disagree: A

(7) My parents think they're lucky to have had me.

   Agree: A   Disagree: B

(8) My life was better in the past than it is now.

   Agree: B   Disagree: A

(9) I was born with a combination of talents few others have.

   Agree: A   Disagree: B

(10) I get upset more with myself than others.

   Agree: B   Disagree: A

Section C   Case

The Scenario

Scan and Listen

Goodnight Kiss

Xiaohong is a graduate student in China and over the last few weeks, she has become friends with Mark, a Western student who is studying Chinese at her university. They have a number of friends in common, so often see each other at various social gatherings. They enjoy talking to each other and have gotten to know each other fairly well.

Last weekend Mark asked Xiaohong if she would like to see a movie with him. Xiaohong said yes, so they had dinner and saw a movie together. After the movie, they talked for a long time as they walked home. When it was time to say goodnight, Mark first took Xiaohong's hand and then he kissed Xiaohong. Xiaohong was a little surprised when he kissed her, but she was not unhappy because she likes him quite a bit.

Now Xiaohong has started to tell people that Mark is her boyfriend. However, when Xiaohong told one of her Chinese girlfriends about all of this, the girlfriend said that Westerners are very casual about relationships between men and women. The goodnight kiss can mean that Mark has fallen in love with Xiaohong and wants to have a more serious relationship. Or Mark was moved more by the romance of the moment than by any deeper feelings, and he doesn't know for sure himself how he feels about Xiaohong. It is also possible that Mark's interest in Xiaohong is more superficial. Perhaps he just finds Xiaohong physically attractive or he is lonely in China and enjoys Xiaohong's company. In order to sort things out, Xiaohong can consider talking to Mark about their relationship. Talking about a romantic relationship in this way may seem somewhat awkward and difficult—even for Westerners—but it will help Xiaohong get a better understanding of what Mark thinks about the relationship.

Exercise

Listen to the case above and answer the following questions.

(1) How did Xiaohong and Mark get along?

(2) What happened to Xiaohong and Mark last week?

(3) How did Xiaohong understand the goodnight kiss?

(4) According to Xiaohong's girlfriend, what are the implications of the goodnight kiss?

(5) What can be done to figure out the genuine meaning of the goodnight kiss?

Unit 15   Intercultural Communication in Education Context

Section A   Video Clip Appreciation

I. Introduction to the Movie *Dead Poets Society*

Dead Poets Society is a 1989 American drama film written by Tom Schulman, directed by PeterWeir and starring Robin Williams. The film evoked an extensive reflection on education.

John Keating is the new charismatic English teacher at Welton Academy, a very traditional New England boarding school. Questioning authority and going against the conformist norm, he challenges his students to live life to the fullest, to "seize the day." He teaches them to act on their impulses and to be spontaneous, free thinkers. Some of the boys are inspired by his idealism and form a secret society based on their mutual appreciation of poetry. Here they learn to express their feelings and to find out who they are and what they really want.

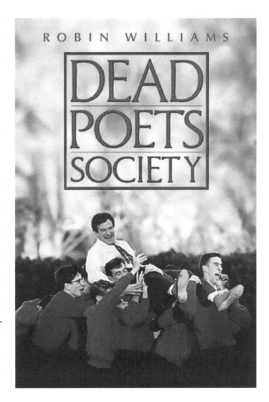

But the school authorities refuse to tolerate this obvious rebellion against their traditional rules, and what follows is a conflict with tragic consequences.

II. Introduction to the Video Clip

Nolan investigates Neil's death at the request of the Perry family. Richard blames Neil's death on Keating to escape punishment for his own participation in the Dead Poets Society, and names the other members. Confronted by Charlie, Richard urges the rest of them to let Keating take the fall. Charlie punches Richard and is expelled. Each of the boys is called to Nolan's office to sign a letter attesting to the truth of Richard's allegations, even though they know they are false. When Todd's turn comes, he is reluctant to sign, but does so after seeing that the others have complied.

Keating is fired and Nolan takes over teaching the class. Keating interrupts the class to collect personal articles; before he leaves, Todd shouts that all of them were forced to sign the letter that resulted in his dismissal and that Neil's death was not his fault. Todd stands on his desk and salutes Keating with the words "O Captain! My Captain!" Knox, Gerard, Steven, and over half of the class do the same, ignoring Nolan's order to sit down. Keating is deeply touched by their gesture. He thanks the boys and departs.

III. Script of the Video Clip

Video Clip

[*Chorus*]

All my life Shall surely Follow me

And in God's house

Forevermore

My dwelling place Shall be

Amen

Nolan: The death of Neil Perry is a tragedy. He was a fine student, one of Welton's best. And he will be missed. We've contacted each of your parents to explain the situation. Naturally, they're all quite concerned. At the request of Neil's family, I intend to conduct a thorough inquiry into this matter. Your complete cooperation is expected.

Charlie: You told him about this meeting?

Meek: Twice.

Charlie: That's it, guys. We're all fried.

Pitts: How do you mean?

Charlie: Cameron's a fink. He's in Nolan's office now, finking.

Meeks: About what?

Charlie: The club, Pittsie. Think about it. The board of directors, the trustees and Mr. Nolan. Do you think for one moment they're gonna let this thing just blow over? Schools go down because of things like this. They need a scapegoat.

Cameron: What's going on, guys?

Charlie: You finked, didn't you, Cameron?

Cameron: "Finked"? I don't know what the hell you're talking about.

Charlie: You told Nolan everything about the club is what I'm talking about.

Cameron: Look, in case you hadn't heard, Dalton, there's something... called an honor code at this school, all right? If a teacher asks you a question, you tell the truth or you're expelled.

Todd: You...

Boys: Charlie!

Charlie: He's a rat! He's in it up to his eyes, so he ratted to save himself!

Knox: Don't touch him, Charlie. You do and you're out.

Charlie: I'm out anyway!

Knox: You don't know that. Not yet!

Cameron: He's right there, Charlie. And if you guys are smart, you will do exactly what I did and cooperate. They're not after us. We're the victims. Us and Neil.

Charlie: What's that mean? Who are they after?

Cameron: Why, Mr. Keating, of course. The "Captain" himself! You guys didn't really think he could avoid responsibility, did you?

Charlie: Mr. Keating responsible for Neil? Is that what they're saying?

Cameron: Well, who else do you think, dumb ass? The administration? Mr. Perry? Mr. Keating put us up to all this crap, didn't he? If it wasn't for Mr. Keating, Neil would be... cozied up in his room right now, studying his chemistry... and dreaming of being called "Doctor"!

Todd: That is not true, Cameron! You know that! He didn't put us up to anything. Neil loved acting.

Cameron: Believe what you want, but I say let Keating fry. I mean, why ruin our lives?

[*Charlie punched Cameron*]

Cameron: You just signed your expulsion papers, Nuwanda. And if the rest of you are smart, you'll do exactly what I did! They know everything anyway. You can't save Keating, but you can save yourselves.

Nolan: Knox Overstreet.

Todd: Meeks.

Meeks: Go away. I have to study.

Todd: What happened to Nuwanda?

Meeks: Expelled.

Todd: What'd you tell'em?

Meeks: Nothing they didn't already know.

Voice Over: Todd Anderson.

Todd's Father: Hello, son.

Todd's Mother: Hello, darling.

Todd: Mom.

Nolan: Have a seat, Mr. Anderson. Mr. Anderson, I think we've pretty well put together what's happened here. You do admit to being a part of this Dead Poets Society?

Todd's Father: Answer him, Todd.

Todd: Yes, sir.

Nolan: I have here a detailed description of what occurred at your meetings. It describes how your teacher, Mr. Keating, encouraged you boys to organize this club... and to use it as a source of inspiration for reckless and self-indulgent behavior. It describes how Mr. Keating, both in and out of the classroom, encouraged Neil Perry to follow his obsession with acting... when he knew all along it was against the explicit orders of Neil's parents. It was Mr. Keating's blatant abuse of his position as teacher... that led directly to Neil Perry's death. Read that document carefully, Todd. Very carefully. If you've nothing to add or amend, sign it.

Todd: What's gonna happen to Mr. Keating?

Todd's Father: I've had enough. Sign the paper, Todd!

Teacher 1: Grass is gramen or herba. Lapis is stone. The entire building is aedificium.

****

Nolan: Sit. I'll be teaching this class through exams. We'll find a permanent English teacher during the break. Who will tell me where you are in the Pritchard textbook? Mr. Anderson?

Todd: Uh, in the, in the Prit...

Nolan: I can't hear you, Mr. Anderson.

Todd: In the, in the, in the Pritchard...

Nolan: Kindly inform me, Mr. Cameron.

Cameron: We skipped around a lot, sir. We covered the romantics and some of the chapters on post-Civil War literature.

Nolan: What about the realists?

Cameron: I believe we skipped most of that, sir.

Nolan: All right, then, we'll start over. What is poetry?

[*Knocking*]

Nolan: Come!

Mr. Keating: Excuse me. I came for my personals. Should I come back after class?

Nolan: Get them now, Mr. Keating. Gentlemen, turn to page 21 of the introduction. Mr. Cameron, read aloud the excellent essay by Dr. Pritchard... on "Understanding Poetry."

Cameron: That page has been ripped out, sir.

Nolan: Well, borrow somebody else's book.

Cameron: They're all ripped out, sir.

Nolan: What do you mean, "They're all ripped out"?

Cameron: Sir, we... Ac...

Nolan: Never mind. Read.

Cameron: "Understanding Poetry" by Dr. J. Evans Pritchard, Ph.D. "To fully understand poetry, we must first be fluent... with its metre, rhyme and figures of speech. Then ask two questions. One: How artfully has the objective of the poem been rendered? And, two: How important is that objective? Question one rates the poem's perfection. Question two rates its importance. And once these questions have been answered, determining a poem's greatness becomes a relatively simple matter. If the poem's score for perfection is plotted on the horizontal of a graph..."

Todd: Mr. Keating! They made everybody sign it.

Nolan: Quiet, Mr. Anderson!

Todd: You've got to believe me. It's true.

Mr. Keating: I do believe you, Todd.

Nolan: Leave, Mr. Keating.

Todd: But it wasn't his fault!

Nolan: Sit down, Mr. Anderson! One more outburst from you or anyone else, and you're out of this school! Leave, Mr. Keating. I said, "Leave, Mr. Keating."

Todd: O Captain, my Captain.

Nolan: Sit down, Mr. Anderson. Do you hear me? Sit down! Sit down! This is your final warning, Anderson. How dare you. Do you hear me?

Knox: O Captain, my Captain.

Nolan: Mr. Overstreet, I warn you! Sit down! Sit down! Sit down! All of you! I want you seated! Sit down! Leave, Mr. Keating. All of you, down! I want you seated! Do you hear me? Sit down!

Mr. Keating: Thank you, boys. Thank you.

New Words

fink [fɪŋk] *n.* someone who informs (on someone), as to the police 向警察告发 (某人) 的人

trustee [trʌ'sti:] *n.* someone with legal control of money or property that is kept or invested for another person, company, or organization 受托人

scapegoat ['skeɪpgoʊt] *n.* someone who is punished for the errors of others 替罪羊

expel [ɪk'spel] *v.* to force to leave or move out 开除

rat [ræt] *v.* to tell someone in authority about things that someone else has done, especially bad things 背叛 , 告密

victim ['vɪktɪm] *n.* someone who has been hurt or killed 受害者

administration [əd,mɪnɪ'streɪʃn] *n.* the group of people who organize and supervise a company or an organization 管理层 ; 行政部门

crap [kræp] *n.* sth that it is wrong or of very poor quality 屎 , 废物

expulsion [ɪk'spʌlʃn] *n.* the act of forcing someone to leave a place 开除

reckless ['rekləs] *adj.* showing a lack of care about danger and the possible results of your actions 鲁莽的 , 不顾后果的

self-indulgent [,selfɪn'dʌldʒənt] *adj.* If you say that someone is self-indulgent, you mean that they allow themselves to have or do the things that they enjoy very much. 自我放纵的

obsession [əb'seʃn] *n.* If you say that someone has an obsession with a person or thing, you think they are spending too much time thinking about them. 迷恋

explicit [ɪk'splɪsɪt] *adj.* expressed or shown clearly and openly, without any attempt to hide anything 明确表达的 ; 公开显露的

blatant ['bleɪtnt] *adj.* sth bad that is done in an open or very obvious way 公然的

abuse [ə'bjuːs] *n.* used in a wrong way or for a bad purpose 滥用

amend [ə'mend] *v.* to change sth in order to improve it or make it more accurate 修正

metre [,miːtər] *n.* the rhythmic arrangement of syllables in verse, usually according to the number and kind of feet in a line (诗歌的) 韵律 ; 格律

rhyme [raɪm] *n.* If a poem or song rhymes, the lines end with words that have very similar sounds. (诗、歌曲) 押韵

objective [əb'dʒektɪv] *n.* sth you are trying to achieve 目标

render ['rendər] *v.* to express or perform sth 表达

horizontal [ˌhɔːrɪ'zɑːntl] *adj.* flat and level with the ground, rather than at an angle to it 水平的；横的

graph [ɡræf] *n.* a mathematical diagram which shows the relationship between two or more sets of numbers or measurements 图表

Phrases and Expressions

blow over: to end without any serious consequences (麻烦、争论等) 平息

dumb ass: a stupid person 笨蛋；傻子

cozy up: to indulge in 沉溺于

rip out: to tear out 撕开，扯下

figure of speech: words that are used together in an imaginative way to mean sth different from their usual meaning 修辞手法

Notes

Nuwanda: It is a made-up name that stems from the African-American trend of making up names for children. 化名，源自美国黑人给孩子的起名。电影中 Charlie 把自己的名字改为 Nuwanda，抛弃父母给的名字，表明他要开始新的人生。

Exercises for Understanding

1. Answer the following questions according to the video clip you have just watched.

(1) What did Nolan ask the students to do after the death of Neil?

(2) According to Cameron, who is to blame for the death of Neil?

(3) Why did some students stand on their desks at the end of the video clip?

(4) Why did students address Mr. Keating as their "Captain"?

(5) What did Nolan threaten to do when he saw students standing on the desks?

2. Decide whether the following statements are true or false according to the video clip you have just watched. Write a "T" for true or an "F" for false.

_____(1) Among the members of the Dead Poets Society, Charlie is a fink.

_____(2) Neil's parents wanted Neil to become a doctor while Neil himself dreamed of becoming an actor.

_____(3) Both the principal Nolan and the students wanted to expel Mr. Keating.

_____(4) Knox is the first guy to stand up against the principal Nolan.

_____(5) Nolan is the temporary English teacher after Mr. Keating.

3. Put the following sentences in the right order according to the video clip you have just watched.

_____(1) Students were required to go to Nolan to sign the description documents concerning Mr. Keating.

_____(2) Students discussed about what their future would be after Neil's death.

_____(3) Mr. Keating came to pick up his personal belongings before he was expelled by the Welton Academy.

_____(4) Students sang in memory of their classmate Neil who killed himself.

_____(5) Some students showed their love and respect towards Mr. Keating by standing on desks and calling him Captain.

Section B Reading

The Chinese and American education systems have different purposes and goals. Many parents and educators view Chinese education as important for foundation, and American education as being helpful for the cultivation of students' creativity. As a matter of fact, Chinese education focuses on the knowledge of accumulation and more importantly on how students manage and use the knowledge they have learned in school. Americans are deeply interested in how students use their knowledge in everyday society.

Educational Differences Between US and China

Furthermore, the American system lets students criticize ideas, challenge as well as create concepts to a larger degree than the Chinese education system. Chinese education focuses on strictness and precision, which helps improve retention whereas American education focuses on assuredness, self-determination, and independence, which aids in improving students' comprehensive thinking. In comparing Chinese with American school approaches, one can easily understand why Chinese students get gold medals in Math Olympics Competitions, but Nobel Prize winners are often from Americans.

On top of that, the ways that American and Chinese students receive knowledge are also different. Memorization is viewed as the norm among Chinese students who generally spend hours trying to remember the content of their textbooks. American teachers would normally assess students' creativity, leadership, and cooperation skills and encourage American students to take part in extracurricular activities. American students strongly believe that every piece of information taught in their curriculum is part of life rather than part of school.

Teachers in America regularly have a bit more freedom, especially when it comes down to building a unique curriculum to meet students' needs. In China, the most noticeable changes have surprisingly come down to advanced technology. Although test scores are still incredibly critical in China and schools continue to place high levels of pressure on students to compete and maintain high grades, students are starting to take part in more diversified activities to prepare for the competitive future that awaits them.

It is worth mentioning that Chinese teachers are responsible for larger student bodies in their classrooms. In fact, the majority of Chinese teachers work with more than 30 to 50 students per class whereas schools in America are more likely to have classes of 25 students or so.

In China's education world, the focus is based more on the collective group of students. Indeed, teachers would ask themselves "What can I do to improve learning as a whole?", while American teachers would rather focus on "What can I do to improve his or her (each student) learning?"

In the American education system, after each year or grade, students will usually move on to a different teacher as they continue their education journey. In the Chinese education system, however, one group of students may have the same teacher (the head teacher) throughout their education journey, especially in their primary school years.

Furthermore, examinations in China hold most substantial weight, and this pressure comes from both the home as well as the country. The expectation for high grades has become ingrained in the Chinese culture, and all citizens take grades and standardized test scores seriously. Grading not only determines the educational level of a student, but also is used to evaluate teachers' performance. As opposed to the latter, there can be slight consequences for teachers in America when it comes to students' outcomes and performances on both oral and written exams.

In America, arts and sports are highly encouraged from a young age. Now China has recognized the importance of these two subjects and has started to implement these as part of its education system.

In Chinese society, there is a high value on learning for future success. Beginning in preschool, Chinese parents communicate early that their children are expected to succeed in school, which has a very competitive environment. Students do not typically have time for extracurricular activities as the school day runs long. American parents tend to view education as just another part of their children's lives. A majority of American children play sports, learn an instrument and socialize with friends from a young age. School typically does not begin for American children until five years, which is usually the first formal school experience. And the American students do not have to strive in a competitive academic environment until late high school and into college as the American educational system is focused on any achievement, not just high grades.

To conclude, education is culture-specific, and different education systems show different social cultures. American education system is good, but it may not be exactly right for Chinese society, and vice versa. Both education systems have room for improvement. Neither system is better than the other. In the world of education, it is important to develop an international awareness and accept different learning approaches, cultures and knowledge.

Exercises for Understanding

1. Answer the following questions according to the passage you have just read.

(1) What are the different focuses of Chinese and American education systems?

(2) What is the difference in receiving knowledge between China and America?

(3) Speaking of middle school education, which is more competitive, China or America? Why?

2. Choose the correct answers to the following questions.

(1) The American education system focuses on improving _____.

    A. Learning as a whole

    B. Students' interests

    C. Students' confidence

    D. Students' creativity

(2) Most children in America usually start school in kindergarten or first grade at the age of _____.

    A. 3

    B. 4

    C. 5

    D. 6

(3) China's sense of _____ in the education system is strong.

    A. Individualism

    B. Strictness and precision

    C. Collectivism

D. Indulgence

(4) American students excel in majors related to comprehensive thinking whereas Chinese students tend to strive in _____.

A. Language-related majors

B. Science and math-related majors

C. Arts-related majors

D. Law-related majors

(5) Asserting that Chinese students take examinations more seriously than their American counterparts would be _____.

A. Accurate

B. Inaccurate

C. A misrepresentation

D. Baseless

3. Decide whether the following statements are true or false according to the passage you have just read. Write a "T" for true or an "F" for false.

_____(1) Chinese education is extremely tolerant and doesn't focus on diligence.

_____(2) Chinese parents place a very high value on China's education system in the early stages of schooling.

_____(3) Teachers in America aim to encourage their students to take part in extracurricular activities.

_____(4) Teachers in China have lots of freedom when it comes to building their own curriculum without the consent of school representatives.

_____(5) In Chinese culture, students' outcomes and performances on both oral and written exams are related to the performance and effectiveness of teachers.

Section C **Case**

The Scenario

Scan and Listen

How Do Students Learn?

Karen Randolph had been teaching high school English in the United States before she accepted a teaching job at teacher's college in China. She found her new environment and her new teaching assignment exciting. Both her students and her colleagues seemed a bit shy of her, but Karen was sure that in time they would all come to be friends.

In the classroom, however, Karen was very frustrated. When she asked a question, the class was silent. Only if she called on a particular student would she get an answer, often a very good one. She could not understand why they wouldn't volunteer when they obviously knew the answers. They were very quiet when she was speaking in front of the class, and never asked questions, let alone interrupt with an opinion. But as soon as the class ended, they would cluster around her desk to ask their questions one by one. They would also offer their suggestions about the lesson at this time.

Karen often asked her students to work in small groups during class, especially when they were editing each other's writing. They were slow to move into groups and when they did, they often simply formed a group with the people sitting next to them. Finally she devised her own system of forming groups to get them interact with students sitting in another section of the classroom.

Most frustrating of all, after she taught her class how to edit essays, she found that the students were likely to write vague and not very helpful remarks on their classmates' papers. They would say nice things about the essays and correct small grammatical errors, but seemed unwilling to criticize them in a way that would help another student revise the essay. They usually accepted her criticism of their writing with good spirits and promised to improve. Karen felt that one hundred percent grammatical correctness was not as important as learning how to correct what they had written on their own and with the help of others.

Exercise

Listen to the case above and answer the following questions.

(1) What was Karen excited about when she arrived in China?

(2) When do Chinese students usually ask questions, in class or after class?

(3) According to this passage, do Chinese students like to study in groups? How do Chinese students find group members?

(4) When editing peer students' papers, what remarks would Chinese students give?

(5) What's Karen's opinion of good paper editing?

References

[1] Bruneau T. J. Chronemics and the Verbal-Nonverbal Interface [M]//Key M. R. The Relationship of Verbal and Nonverbal Communication. Mouton Press, 1980.

[2] Charles Mitchell. 国际商业文化 [M]. 上海：上海外语教育出版社，2009.

[3] Davis L. Doing Culture: Cross-Cultural Communication in Action [M]. Beijing: Foreign Language Teaching and Research Press, 2001.

[4] Gudykunst W. B., Kim Y. Y. Communicating with Strangers: An Approach to Intercultural Communication (4th ed.) [M]. Boston: McGraw-Hill, 2003.

[5] Hall E. T. Beyond Culture [M]. New York: Doubleday Anchor Press, 1976.

[6] Hall E. T. The Silent Language [M]. New York: Doubleday & Co., 1959.

[7] Hirschberg S. One World, Many Cultures [M]. Needham Heights: Allyn & Bacon, 1995.

[8] Hofstede G. J., Minkov M. Cultures and Organizations: Software of the Mind [M]. New York: McGraw-Hill, 2010.

[9] Lewis N. Chronemics [M]. Fort Collins: Colorado State University, 2003.

[10] Samovar L. A., Porter R. E., McDaniel E. R., et al. Cross-Cultural Communication [M]. Beijing：Beijing University Press, 2017.

[11] Snow, Don. 跨文化交际技巧——如何跟西方人打交道 [M]. 上海：上海外语教育出版社，2014.

[12] Varner I., Beamer L. Intercultural Communication in the Global Workplace (3rd ed.) [M]. McGraw-Hill Companies, Inc., 2005.

[13] 杜平，姚连兵. 跨文化交际教程 [M]. 北京：中国人民大学出版社，2015.

[14] 樊葳葳. 跨文化交际视听说 [M]. 北京：高等教育出版社，2009.

[15] 刘凤霞. 跨文化交际教程 [M]. 北京：北京大学出版社，2009.

[16] 盛湘君. 英语实训教程——文化与交际 [M]. 杭州：浙江大学出版社，2009.

[17] 许力生. 跨文化交流入门 [M]. 杭州：浙江大学出版社，2017.

[18] 许力生. 新编跨文化交际英语教程 [M]. 上海：上海外语教育出版社，2013.

[19] 叶朗，朱良志. 中国文化读本（英文版）[M]. 北京：外语教学与研究出版社，2008.

[20] 郑晓泉. 跨文化交流 [M]. 杭州：浙江大学出版社，2010.

[21] 庄恩平. 跨文化商务沟通案例教程 [M]. 上海：上海外语教育出版社，2004.

Appendix
Key to the Exercises

Unit 1

Section A

1. (1) T   (2) T   (3) F   (4) T   (5) F

2. (2)—(4)—(6)—(5)—(1)—(3)

3.

(1) Undoubtedly, Sully is a real-life hero. His split-second decision not to attempt to return to the airport but instead to land the plane on the Hudson saved 155 lives on board. Only a man with the combination of skills, temperament and expertise could perform such an astonishing and almost unlikely emergency landing in aviation history. Sully is conscientious. He was the last to leave to make sure no one remained on the plane. He is modest, insisting that he was just doing his job and paying tribute to his co-pilot as well as the crew, first responders and the passengers. He is dignified, which was manifested in word and deed.

(2) Heroism exists in almost every place of the world. Different cultures have different definitions of heroism, which shape their own unique heroes. In America, people have the greatest esteem for individualism, humanism and democracy. Even if the heroes are deified, the subjects are still human beings, who have feelings and emotions, personality and shortcomings all the time. They lay down their lives for honor and ideal, love and freedom. Even when the justice conflicts with the interest of the nation, they will resolutely select justice. However, heroes are covered with a layer of idealism in Chinese culture. In the circumstance of collectivism in Chinese culture, what is amplified is the loyalty and devotion to the nation and the sacrifice of individuals. The heroes die for the interest of the country or community. Thus, heroes in China usually don't have private desire. Furthermore, Chinese heroes tend to be godlike, perfect and supernatural. Even so, heroes all over the world share sth in common. Heroes from both countries usually have characteristics superior to ordinary people, both physically and psychologically. Besides,

they always have noble qualities, such as unbelievable courage, unswerving pursuance, and rich sympathy.

Section B

1.

(1) What I prefer is "Culture is like the water a fish swims in." This metaphor is vivid. Culture to humans is like water to fish—the fish never stops to reflect on what it means to live in the water. It just swims and goes about its normal routine. But if the fish swims into unfamiliar water, it would need a long time to adapt.

(2) In the iceberg analogy of culture, only some aspects of culture are visible. These can include language, art, music, dance, dress, food, celebrations and many others. The majority of the culture lies beneath the surface. These aspects are not immediately visible. They can include wordviews, religions, spiritual beliefs, power relationships, respect for authority, concepts of time, status and so on.

2.   (1) A   (2) D   (3) D

3.   (1) F   (2) T   (3) T   (4) T   (5) F

Section C

(1) Janice is a young American engineer working for a manufacturing joint venture near Nanjing and Liu Lingling is Janice's young co-worker.

(2) Janice and her husband George who both come from America were pleased because they have been eager to get to know about Chinese people better.

(3) They were busy preparing meals and barely had time to sit down and talk to the guests. Janice and her husband felt slightly depressed.

(4) They treated them in a typically American way—a simple Western meal and a talk.

(5) There are many fundamental differences concerning inviting people to dinner between China and America. The Chinese emphasize ostentation of food because abundant and valuable food can reflect the hospitality of hosts. Usually the amount of food is more than what the host and guests can consume. In contrast, hosts in America do not focus on preparing food excessively and regard eating as a chance to exchange information, renew old friendship or make new friends.

Unit 2

Section A

1. (1) 1) shinning   2) embrace   3) come true

(2) 1) wanted   2) *Jingle Bells*   3) club   4) passionate   5) remind

(3) 1) give   2) dream   3) follow   4) Paris   5) wait and see

6) love   7) love

2. (1) F   (2) F   (3) T   (4) T   (5) T

3.

(1) Sebastian gave up his ultimate dream because he thought he needed a steady gig for Mia to accomplish her goals. So he started playing with the band. It was hard at first, but he got accustomed to it. When he cooked a surprise dinner for Mia, she started to question his happiness with the band. She couldn't see it from his point of view how supporting her and being a part of sth that people enjoy at the same time could make him happy. She didn't see how it wasn't exactly about caring what others thought. He was enjoying creating joy for people. She wanted him to be a "dreamer" again. He overreacted, and they fought, and she left without much of a second thought.

(2) Although they always loved/will love each other, they decide they should each follow their own paths and see what happens. Both of them have to do what they need to make their first dreams come true.

(3) They exchange the look at each other, nod, acknowledge and thank each other graciously for the wonderful time they had when they were together. Like mature adults, they understand that while it would have been great if things worked out, life isn't rosy all the time. Despite the amazing chemistry they shared, they just weren't meant to be together. Even though they aren't romantically involved in the end, they continue to hold great admiration and respect for each other and remain to be important figures in their life.

Section B

1.

(1) Of the variety of sensory channels, I prefer sight. As the old saying goes, words are but wind, but seeing is believing.

(2) For example, when asking a day for a date, a young man may wear an formal suit and spray

some perfume to show that he highly values this date with her. In this case, sight and smell are definitely more effective than words for conveying particular message.

(3) Sights, sounds, and other stimuli in the environment that draw people's attention away from intended meaning are known as external noise. Thoughts and feelings that interfere with the communication process are known as internal noise. Unintended meanings aroused by certain verbal symbols can inhibit the accuracy of decoding. This is known as semantic noise.

(4) Feedback is very important because it serves useful functions for both senders and receivers: it provides sender with the opportunity to measure how they are coming across, and it provides receivers with the opportunity to exert some influence over the communication process.

2. (Just for reference)

(1) 龙

It is a legendary creature which is honored as a godlike creature in the Chinese culture. It is valued so much that it becomes the token of China. In sharp contrast, it is often a symbol of evil, a fierce monster in English culture.

(2) 望子成龙

It is a four-character idiom which means longing for one's son to be successful.

(3) 红色

It is a kind of color which is often connected with celebrations and joyful occasions. It is symbolic of good fortune as well.

(4) 铁饭碗

It is a metaphor which means a stable, lifelong job regardless of one's performance.

(5) 抓周

It's a traditional Chinese custom. A child is told by his or her parents to choose one thing among others to show his or her future.

(6) 母老虎

It's a slang which means a fierce and tough woman. And the wife of Camel Xiangzi is a case in point.

(7) 打酱油

It a kind of cyber language which means to be a standby or just pass by.

3. (1) B   (2) C   (3) D   (4) A

4. (1) T   (2) T   (3) F   (4) F   (5) F

5. Open

Section C

(1) On the National Day.

(2) They were accompanied by a number of mostly monolingual Chinese guides from the Foreign Affairs Office as well as some young teachers from the English, German, French and Russian faculties who accompanied their colleagues to act as interpreters.

(3) They got to Hangzhou by a touring bus and stayed at a hotel on the outsides of the city.

(4) Because the Foreign Affairs Office had found out only after they got there that the city of Hangzhou had passed an Emergency Traffic Control Regulation prohibiting buses without Hangzhou registrations from entering the city for the few days before, after, and including the holiday.

(5) They weren't told the truth because they were thought not to be able to understand the reasons.

(6) They were annoyed, thinking they had been deceived.

(7) It is widely acknowledged that people from different cultures communicate differently. In the mainstream American culture, the ideal form of communication includes directness while in Chinese culture indirectness is held in esteem. And the difference in communication styles can become a source of misunderstanding, frustration, and conflict in intercultural communication.

Unit 3

Section A

1. (1) T   (2) F   (3) T   (4) F   (5) T

2.

(1) let alone   (2) worth the wait (3) From the heart (4) counts (5) behold (6) reception

(7) honeymoon (8) leave the story (9) co-manager   (10) present like the time

3.

(1) Because she thinks that Sonny Kapoor may be too nervous and too eager when communicating with the investor and screw up the negotiation.

(2) She wants to demonstrate that she, as an experienced co-manager of a hotel, is professional enough in serving hotel guests.

(3) He conducts morning rollcall.

(4) She thinks that Sonny Kapoor is penny foolish and pound wise.

(5) Because Madge Hardcastle is tired of flirting with two men and decides to follow her will.

Section B

1.

(1) There are mainly three reasons, namely, the rise of new technology and information systems, the changes in the world's population and a shift in the world's economic, political and cultural arena.

(2) The 4 variables in intercultural communication are perception, verbal processes, nonverbal processes, and contextual elements.

(3) Spanish people understand the meaning of being "embarrassed" as pregnant.

(4) The hum and buzz of implication is mainly cultural, which shows that people in different cultural contexts have different interpretations about the same thing.

(5) Because the subjective world is interpreted by people from different cultures who abstract whatever fits into their personal world of reorganization and then interpret through the frame of reference of their own culture.

2.

It should be noted that knowing a country's language, while clearly helpful, is no guarantee of understanding its cultural mindset, and some of the most difficult problems may be created by individuals who have a high-level of fluency but a low level of cultural understanding. In most cases, cultural mistakes are more serious than linguistic mistakes. The linguistic mistakes mean someone is not fully expressing his or her idea while cultural mistakes can lead to serious misunderstanding and even ill-feeling between individuals.

Section C

(1) Jeff thinks that Ji Bing is easy-going, warm-hearted, and always ready for a new experience.

(2) Ji Bing suspects that Jeff is angry because Jeff is too polite when he borrows things from him. He thinks that friends don't have to ask so frequently when borrowing small things from each other. For example, Ji Bing himself sometimes borrows Jeff's things without asking first. Ji Bing feels impatient with Jeff's asking.

(3) Ji Bing would probably answer as follows: your politeness makes me think that you

haven't treated me as a friend. Now that we are roommates and friends, please feel free to use these tools and you don't have to buy me another one.

(4) Americans expect friends to be independent, provide emotional support and spend time together. The individual belongs to many groups but his attachment to these groups is relatively weak. Chinese have enormous responsibility for their friends. They give each other much concrete help and assistance. Close friends share most aspects of their life, including material wealth. Individual Chinese feels strongly attached to group members.

(5) Both Ji Bing and Jeff should learn about each other's culture and etiquettes and communicate with each other more often.

Unit 4

Section A

Video Clip 1

1.

(1) No. Because Dubey hasn't come yet and Lalit has to urge him to come to do his work.

(2) Because the wedding is about to take place and Lalit is doing everything single-handedly. He is angry about the wedding contractor for not doing his job properly.

(3) It is falling apart and flowers are everywhere.

(4) Because they should get ready before the guests arrive.

2.   (1) T   (2) F   (3) F   (4) T

Video Clip 2

1.

(1) No. From the way they greet each other we can see this is the first time they meet each other.

(2) Yes. We can tell this from the way the groom's father and grandmother talk to Aditi.

(3) In this movie, the groom's family come to the bride's house. The bride and groom meet each other's family members. They exchange wedding rings in the presence of both families and guests. It's a warm and lively scene.

2.   (1) T   (2) F   (3) T   (4) T

Video Clip 3

1.

(1) She wants to study creative writing in America.

(2) Ria's mother is worried about the money for studying in America. Others think it might be possible to make a lot of money through writing.

(3) He tried to refuse at first. Later he was overjoyed at the idea. He was happy that the whole family was together for the wedding.

2. (1) F (2) T (3) F

Video Clip 4

1.

(1) Because she doesn't want to lose both her children. Her daughter will get married and leave the family soon.

(2) Because he thinks his son is wasting time by staying home watching TV the whole day. He believes boarding school is good for his son.

(3) He wants to be a chef.

(4) He wants his son to be an educated professional. Because he doesn't want his son to become an entertainer, singing and dancing at people's wedding.

(5) Lalit has the final say. Pimmi tries to persuade her husband into giving up the idea of sending their son to boarding school, but in vain.

2. (1) T (2) F (3) T (4) T

Section B

1.

(1) The proverb means "单梁难撑房" in Chinese. No matter how strong, one single beam can hardly support a house. The proverb shows the importance of group orientation in Chinese culture. There are many Chinese proverbs which demonstrate the collective sense in Chinese culture, for example: "众人拾柴火焰高（The fire burns high when everybody adds wood to it）", "人多力量大（Many hands make light work）", "团结就是力量（Unity is strength）", "滴水不成海，独木难成林（A drop of water does not make a sea, and a single tree does not make a forest）", "三个臭皮匠，顶个诸葛亮 (Two heads are better than one)", etc.

(2) The four pairs of values identified in Hofstede's research can be understood as follows:

1) Collectivist cultures emphasize community, collaboration, shared interest, harmony, the public good, and maintaining face. Individualistic cultures emphasize personal rights and responsibilities, privacy, voicing one's own opinion, freedom, innovation, and self-expression. For example, in Korean culture, traits such as indirect communication, saving face, concern for others, and group cooperation are linked to Korea's collective orientation. In a learning environment, a collective classroom will stress harmony and cooperation rather than competition.

2) Power distance defines the extent to which the less powerful person in society accepts inequality in power and considers it as normal. In high-power distance cultures, people believe that power and authority are facts of life. In low-power distance countries, people hold that inequality in society should be minimized. For example, in high-power distance societies, the educational process is teacher centered. The teacher initiates all communication, outlines the path of learning students should follow, and is never publicly criticized or contradicted. In a business context with low-power distance you might observe decisions being shared, subordinates being consulted, bosses relying on support teams, and status symbols being kept to a minimum.

3) Uncertainty avoidance deals with the fact that the future is unknown. People can never predict with 100 percent assurance what someone will do or what might happen in the future. Different cultures deal with the fact that the future is uncertain differently. People in some cultures experience relatively high level of anxiety and stress, while others are willing to take risks and are more flexible. High-uncertainty avoidance cultures try to avoid uncertainty by providing stability for their members through rules, regulations, rituals, etc. In low-uncertainty avoidance cultures, people accept the uncertainty inherent in life more easily, tend to be tolerant of the unusual, and are not as threatened by different ideas and people. Differences in uncertainty avoidance influence intercultural communication. For example, in a classroom composed of children from low-uncertainty avoidance cultures, we might expect to see students feeling comfortable in unstructured learning situations, being rewarded for innovative approaches to problem-solving, and recognizing that truth is relative. In high uncertainty avoidance cultures, students expect structured learning situations and seek right answers.

4) Masculinity stands for a society in which social gender roles are clearly distinct. Men are supposed to be assertive, tough, and focused on material success, while women are supposed to be more modest, tender, and concerned with the quality of life. Femininity stands for

a society in which social gender roles overlap: both men and women are supposed to be modest, tender, and concerned with the quality of life. For feminine society, quality of life is a high priority in life, and one works in order to live. Work is less central in people's life. Nations such as Sweden, Norway, Finland, Denmark, and the Netherlands tend toward a feminine world view. In Sweden, which had the highest ranking in Hofstede's femininity category, women occupied 47.3 percent of the 349 legislative positions following the 2006 election, which suggests a high level of political empowerment.

(3)

1) There are many co-cultures within the American society, and some co-cultures have collective traits.

2) Hofstede's research ranked the United States No.1 in the individualism value orientation.

3) Hofstede's research only showed differences in national value orientations, while within each nation, there are many layers of cultures. So Hofstede's finding applied to the dominant culture of a country.

2.

In high-context cultures, an important purpose in communicating is to promote and sustain harmony among the participants in these cultures. It is generally true that direct confrontation of another person is considered rude and undesirable in Chinese culture. It is related to the concept of "face" in Chinese culture. Chinese people are cautious about speaking, because they are cautious about the impact of their words when they communicate with others. They don't want to lose face or threaten the face of others. Making a request is a somewhat face-threatening speech act. A direct "no" is face-threatening to the other party. By saying "you may be right" or "we'll think about it," the speaker's real meaning is expressed without saying "no" directly. And the listener who grows up in the same culture will understand the answer as a tentative decline or a half-decline at least. In this way, the speaker does not have to say "no," and the listener is not refused directly. Hurting the other party's feelings is avoided at all costs with great emphasis on saving face.

Section C

(1) The author teaches in a Chinese university.

(2) Most of the Chinese classrooms have large raised podiums with students sitting in rows below.

(3) The author prefers classrooms with movable tables and chairs, so it is easier for the author

to arrange students into work groups.

(4) A facilitator defines tasks and goals and arranges activities to achieve them. Because the author believes the teacher is not the main source of knowledge for the students but the leader of their learning activities.

(5) According to Hofstede's research, China is a high power distance society while the United States is a low power distance society. This could be observed in classroom patterns in both countries. A typical Chinese classroom has large raised podium for the teacher with students sitting in rows below. This classroom pattern helps to emphasize the teacher's authority, indicating larger power distance between the teacher and students. The teacher is believed to be the core of Chinese classroom, and his or her role is to teach, to solve problems and puzzlement of the students. The author comes from the United States where there is smaller power distance between the teacher and students. In a Western classroom, the teacher is a facilitator, a leader of students' learning activities. With movable tables and chairs, teachers can arrange students to work in groups and monitor their work and offer advice. So the author find the physical arrangement of the Chinese classroom a problem in conducting the Western-style teaching.

Unit 5

Section A
Video Clip 1
1.

(1) Rachel says her father died before she was born and her mother didn't go to college. Her mother worked really hard and became a top real estate broker. She was proud of her mother.

(2) She thinks Rachel's mother is very open-minded.

(3) Because she feels that way. Nick's mother was kind of serious in the talk. It seems as if she is not so happy to see Rachel.

(4) Probably not. Because she doesn't seem happy to see the girl her son brought home. When Rachel talks about her passion, Nick's mother says that's typical American style. She also hints that Nick's parents are different from Rachel's mother. She didn't show approval in the conversation.

2. (1) T (2) T (3) F (4) Γ (5) Γ

3.

(1) challenging　　(2) immigrated　　(3) license　　(4) waiting tables　　(5) broker

(6) proud　　(7) passion　　(8) open-minded

Video Clip 2

1.

(1) She says the dumplings don't look very good.

(2) No. Because she kind of criticized Eleanor in front of the whole family by commenting negatively on the dumplings made by Eleanor. In the later part of the video clip, Eleanor said she was not Ah Ma's first choice.

(3) Because Ah Ma didn't like Eleanor.

(4) Because she hints that Rachel is not good enough for her son.

(5) She says the shape of Rachel's nose is auspicious, and Rachel is nice looking. I think she likes Rachel.

2.　(1) T　　(2) F　　(3) F　　(4) F　　(5) T

3.　(1) adequate　　(2) concerned　　(3) sacrifice　　(4) measure up　　(5) worry

Section B

1.

(1) In high-context culture, much information is implied in the context. In low-context cultures, the majority of the information is contained in the verbal code, and the message is stated clearly and explicitly without depending on the context of the communication.

(2) An important difference between high-context and low-context communication is that with high-context communication, the burden of interpreting the meaning falls on the listener, while with low-context communication the speaker has the responsibility for making the meaning clear. For example, the Asian mode of communication (high-context) is often vague, indirect and implicit, whereas Western communication (low-context) tends to be direct and explicit. Americans depend more on spoken words than on nonverbal behavior to convey messages. They think it is important to be able to "speak up" and "say what's on their mind."

(3) Silence is often regarded as a very important nonverbal code highly valued by people in high-context cultures. Just as the Indonesian proverb says, "Empty cans clatter the loudest (罐空声高)," high-context people may perceive talkative low-context people

as less credible. Chinese culture is a typical example of high-context culture. Silence is often regarded as an important nonverbal code in communication. In Chinese language, there are some proverbs or sayings concerning Chinese people's view on silence. For example, "沉默是金(Silence is golden)" "言多必失(He that talks much errs much)" and "祸从口出(Careless talk leads to trouble)." There are many other sayings about Chinese communication styles or rules of communicating. For example, "一言既出，驷马难追 (A word spoken is past recalling)" "言不尽意 (What I have said or written does not convey all I have on my mind)" "言外之意 (Meaning beyond words, or hidden meaning between the lines)" "只可意会，不可言传 (The subtlety is beyond description though it can be sensed)," etc.

2. Open

Section C

(1) Because her neighbor's opera singing was disturbing her sleep. She wanted to get a good night's sleep because she would have an important job interview the next morning.

(2) She wanted to let the mother know that her daughter's piano practice was disturbing at night.

(3) The dispute between two European American neighbors in Scene 1 is an example of low-context communication interaction.

(4) The dialogue in Scene 2 between two Japanese housewives illustrates their use of high-context communication style.

(5) High-context communication is indirect and the responsibility of interpreting the meaning falls on the listener. In Scene 2, Mrs. A has not directly expressed her concern over the piano noise with Mrs. B. Rather, Mrs. A only uses indirect hints and nonverbal signals to get her point across. However, Mrs. B. correctly "reads between the lines" of Mrs. A's verbal message and apologizes appropriately and effectively before a real conflict can bubble to the surface. Scene 2 represents one possible high-context way of approaching interpersonal conflict.

(6) Low-context communication is direct and to the point. In Scene 1, Jane and Diane spell out everything that is on their minds with no restraints. Their interaction exchange is direct, to the point, bluntly contentious, and full of face-threat verbal messages. Scene 1 represents one possible low-context way of approaching interpersonal conflicts.

Unit 6

Section A

1. (1) T   (2) F   (3) T   (4) F   (5) F

2.

Video Clip 1

(1) personal business   (2) tricked   (3) mechanical   (4) do your part   (5) strengthen your tongue

Video Clip 2

(1) in vain   (2) stripped of all disguise   (3) make our cause their own

(4) in this time of trial   (5) prevail

3.

(1) I think language is powerful. Language is central to our lives, which sets us apart from other species. Ever since the invention of language, it has been helping name objects and people , resulting in its leverage over the action of others. Language can also populate worlds of meaning. People can use language to love or hate, to persuade or dissuade, and so on.

(2) Firstly, Bertie has overcome his stammering. Secondly, with his improvement of language skills, he has picked up confidence in himself. Thirdly, as a leader, he is courageous and determined to lead his people in the fight against the Nazis.

Section B

1.

(1) "The limits of my language are the limits of my world" means that when you become fluent in one language, you can see things through a different lens. People's ability to express themselves in a certain language is the limit of their epistemology.

(2) The metaphor used to describe the relationship between language and culture is living organism in which life is flesh and culture is blood.

(3) We use language to practice culture and shape our lives. We need language to express ourselves and to communicate with members of the culture properly. We need language for self-expression, communication, and social interaction.

(4) Weasel words refer to the words that appear to have substance and appear to make a claim,

but in fact do not. Advertisers deceptively use these words. Some examples are listed as follows.

1) help: help relieve the pain (The product aids in the relief of pain but may not relieve the pain all by itself. Also, the degree to which it helps relieve pain is unknown.)

2) virtually: virtually spotless dishes (Dishes that are not in fact or not entirely spotless.)

3) new and improved: a new and improved floor cleaner (could simply be the same cleaner with a different color dye added to it)

4) act fast: a cold medicine that "acts fast" could simply make the user sleepy within 12 hours.

5) like magic: a product that works "like magic" could be claiming that the product functions accurately because that could be how magic functions.

(5) Denotative meanings are the basic meanings of words while connotative meanings are the implied meanings of words.

2. Open

3.

(1) green　　(2) brown　　(3) blue　　(4) white　　(5) black

(6) yellow　　(7) green　　(8) yellow　　(9) black　　(10) blue

(11) white　　(12) red　　(13) black　　(14) white　　(15) yellow

4.

(1) lover: 情人（不是"爱人"）

(2) busboy: 餐馆勤杂工（不是"公共汽车售票员"）

(3) busybody: 爱管闲事的人（不是"大忙人"）

(4) dry goods:（美）纺织品；（英）谷物（不是"干货"）

(5) heartman: 做心脏移植手术的人（不是"有心人"）

(6) blind date:（由第三者安排的）男女初次会面（并非"盲目约会"或"瞎约会"）

(7) dead president: 美钞（上印有总统头像）（并非"死了的总统"）

(8) sweet water: 淡水（不是"糖水"）

(9) confidence man: 骗子（不是"信得过的人"）

(10) criminal lawyer: 刑事律师（不是"犯罪的律师"）

(11) dressing room: 化妆室（不是"试衣室"或"更衣室"）

(12) horse sense: 常识（不是"马的感觉"）

(13) familiar talk: 庸俗的交谈（不是"熟悉的谈话"）

(14) black stranger: 完全陌生的人（不是"陌生的黑人"）

(15) white man: 忠实可靠的人（不是"皮肤白的人"）

(16) yellow book: 黄皮书 (法国政府报告书，以黄纸为封，不是 "黄色书籍")

(17) red tape: 官僚习气 (不是 "红色带子")

(18) blue stocking: 女学者，女才子 (不是 "蓝色长统袜")

(19) American beauty: 红蔷薇 (不是 "美国美女")

(20) English disease: 气管炎 (不是 "英国病")

(21) Indian summer: 愉快宁静的晚年 (不是 "印度的夏日")

(22) Greek gift: 害人的礼品 (不是 "希腊礼物")

(23) Spanish athlete: 吹牛的人 (不是 "西班牙运动员")

(24) French chalk: 滑石粉 (不是 "法国粉笔")

Section C

(1) The Chinese student sat on the steps of foreign students' building because she wanted to be close to foreign students and found opportunities to practice her English with foreign students.

(2) The two foreign students were not eager to keep the conversation going on because each time they answered with only one or two words.

(3) Because she was determined to practice her English.

(4) The implied meaning of "fishing" is walking on the street and waiting for some girls to come up.

(5) The main cultural difference is the different interpretations of the word of "fishing". Chinese students are taught with its literal meaning without the awareness of its implied meaning. The other cultural difference is Chinese and foreign students' attitudes towards keeping on the conversation. Foreign students showed little interest in the conversation probably because they felt they were pushed too hard.

Unit 7

Section A

1.

(1) Toula means that her parents want to keep the Greek tradition so much that children are likely to have no privacy, which may hurt both the parents and the children.

(2) According to Gus, the Greeks invented the Facebook. In fact, Facebook was invented by Mark Zuckerberg in 2004 in the United States. Gus said so because in his opinion, everything in the world can be traced back to the great Greek culture.

(3) Toula gave up her dream as a travel agent because the economy in her time was stagnant and few people chose to travel. Tourism industry was sluggish.

(4) Paris thinks that her parents always don't say what they mean. On the one hand, they hope Paris to dream big. On the other hand, they strongly suggest they Paris study in a local university. In this way, they can keep an eye on her. Mother is too needy, while father wants Paris to get married soon.

(5) The family wants Paris to choose a local university because they want her to be close to family members who will exert Greek influences on her more easily.

2. (1) T (2) T (3) F (4) F (5) T

Section B

1.

(1) The time for the main meal during a day in Mexico is 2 p.m. to 4 p.m.

(2) No. It is considered to be impolite to eat all the food on the plate in Egypt.

(3) Yes. There are food taboos in certain cultures. For example, strict Muslims do not consume pork or alcohol. Orthodox Jews eat neither pork nor shellfish. Hindus do not eat any beef.

(4) Alcohol still maintains its important role in China, Japan and ROK.

(5) In Middle Eastern cultures, seating is usually circular. Guests might sit on the floor. Someone's right-hand side is the preferred side. Women usually sit separately.

(6) In a tipping culture, leaving a few coins is rude because this shows a lack of respect for the servants. The proper way is to report the situation to the manager.

2. Open

3.

(1) Learn the Chinese language.

(2) Travel or do sports with Chinese. Learning Chinese greetings like ni hao (hello) and ni hao ma (How are you?) will help your relationships and make a good impression. It is acceptable to give a compliment. When receiving a compliment, the typical response should be one of modesty. Instead of saying thank you, it is better to downplay the compliment.

(3) Choose proper topics. Any normal topics are okay, but avoid talking about work, money and apartments.

(4) Follow common customs of China and be aware of cultural taboos.

(5) Get a QQ or Wechat account.

(6) Learn to use chopsticks.

(7) Understand and choose Chinese names. When doing business in China, it is a good idea to select a Chinese name. It can be a simple translation of your English name into Chinese or an elaborately chosen name given with the assistance of a Chinese teacher or fortune teller. Going to a fortune teller to pick a Chinese name is a straightforward process. All that is needed is your name, date of birth, and time of birth. Do not assume that a married Chinese man or woman has the same surname as his or her spouse. While it is becoming more popular in Hong Kong and Taiwan to take or add the man's name to a woman's name, most Chinese women typically retain their maiden last names after marriage.

(8) Be conscious of personal space. The concept of personal space in China is vastly different than in the West. On crowded streets and malls, it is not uncommon for people to bump into strangers without saying "Excuse me" or "sorry." In Chinese culture, the concept of personal space is much different than the West, especially when standing in line to buy something like train tickets or groceries. It is typical for people in a queue to stand very close together. Leaving a gap just invites other people to cut in line.

(9) Making a great first impression. It is becoming more and more popular to shake hands upon meeting, but oftentimes, a simple nod is how Chinese will greet each other. When a handshake is given, it may be firm or weak but don't read into the firmness of the handshake as it's not a sign of confidence like in the West but a simple formality. Avoid hugging or kissing during greetings and farewells.

(10) Observe Chinese banquette etiquettes. 1) The seating arrangement is determined by the host. Always wait to be seated rather than seating yourself. 2) A banquet is an opportunity, a time to get to know your hosts on a personal level, not to discuss serious business issuers, so ask about their family, hobbies, children's schooling etc. 3) Do not eat or drink anything (except tea) until the host has delivered the welcoming toast and begins eating. If you are the guest of honor, you should also make a toast a few minutes after everyone has begun eating. Never drink your alcoholic drink alone, if you want to take a sip from it, find someone else at the table that you can toast with and then you can drink. 4) During the meal, your hosts may place food on your plate for you as a sign of respect. Don't feel obliged to finish everything in your plate, and its best to finish the meal with sth left in your plate to show that you have eaten so much you can't possibly eat another thing. 5) The host is the only person who can signal that the meal has ended—guests must not leave early. All guests should wait for direction from the host, and then

leave in order of importance. The host will first escort the head guest out of the room and others can then follow.

Section C

(1) In the beginning, they are friendly with each other and always ask each other for advice.

(2) Yang Ruifang visited Cathy several times at home but did not invite Cathy to her apartment.

(3) Because they kept on talking on the telephone if they could not see each other over the weekend.

(4) The meanings of "friends" in two cultures are not equivalent. According to *Contemporary Chinese Dictionary* (7th edition), "friend" in Chinese context, has two denotations. One is "acquaintance," which frequently refers to the person you know from your work or living places. Another is "companion," who shares with you the common life goals and will support you emotionally. And in Chinese culture, the implication of "friend" actually often refers to the second definition. That is, one may have many acquaintances but only a few friends. "Friend" in Australian Culture has been defined as 1) a person you know well and like, and who is not usually a member of your family; 2) a person who supports an organization, a charity, etc.; 3) a person who has the same interests and opinions as yourself, and will help and support you. From the above definitions of "friend," it can be summarized that the foundations of friendship in two cultures are not always the same. In Chinese culture, friendship is based on similar pursuit in life and mutual caring and support. On the contrary, the similar goals and values in life lay foundation to Australian concept of friendship. It depends on trust, sincerity and the mutual matters the friends are sharing. What's more, the most striking distinctions are the classification and the duration of Chinese and Australian friendships. Australians tend to establish and forget their friendship more easily and quickly than their Chinese counterparts. It is apparent that Australians seem to have various kinds of friends. One may find acquaintance, casual friend, good friend, intimate, close friend, best friend and many other expressions which contain diverse levels and closeness. However, more often than not, Australians may have a particular partner in their school, neighborhood, army, and church; even when they are in hospital, they may have found a new friend there. This means most Australians tend to have more general friends rather than small quantity of lifelong friends. Australian friends may be close, durable, generous and sincere at one time. But when the situation changes, for instance, moving to another district or finishing a certain course in the university, the

newly-established friendship may disappear soon. No wonder many non-Australians regard Australians are easy to get to know but difficult to maintain friendship. When Australians are doing the same thing together, they seem to be very good friends; however, when the shared matter finished, their friendship will end at the same time. For them, friends are out of sight, out of mind. Unlike Australians' pragmatic attitude to friendship, Chinese think highly of lasting closeness between friends. The process to establish friendship is quite slow and once established, the friendship perhaps will last quite long, even for lifelong time.

(5) Open

Unit 8

Section A

1.

(1) Because she has finished her course work in S. P. R.

(2) Ria notices that Jane has her head and eyes down and blocks her eyes with her hand, which manifests that she feels ashamed of herself.

(3) She felt outraged because she was replaced by a younger women in the S. P. R.

(4) When she stayed with John Stafford as a member of S. R. P., at first she was favored by John and she liked this. Then she began to hate this way of living.

(5) Because John Stafford had undergone some facial operations, making it hard for policemen to get a read on him.

2. (1) F   (2) F   (3) F   (4) T   (5) T

3. (1) C   (2) A   (3) D   (4) E   (5) B

Section B

1.

(1) Kinesic behaviors include gestures, head movements, facial expressions, eye behaviors, and other physical movements that can be used to communicate.

(2) People who walk confidently with swinging foot movements are less likely to be attacked.

(3) Firstly, nonverbal communication is important because we use the actions of others to learn their affective or emotional states. Secondly, it is significant in human interaction because it is usually responsible for first impressions. Thirdly, it is valuable in human interaction because it is relatively free of distortions and deception.

(4) Emblems are nonverbal behaviors that have a direct verbal translation, which are direct

replacements for words, while illustrators are nonverbal behaviors that are directly tied to or accompany verbal messages.

(5) In beckoning people to come over, one moves the finger back and forth with the palm down in Thailand. In the United States, people hold the palm up and move the fingers toward their body.

(6) Nonverbal messages cannot be judged in isolation because people usually send nonverbal cues simultaneously and these cues are linked to both verbal messages and the settings in which we find ourselves.

2.

Signs	Meanings of Signs	Countries and Areas
THE OK SIGN	Everything is great.	United States, Germany
	Things are good (not excellent).	Mexico
	Worthless (zero)	France, most of Europe
	Symbol for money	Japan
	Vulgar gestures	Spain, Russia, Paraguay, Brazil, Uruguay
	Threat of bodily harm	Tunisia
THUMBS UP	Approval	United States, Great Britain, Russia
	Highly offensive	Iran
	Rude	Australia
THUMBS DOWN	Disapproval	United States, Cananda
	Rude	Greece
CLOSED FIST	Obscene gesture	Pakistan
	If raised in air, it is obscene.	Lebanon
THE V SIGN	Victory	Great Britain, United States, most of the world
	Peace	United States (from the 1960's)
TO HELLWITH YOU	Offensive gesture	Great Britain, South Africa
THE FINGER	Highly offensive	United States, most of Europe, many parts of the world
THE FIG	Highly rude	Central America, Turkey

Signs	Meanings of Signs		Countries and Areas
NODDING HEAD UP AND DOWN / SHAKING HEAD LEFT TO RIGHT	Shaking head left to right	No	United States
		No	Most of the world
		Yes	Bulgaria, Saudi Arabia, Malaysia
	Nodding head up and down	Yes	United States, most of the world
		No	Bulgaria
PAT ON THE SHOULDER	Encouragement/sympathy		United States
	Offensive		Thailand
RAISED EYEBROW	Surprise		United States
	Hello or general greeting		Philippines
BLINKING	Disbelief		United States
	Boredom		China
TAPPING YOUR TEMPLE WITH YOUR FINGER	Person is crazy.		North America, Europe, Germany (especially)
	I'm thinking about it.		Africa, Peru, Argentina
HANDS ON HIPS	Hostility		Mexico
	Anger		Malaysia
	Impatience		United States
	A challenge		Argentina
SLAPPING THE INSIDE OF THIGNS	Rude and suggestive		Argentina
PINCH OF THE EARLOBE	Enjoyed a meal		Brazil
	Sign of humility		India
CHIN FLICK	I don't know.		Portugal
	Dull or boring		France
	Get lost		Italy
HANDS IN A POCKET(S)	Rude		All Europe, Japan, China

Signs	Meanings of Signs	Countries and Areas
NOSE BLOWING	Extremely rude	China, Japan
	Bad upbringing	France
TAPPING THE INSIDE OF THE ELBOW WITH THE OPPOSITE HAND	Cheap or stingy	Colombia
	Untrustworthy or unreliable	Netherlands
ARMS FOLDED	Boredom or disapproval	United States
	Arrogance	Finland
SNAPPNING THE FINGERS OF BOTH HANDS	Vulgar gesture	France
FORMING A CIRCLE WITH YOUR THUMB AND FOREFINGER AND PLACING IT OVER YOUR NOSE (PINCHING YOUR NOSE)	Drunk	France
	Deal is no good. (It stinks.)	United States
PLAYING THE IMAGINARY FLUTE	Talking too much	France
SHOULDER SHRUG	Don't know. / Don't care.	Italy
	Reluctance to agree	United States
	Ridiculous	France
SHOWING THE SOLE OF YOUR FOOT OR SHOE	Highly offensive	Thailand, Myanmar, Middle East

3. Open

4.

(1) "兔耳"手势：这个手势的英文名叫"finger quote-mark gesture"，用法和双引号完全一样，表示反义、讽刺、重点、引用等。一般做"兔耳手势"都是在正在说话的情况下，不会单独使用。

(2) "我爱你"手势："我爱你"手势应该是美剧和生活中最常见的手势之一。"我爱你"手势由三个部分组成：只伸出食指表示"I"；伸出食指和大拇指，表示"L"（LOVE）；伸出大拇指和小指，表示"Y"（YOU）；一起伸出大拇指、食指和小指就是"I Love You"。

(3) "瓦肯"手势：《星际迷航》里瓦肯人（Vulcan）的问候手势，意思是生生不息、繁荣昌盛。

5.

(1)	1) B	2) D	3) C	4) A
(2)	1) C	2) A	3) D	4) A
(3)	1) C	2) D	3) A	4) B
(4)	1) C	2) A	3) D	4) B
(5)	1) B	2) C	3) D	4) A
(6)	1) C	2) A	3) D	4) A
(7)	1) B	2) D	3) C	4) A
(8)	1) C	2) A	3) A	4) D

6. Open

Section C

(1) To the Chinese group, the car should be driven by authorized Chinese drivers for senior Chinese project members. To the American group, having the car means they should be able to drive it.

(2) They cited the Memorandum of the Understanding, Chinese law and precedent to show it was possible to change the registration of the car.

(3) The Chinese authorities acknowledged the Americans' right to drive the car, but mentioned a number of practical difficulties and promised to look into the matter. But nothing changed after a year.

(4) When the Chinese authorities mentioned a number of practical difficulties, they were indicating it was a tough problem to solve, probably involving the efforts of different government sectors. They promised to look into the matter but didn't promise a deadline of working out the problem. If the Americans want to get the problem solved, they should check the progress with the government regularly.

Unit 9

Section A

1.

(1) In the real world, time is the manifestation of motion, the continuity of variation and the succession of events and existences. While in the movie, time is used as the currency.

(2) She is 50.

(3) Because in the movie, the physical aging of the human body stops when people turn to 25.

(4) Because he thinks he should have got more money.

(5) He is the leader of the Minutemen. He comes to rob the rich man's time.

2. (1) T   (2) T   (3) F   (4) F   (5) F

3.

(1) whole	(2) bills	(3) a cup of coffee	(4) shifts	(5) excited about
(6) fortune	(7) the rest	(8) units	(9) joke	(10) taking forever

Section B

1.

(1) For me, time is monochromic, since I find it extremely difficult to do several things simultaneously and I usually do one thing at a time.

(2) China owns a history of over 5,000 years. There are hundreds of time-honored brands in China. The Chinese people respect and treasure the ancient Chinese traditions.

(3) Open

2. Open

Section C

(1) He was the supervisor of a clothing factory on the island.

(2) The natives of the island had some disagreements on the number of people who were hired.

(3) They thought it broke the existing status system and the balance of power.

(4) Because they had just reached an agreement and were too excited to wait until the next day.

(5) Because he mistakenly thought sth extremely urgent happened after the phone call at 2 o'clock in the morning.

Unit 10

Section A

1.

(1) evil	(2) zone	(3) mean	(4) normal	(5) weird
(6) bouncing	(7) material	(8) medium	(9) bending	(10) Pop quiz

2. (1) T   (2) F   (3) F   (4) T   (5) F

3.

(1) Auggie tries to hide himself not to be included in the photo, because he feels self-abased and lacks a sense of belonging to his peers.

(2) Because his classmates think Auggie is different so they keep a distance from him.

(3) Jack chooses this school because he has been offered the scholarship.

(4) She is surprised, touched and gratified.

Section B

1.   (1) T   (2) F   (3) F   (4) F   (5) F

2.   (1) A   (2) C   (3) C   (4) D   (5) B

3. Open

Section C

(1) Bill came to China to study engineering.

(2) Bill got along well with his Chinese roommates. They studied engineering together and went to the student cafeteria together. The Chinese students also showed him around and help correct his classroom Chinese.

(3) They huddled over a radio to listen to a broadcast. Zemin was draped over the back of the boy seated in front of the radio. And that boy had his feet propped up on his roommate who was seated nearby.

(4) Bill felt uncomfortable because in Western countries, if people of the same sex stay so close to each other, it is a sign of homosexuality.

Unit 11

Section A

1.

(1) Detective Graham Waters says so because he thinks people in the city tend to be indifferent to each other in their daily lives. They need to be awakened by sth dramatic.

(2) Farhad is an American with Muslim background, and the gun store owner has racial prejudice against him.

(3) Anthony guesses that black waitress has stereotypes, thinking that black people don't tip. So the waitress didn't want to waste her time on him.

(4) I don't think that the robbery of car of Jean Cabot was an intended one. It was triggered

by a white woman's reaction on seeing the 2 black guys of Anthony and Peter Waters on a street at night.

(5) She complains about the possibility of being attacked by a black gangbanger and insists that the lock be changed again. I think it is a negative stereotype based on her prejudice against the black. On seeing the black guy with shaved head, pants and tattoo, she cannot help connecting him with black gang member.

2. (3)—(2)—(1)—(5)—(4)

Section B

1.

(1) Ethnocentrism is the tendency to think of one's own culture as being at the center of the world. People are born to be ethnocentric to some degree. As we grow up, we naturally learn to view the world as our culture views it and the ideas about the world formed in childhood are so deeply rooted in our minds that we feel quite strongly about many of them and are not likely to change them.

(2) Because people naturally feel that the ways and ideas of their culture are more natural and correct than those of other cultures. They tend to use the norms of their own culture as standards when judging the behaviors of people from other cultures, thus making it possible to cause cultural barriers in intercultural communication.

(3) One of the best ways to overcome ethnocentrism is to cultivate the habit of learning about other cultural perspectives and understand the world from other cultural perspectives.

(4) Stereotypes are a set of assumed characteristics about a certain group of people whose actual beliefs, habits and realities more often than not disagree with the imposed assumptions. Stereotypes, based on exaggeration, distortion, ignorance, racism, cultural factors or even historical experiences, are misleading to individuals and can influence people positively and negatively.

(5) We must develop our cultural competency and learn to perceive the world from other cultures' standpoints.

2. Open

Section C

(1) Anna used her friendship with one of the women in another department, Gu Ming, to borrow English novels and reference books.

(2) The memo was about collecting all the English language materials together into a single collection and then put them in a small room so that all employees could have equal access to English materials.

(3) I think Gu Ming would probably explain that the English materials have all been borrowed by her colleagues in her department.

(4) The main problem would be that the outsiders' offers are likely to be turned down. Generally Chinese people are collectivistic, in which to share resources is based on the relations within group members.

Unit 12

Section A

1.

(1) 15 brands of luxuries are mentioned in Clip 1.

(2) Shashi thinks Manhattan is a place of wonder, color and wealth.

(3) Shashi is a loving mother and a good wife. She misses her husband and children a lot when in a foreign country.

(4) Because her English was so poor that she could not make herself understood by the saleswoman.

(5) In the eyes of Shashi, family is a place that never puts people down and makes people feel small. Family members should never laugh at each other's weaknesses. Family is a place of love and respect.

2.　(1) T　　(2) T　　(3) T　　(4) F　　(5) T

3.

(1) touching heaven　　(2) full of dreams　　(3) speechless　　(4) legs and shoes

(5) straight and gay

4.　(1) B　　(2) E　　(3) D　　(4) C　　(5) A

Section B

1.

(1) The traditional explanation for culture shock is lined with the sorrow people feel after losing their beloved ones. Today culture shock is mainly due to three reasons: the theory of negative events, the theory of decrease in social support and the theory of different values.

(2) The mental discomfort includes loneliness, helplessness, anxiety, unease and withdrawal.

The physical discomforts include insomnia, inattentiveness, loss of appetite and headaches.

(3) There are many ways to deal with culture shock. Firstly, be patient. Secondly, keep in touch with home country. Thirdly, take care of yourselves. Fourthly, have fun and relax.

(4) The second period is called the culture shock period. People at this period usually feel anxious, restless, impatient, and disappointed.

(5) To put it simple, developing empathy is to put oneself in others' shoes, to see things from the point of view of others so that one can better know and adjust to other people.

2. Open

3. Open

4. Open

5.

How to Tell If You Are an American

The following is a first crack at an ostensive definition of "American culture" —things shared by the vast majority of native-born Americans.

(1) You know how baseball, basketball, and American football are played. If you are a male, you can argue intricate points about their rules. On the other hand (and unless you are under about 20), you don't care that much for soccer.

(2) You are fairly likely to believe in God; if not, you've certainly been approached by people asking whether you know that you are going to Heaven.

(3) You think of McDonald's, Burger King, KFC, etc. as cheap food.

(4) A bathroom may not have a bathtub in it, but it certainly has a toilet.

(5) It seems natural to you that the telephone system, railroads, auto manufacturers, airlines and power companies are privately run; instead, you can hardly picture things working differently.

(6) The train system, by contrast, isn't very good. Things don't go any faster than cars; you're better off taking a plane.

(7) You take a strong court system for granted, even if you don't use it. You know that if you went into business and had problems with a customer, partner, or supplier, you could take them to court.

(8) It is not all that necessary to learn foreign languages anyway. You can travel the continent using nothing but English, and get by pretty well in the rest of the world, too.

(9) School is free throughout high school. At least, it's an option, even if you went to the private school; college isn't, unless you get a scholarship.

(10) Mustard comes in jars. Shaving cream comes in cans. Milk comes in plastic jugs or cardboard boxes, and occasionally in bottles.

(11) You expect marriages to be made for love, not arranged by third parties. Getting married by a judge is an option, but not a requirement; most marriages happen in church. You have a best man a maid or matron of honor at the wedding—a friend or a sibling. And naturally, a man gets only one wife a time.

(12) Once you're introduced to someone, you can call them by their first name.

(13) You'd rather a film be subtitled than dubbed if you go to foreign film at all.

(14) You seriously expect to be able to transact business, or deal with the government, without paying bribes.

(15) Your country has never been conquered by a foreign nation.

(16) You still measure things in feet, pounds, and gallons.

(17) The biggest meal of the day is in the evening.

(18) There are parts of the city you definitely want to avoid at night.

(19) The normal thing, when a couple die, is for their estate to be divided equally between their children.

(20) If you're talking to someone, you get uncomfortable if they approach closer than about two feet.

Section C

(1) He always felt tense and slept over 12 hours a day. He missed his family very much and isolated himself from the outside world.

(2) Because he has severe headaches after shutting himself inside for 3 months.

(3) After he learned about culture shock, he began to see things from a new point of view and was able to accept himself in a better way.

(4) Because they felt the defensiveness, aggressiveness and avoidance from the local Peruvians. In order to seek safety and comfort, they chose to stay in the familiarity of the embassy compound.

(5) They thought that it was the Peruvians that brought about their discomfort.

Unit 13

Section A

1.

(1) Because the company's top client—Groff Technologies has just moved its headquarters to Shanghai. And Powell and Davis think Sam, a Chinese single go-getter, is the most suitable person to head it up.

(2) Because he has a lot of things at hand. For example, in order to celebrate his thirtieth birthday, he has rented a restaurant with a DJ coming. Besides, he is very familiar with his American life rather than the Chinese one. He knows the ins and outs of New York and nothing about Shanghai.

(3) Amanda is Sam's relocation specialist. She was late to receive Sam because her Ayi was sick in the morning and she had to find a temporary babysitter.

(4) Because Amanda is more familiar with Chinese culture than Sam. Maybe she has encountered similar situations.

(5) The culture shock is mainly about language. Sam looks like a Chinese, but he knows nothing about Chinese language. So he cannot communicate with the taxi driver properly. What's more, as a newcomer in Shanghai, he hasn't developed a good sense of direction, which makes him confused and frustrated.

2. (1) F (2) F (3) F (4) T (5) T

3. (2)—(4)—(1)—(5)—(3)

Section B

1.

(1) The very concept of community is undergoing a fundamental transformation in today's world.

(2) Because the integrated markets and global networks bind people together. The study of intercultural and international communication will bring about apparent and real-world consequences.

(3) Because the integration of markets and community has penetrated the daily lives of nearly everyone on the planet, regardless of language or culture.

(4) A list of where components were made and assembled and what percentage corresponds to each nation is included in "Made in X."

(5) Business communication values clear, concise interaction that promotes efficiency and effectiveness. In intercultural business communication, one should be aware that his role as business communicator crosses cultures, languages, value and legal systems, and borders.

(6) The author implies that people may learn different things from different cultures. Different cultures reflect the inequality, diversity, and divergent range of values, symbols, and meanings across communities.

(7) Theory X holds that workers are motivated by personal interest, while Theory Y views employees as ambitious, self-directed, and capable of self-motivation.

(8) Theory Z combines elements of both Theory X and Theory Y and draws from American and Japanese management style. It promotes worker participation and emphasizes job rotation, skills development, and loyalty to the company.

2. Open

Section C

(1) The goal of a cocktail party in the United States is to meet as many people as possible.

(2) No. People don't have deep discussions at cocktail parties in the United States. They just make small talks and walk around the room, exchanging business cards and phone numbers so that they can get into contact later and establish future business relationships.

(3) The Europeans regard the cocktails in the United States as superficial and lacking sincerity. People at parties in European countries are supposed to sit and talk.

(4) Because in Japan, a country of hierarchy and protocol, it is improper to introduce oneself without knowing the age and status of the other person, while at American cocktail parties, it is quite acceptable to walk up to anyone in the room and introduce oneself. That's why a US firm that hosts a cocktail party in Japan can create problems.

(5) The cultures that emphasize hospitality would think of Americans' set length of cocktail party as rude.

Unit 14

Section A

1.

(1) The documents include: death certificate, a report of the death and an ME pink slip.

(2) Richard would drive another 2 hours to California with his father's remain in the trunk and call a funeral home once the family get there. In the meantime he would arrange Olive to

perform in the pageant held in California. Thus he can handle his father's death affairs and Olive's performance properly.

(3) Because the horn seemed to get stuck and keeps honking.

(4) Frank found that Dwayne could not recognize the dark green "A" in the circle.

(5) Olive said nothing. She just gave Dwayne a hug, which was powerful enough to persuade Dwayne into joining the family again.

2. (1) F (2) F (3) F (4) F (5) T

3. (1) D (2) E (3) A (4) B (5) F (6) C

Section B

1.

(1) Because tourists usually spend limited period of time (2 weeks for example) staying in one city. Their intercultural encounters are short and their consciousness of different behavioral rules and patterns are superficial.

(2) The key to successful intercultural communication lies in 4 aspects: understanding cultural diversity, developing awareness of individual cultures, having tolerance and keeping the communication clear and simple.

(3) Patience, courtesy and a bit of curiosity are the solutions to different needs.

(4) About 400 million people around the world speak English as a first language. When speaking English, it is suggested that speakers make it clear, simple and unambiguous.

(5) Because humor is culture-specific, so try to avoid humor until you know that the person you're communicating will "get it" and isn't offended by it.

2. Open

3.

(1) In Chile, it is good manners to open a gift immediately and express delight and thanks. But in Japan it is a traditional custom not to open a gift in the giver's presence.

(2) In the United States, shoppers typically touch, hold, and even smell fruits and vegetables before buying them. But in northern Europe this is strongly frowned upon.

(3) In mainstream North American culture, people are expected to look directly at each other when having a conversation. But a cultural norm for many native Americans involves keeping one's eyes lowered as a sign of respect when speaking to an instructor or supervisor.

Comment: No one can be expected to learn all the "dos and don'ts" of the world's myriad cultures. Instead, the key is to keep an open mind, be sensitive to other cultures, and remember that the way you'd like to be treated is not necessarily the way others would appreciate.

4.

8 or more As: You are scoring very high for happiness. However, one problem with being so happy is that it may lead to complacency. You are less interested in changing yourself, or improving certain aspects of your character, than most people.

6-7As: You are just above average for happiness, either because you're basking in the glow of some recent positive life event or because you have a long-term tendency to feel good. Your happiness dips when you become self-critical—at these times you need to be kinder to yourself if you want to improve your happiness.

3-5 As: Your average score means that you tend to dwell on times when you have invoked (招致) the disapproval of others. You need to realize these negative messages may say more about those saying them than about you. Greater happiness will not depend others' approval for your self-worth.

0-2As: You're scoring low on happiness, which means you're confusing the pursuit of short-term happiness (through comfort eating, alcohol or other self-destructive habits) with what would bring you lasting happiness—the pursuit of a meaningful long-term goal. You need to stop putting off working toward an achievement that would make you truly happy.

Section C

(1) Xiaohong and Mark got along with each other well because they enjoyed talking with each other and attended various social gatherings together.

(2) Last week Xiaohong and Mark had dinner and watched a movie together. During their way back home, Marked kissed Xiaohong.

(3) Xiaohong understood the kiss as a sign of Mark's affection toward her.

(4) There are three possible implications. Firstly, Mark has fallen in love with Xiaohong and wants to have a more serious relationship. Secondly, Mark was moved more by the romance of the moment than by any deeper feelings. Thirdly, perhaps he just finds Xiaohong physically attractive or he is lonely in China and enjoys Xiaohong's company.

(5) To figure out the real meaning of the goodnight kiss, Xiaohong can consider talking to Mark about their relationship directly.

Unit 15

Section A

1.

(1) Nolan asked the students to sign a letter attesting to the truth of Richard's allegations.

(2) Cameron thinks that Mr. Keating is responsible for Neil's death. In his opinion, if it wasn't for Mr. Keating, Neil would be in his room right now, studying his chemistry and dreaming of being called Doctor.

(3) The students stood on the desks to show their respect for Mr. Keating and their dissatisfaction with the school authorities.

(4) Captain is the person to inspire and lead a group. The students think Mr. Keating, just like a Captain, is the right person for them to follow and enlighten them.

(5) Nolan threatened to expel the students standing on the desks out of school.

2. (1) F (2) T (3) F (4) F (5) T

3. (4)—(2)—(1)—(3)—(5)

Section B

1.

(1) Chinese education system focuses on knowledge accumulation while American education system focuses on the application of knowledge in students' daily lives. Chinese education focuses on strictness and precision, whereas American teachers focus on improving student assuredness, self-determination, and independence.

(2) In terms of receiving knowledge, Chinese students usually spend many hours trying to remember the content of their textbooks, while American students' pay more attention to the cultivation of creativity, leadership and cooperation skills and are more eager to take part in extracurricular activities.

(3) According to this passage, China's middle school education is more competitive because school days run long and students don't have enough time for extracurricular activities. What's more, Chinese parents have higher expectations on their children and grades are important in evaluating students. In America, however, parents view education as just another part of their children's lives. A majority of American children play sports, learn an instrument and socialize with friends. American students do not have to strive in a competitive academic environment until late high school and into college.

2. (1) D (2) C (3) B (4) B (5) A

3. (1) F (2) T (3) T (4) F (5) T

Section C

(1) She was excited about the new environment and her new teaching assignment when she arrived in China.

(2) Chinese students usually ask questions after class one by one.

(3) According to the passage, Chinese students are reluctant to move into groups. When they do this, they usually form a group with the people sitting next to them.

(4) When editing peer students' papers,Chinese students are likely to say nice things about the essays and correct small grammatical errors.

(5) Karen feels that good paper editing should not only correct grammatical mistakes but also learn how to correct. The editing is supposed to be helpful for peers to revise.